THE
LONDON
COOKBOOK

THE
LONDON
COOKBOOK

LIZ TRIGG

Kyle Cathie Ltd

First published in 1996
by Kyle Cathie Limited
20 Vauxhall Bridge Road
London SW1V 2SA

Text © 1996 by Liz Trigg
Artwork © 1996 by Julie Westbury
Design Ruth Prentice
Design Assistant Claire Graham

ISBN 1 85626 188 3

A Cataloguing in Publication record for this book is available from
the British Library.

Printed and bound in Spain by GraphyCems.

Contents

Introduction

FANNY CRADDOCK WROTE 'Bon Viveur in London' for the *Daily Telegraph* in the years 1950-55. In writing about restaurants of the day, she explained in her introduction that 'it must be realised that we faced and still face a task which is as endless as painting of the Forth Bridge. Just as soon as the painters finish at one end, the opposite end requires fresh attention. So it is with the hotels and restaurants – to what extent we had no clue until we began the job'.

This is true about my search for recipes in London today. As soon as I started my research I realised that recipes, cooks, ideas and restaurants were constantly changing. The food they produce evolves, is created and eaten every day – and the next day provides an opportunity to cook something entirely new. So it is with a great humility that I am able to portray a selection of recipes that represent cooking in London today. Cooks are constantly on the move, travelling around the city cooking business lunches, domestic dinner parties, meals in restaurants, suppers at home; and once they have used up all their ingredients from around London, they have to start again the next day with a fresh delivery of food. Back in the days of eight years ago when I used to work for Leiths Good Food, it was a much smaller establishment off the Goswell Road in the City. Most jobs like washing lettuce were done by hand, cooking lasted a 12-hour day, and the quantities of fruit, vegetables, meat, fish and dry store goods that used to come into our relatively small kitchen were, I used to think, enormous. I was sure that in the course of the day's cooking we could never use it all up – naturally we did and often ran out! Nowadays, Leiths boasts lettuce jaccuzis (or washers) and huge amounts of catering equipment we would have died for.

There is a far greater variety of fresh ingredients available, too, and new and exciting recipes and culinary styles have developed to reflect this.

Having lived and worked in London for nine years, in daily contact with food suppliers, shops, chefs and restaurants, I thought I knew what was happening in and about the food scene in London pretty well. However, the more delving into the food life of the capital I did, the more I realised just how much I didn't know: people, places, ideas and concepts relating to what was happening in London crept out of the most unusual and often unexpected knooks. Accidentally discovering an Iranian restaurant, for example, only to be sworn to secrecy, as the owner is terrified he'll be inundated with numbers of customers he just can't accommodate in his 20-seater caravan. Equally accidental was the discovery of a great British Institution, The W.I., holding a very village-style food market every Friday in Barnes, southwest London. Many of the foreign Embassies in London have excellent traditional cooks lurking in their offices, bringing an exotic flavour to London's food scene. The market traders too, perhaps those most acutely aware of changing consumer demand, gave their best and realistic comments as to how significantly they thought food in London had changed in the last 10 years.

Food in London since the War

If the last decade has brought about changes, the last half-century has seen nothing short of a transformation in the quality, variety and affordability of food on offer in the capital. The rationing restrictions of the Second World War had resulted in food in Britain, and London, becoming unimaginative, in short supply and generally staid. Rationing was not lifted until

1954, with sweets being the last product to come off rationing.

People's attitude towards cooking was not as exciting or enlightened as it is today, and as a result the writer and historian Raymond Postgate took drastic measures. In 1949 he founded the 'Society for the Prevention of Cruelty to Food'. In an article in the *Leader* magazine he reflected on the standard fare which was at that time being offered in the average London eating establishment. The article read thus:

'Sodden, sour, slimy, stale or saccharined – one of these five things (or all) it would certainly be, whether it was fish, flesh, vegetable or sweet. It would be over-cooked, it might be reheated. If the place was English, it would be called a teashop or caffy, if foreign it would be called a restaurant or a caffy. In the second case, it would be dirtier, but the food might have some taste.'

It was from this article that the **Good Food Guide** eventually developed, with the first issue being published in 1951. It sold with great success. This led to increased awareness and enjoyment of food, especially in London.

A Frenchman, André Simon, had also been trying to raise the awareness of good food and wine, by setting up 'The Wine and Food Society'. He was very interested in monitoring the standards of wine and food in hotels, restaurants and private homes.

Elizabeth David's books *A Book of Mediterranean Food*, published in 1950, and *French Country Cooking*, which followed in 1951, had an enormous impact on directing people's thoughts on cooking, in particular towards a more open, European approach. Enjoyment in eating out and experimenting with new ingredients developed as the British people started to travel again after years of war-time restrictions. London attracted many more foreigners to work or study, and they came in large numbers. The Italian influx of waiters, chefs and café workers introduced one of the symbols of London in the late Fifties and early Sixties – the Gaggia Espresso coffee machine. Cafés became the most popular meeting places. The best ones had their own character; El Cubano, for example, in the Brompton Road was lively and noisy, whereas the Partisan in Charlotte Street was quiet and frequented largely by young, left-wing intellectuals. Food didn't feature highly in these bars, but snacks such as beans on toast were generally available.

The *Companion Guide to London* by David Piper, published in 1964, contains a section on restaurants in which he describes the development of all kinds of European and Oriental cooking in London. It was at this time, too, that Egon Ronay's Guide to *1,000 Eating Places in Great Britain* was published, advising the best places to eat in London.

The Indian and Chinese restaurants noted by Piper were now flourishing, and so-called 'ethnic' foods have continued to become popular in London, challenging the traditional monopoly of French and Italian chefs. For example, West Indian and Asian ingredients and food traditions have become integrated into London food life. Ethiopian, Portugese, Jewish, Sardinian, Dutch, Czech, Austrian, Japanese, Californian, Greek, French, Italian, German and Spanish establishments all exist around London. In the 1980s and 1990s all kinds of culinary traditions and ingredients are to be found alongside one another. This continued change and development is characteristic of the most diverse and exciting food capital of all.

British Cooking

Brit ish food in London has changed enormously even in the last ten years, and now offers a thriving culinary heritage of which the capital's inhabitants can be proud. Increasing numbers of top chefs use British ingredients and give classic recipes a modern twist to suit today's tastes and health concerns. Celebrated eating places, such as the Savoy, the Dorchester, the Ritz and Simpson's, continue to feature staple British dishes on their elegant menus. 'Nursery food' like oxtail stew and sticky, steamed toffee pudding has also emerged from the domaine of gentleman's clubs to become a fashionable item for the modern palate.

The Modern British style of cooking has a strong international style and flavour. European influences bring additional texture and interest to the traditional, for example French brioche and Italian panettone transform the traditional bread and butter pudding. Modern British menus offer chefs and cooks great flexibility in adapting recipes to imaginative new ingredients. New methods of cooking like char-grilling have also led to varied methods of visual presentation.

The Savoy hotel restaurant is arguably London's most famous and celebrities fight to book there.

The Blenheim

21 Loudoun Road, St. John's Wood, London NW8 0NB. Tel: 0171 625 1222

CAROLINE SYMMONDS IS THE VERY YOUNG head chef at the new Blenheim in St. John's Wood. Country cooking in town is one of her ideas, buying seasonal ingredients from her parents' farm in Shropshire. Her ideas are dictated by availability and season, with dishes changing daily. The

Baked Cod on a Bed of Vegetables with a Red Wine Sauce

Serves 4

For the sauce:
2 fennel bulbs
12 shallots
3 cloves garlic
2 tablespoons olive oil
25g (1oz) butter
1 bayleaf
3 sprigs of fresh thyme
3 sprigs of fresh parsley
200ml (7fl.oz) Noilly Prat
1 bottle red wine
10 tomatoes, seeded and chopped
1 sprig fresh basil
225g (8oz) mushrooms, sliced
1.4 litres (2½ pints) water
1 tablespoon caster sugar

For the vegetables:
1 red pepper
3 sticks celery
2 fennel bulbs
300g (10oz) courgettes
2 red onions
2 cloves garlic
1 aubergine
3 tablespoons olive oil
3 tablespoons sugar
salt and pepper
ground cinnamon
4 x 225g (8oz) cod fillets
lemon juice
butter
garden herbs, to garnish

Preheat the oven to 180°C/350°F/gas mark 4.

Slice the fennel, shallots and garlic cloves. Heat the olive oil and butter in an ovenproof casserole and add the fennel, shallots and garlic. Cook until soft but not coloured. Add the bayleaf, thyme and parsley and mix well. Add the Noilly Prat and cook rapidly until the sauce is reduced in volume and becomes syrupy.

Add the red wine, mix well, then boil rapidly to reduce the sauce to half its volume. Add the tomatoes, basil and mushrooms and mix well. Add the water and bring the mixture to the boil. Cover and place in the preheated oven for 30 minutes.

Remove from the oven and strain the sauce through a sieve. Discard the pulp in the sieve. Return the liquid to the casserole dish, add the sugar, then cook rapidly until the sauce is reduced to 600ml (1 pint) and thickens. It will be a very rich, dark sauce.

Slice all the vegetables into matchstick strips and place them in a roasting tin. Add the olive oil, sugar, seasoning and cinnamon and toss all the ingredients together. Cook in a preheated oven for 1½ hours, until all the liquid has evaporated. The vegetables will begin to caramelise and go soft.

To serve: Wrap the cod fillets in foil with a little lemon juice, butter and seasoning. Bake in a preheated hot oven at 220°C/425°F/gas mark 7 for 10-15 minutes until cooked.

Reheat the vegetables in a pan and arrange them in the middle of 4 plates. Lay the cod fillets carefully on top. Reheat the sauce and whisk in a little butter to make it shiny. Pour the sauce around the fish and vegetables. Garnish each portion with garden herbs.

Baked Jersey potatoes tossed in melted butter and parsley would be a delicious accompaniment.

Blenheim is one of the groups of restaurants around London, based in a pub. This particular venture is located in a large old pub and has a very relaxed, informal atmosphere, providing the ideal backdrop to Caroline's tasty food. Freshness is essential, and the recipes reflect this.

Hot Apricot Soufflé

Serves 8

600ml (1 pint) water
225g (8oz) caster sugar
juice of 1 lemon
450g (1lb) fresh apricots
25g (1oz) butter
25g (1oz) plain flour
225ml (8fl.oz) milk
1 tablespoon kirsch
3 eggs, separated
225g (8oz) fresh apricots, stoned and chopped
450ml (³/₄ pint) apricot sauce (apricot purée)
150ml (¹/₄ pint) double cream

Preheat the oven to 190°C/375°F/gas mark 5.
Place the water and sugar in a saucepan and heat gently, stirring, until the sugar has dissolved. Add the lemon juice and apricots and cook gently until the apricots are soft. Remove and discard the apricot stones.

Purée the apricots with a little sugar syrup to make a thick purée. Measure out 225g (8oz) apricot purée and set aside.

Add some more sugar syrup to the remaining purée to make a pouring consistency.

Melt the butter in a pan and stir in the flour. Cook for 1 minute, stirring. Add the milk, return to the heat and simmer for a few minutes, stirring. Remove from the heat and stir in the 225g (8oz) thick purée. Add the kirsch. Taste and add more lemon juice if necessary. Mix in the strained egg yolks.

Whisk the egg whites until stiff and fold into the soufflé mixture. Divide equally between 8 well-greased dariole moulds and place in a bain marie. Bake in the preheated oven for 25-30 minutes, until they are set.

Allow them to cool, then carefully turn out each soufflé and place in a gratin dish. Spoon some chopped apricots over each one, together with some apricot sauce and a tablespoon of double cream. Bake in a preheated oven at 230°C/450°F/gas mark 8 for 6-8 minutes, until the sauce is puffy and bubbling.
Serve immediately.

Books for Cooks

4 Blenheim Crescent, London W11 1NN. Tel: 0171 221 1992

ROSIE KINDERSLEY is the able assistant to Heidi Lascelles, owner of Books for Cooks. This shop provides the largest array of books about food and drink in London, with about 8,000 titles in all. It is a real magnet for all foodies who visit London, a unique place in which to experience the fabulous crammed shelves of food history, science, recipes and flavours.

Books for Cooks has frequently been called 'the best smelling bookshop in the World', a reputation which it owes entirely to its tiny test kitchen and café sandwiched between shelves of food books at the back of the shop. Crossing the threshold, customers exclaim with delight as the sweet scents of baking cakes, mingled with the more earthy aromas of frying garlic and onion, waft across the shop. Rosie says that they are proud that these culinary assaults on the senses have lured many a defenceless customer into eating lunch and becoming a purchaser. The menu changes daily as the cooks test recipes from the books on the shelves.

Here Rosie shares the secrets of one of her and her customers' favourite recipes.

Poached Breast of Chicken with a Green Herb Sauce

Serves 6

1 onion, peeled and quartered
1 carrot, peeled and chopped
1 celery stick, chopped
parsley sprigs
6 chicken breasts (preferably free-range)

For the sauce:
2 bunches of fresh parsley
2 bunches of fresh mint
2 garlic cloves, peeled
3 anchovy fillets, drained
2 tablespoons capers, rinsed
3 tablespoons red wine vinegar
2 tablespoons lemon juice
175ml (6fl.oz) good olive oil
salt and pepper

Preheat the oven to 180°C/350°F/gas mark 4.

Put the chopped vegetables, parsley sprigs and chicken into a roasting tin and add enough water to cover the breasts completely. Cover with a sheet of foil, place it in the preheated oven and bake for 20 minutes. Remove the foil; leave the chicken to cool in its poaching liquid.

To make the sauce, put all the ingredients except the olive oil into a food processor and blend together into a paste. Trickle in the olive oil, with the blade still turning quickly. Adjust the seasoning to taste.

Remove the chicken from the liquid and drain. Cut each breast across on the diagonal into 1cm (½ in) slices. Arrange the chicken on 6 plates and pour some sauce over each breast. Serve with a roasted pepper salad and the best new potatoes, scraped and not scrubbed.

VICTORIA BLASHFORD SNELL is one of the present cooks who creates tasty morsels in the test kitchen and café at the back of Books for Cooks. She has been cooking since she was very young, initially as a way to supplement her acting career. Now completely enveloped in the food world, she cooks daily at the shop.

As a result of her food being so popular, Victoria now demonstrates the dishes that customers have tasted in the small flat above the shop. Her style of teaching is, reassuringly, from the 'slosh it in' school of cookery, coupled with lots of professional tips which actually make the informality work.

Victoria often cooks this pistachio meringue for the customers. Books for Cooks is well known for meringues and this recipe is actually an idea of Annie Bell's, the instigator of the test kitchen in 1988. Annie has now moved and she is currently the chief food writer for British *Vogue* magazine.

Pistachio Meringues

Serves 6

5 egg whites
salt
300g (10oz) caster sugar
100g (3½oz) pistachio nuts, shelled and ground
300ml (½ pint) double cream
225g (8oz) raspberries
sprigs of mint, to decorate

Preheat the oven to 180°C/350°F/gas mark 4.

Line two baking sheets with parchment paper (also known as waxed or baking paper). Whisk the egg whites with a pinch of salt until stiff. Add the sugar, a tablespoon at a time, whisking well after each addition. When the mixture is very thick and glossy, fold in the pistachio nuts.

Divide the meringue mixture between the 2 baking sheets to form 2 rounds of 20cm (8in) in diameter. Bake for 5 minutes in the preheated oven, then lower the temperature to 140°C/275°F/gas mark 1 and bake for 1 hour. Leave to cool on the parchment paper.

Whisk the double cream until thick. Sandwich the two meringues together with about three-quarters of the cream and the raspberries, reserving a few for the top. Spread the top of the meringue with the rest of the cream. Decorate with the remaining raspberries and a few sprigs of mint.

The Bishop of London

London House, 8 Barton Street, Westminster, London SW1P 3NE.

THE FORMER BISHOP OF LONDON, Dr Daniel Hope, gave me this simple recipe just before the announcement of his appointment as Archbishop of York. I've included it as an example of how one of the busiest men in London adds sweetness to life! Thick full-fat Greek yogurt or set natural yogurt work best for this recipe. Granulated sugar is best used for the extra sugar sprinkled over the top, to give a little crunch to the pudding.

Yogurt Ambrosia

Serves 6

300ml (¹/₂ pint) Greek yogurt
300ml (¹/₂ pint) double cream
about 4 tablespoons soft,
light brown sugar
extra granulated sugar, to serve

Whip the yogurt and cream together until they become light and thick. Pour the cream mixture into 6 ramekin dishes and sprinkle each one fairly thickly with brown sugar.

Either put the dishes on a large plate and put the plate inside a plastic bag, or cover each dish with cling film. Leave to chill in the refrigerator all day or overnight.

This dessert must be left for about 6-8 hours, to allow the sugar to go to syrup and mingle with the cream. Sprinkle each dish with more sugar just before serving.

The British Museum

Great Russell Street, London WC1B 3DG. Tel: 0171 636 1555

THE CAFÉ AT THE British Museeum has a good selection of dishes, with the menu changing daily to incorporate the special dishes of the day – created by the chef according to season.

The more formal setting of the restaurant will charge the same prices for similar dishes if the café is full, as it often is. The dish below is a popular main course dish from the cold buffet.

Avocado Filled with Caponata and Feta Cheese

Serves 6

For the caponata:

1 large aubergine, chopped
salt
6 tablespoons olive oil
6 sticks celery, chopped
1 onion, chopped
400g (14oz) can tomatoes or 450g (1lb) tomatoes skinned and chopped
2 tablespoons caster sugar
4 tablespoons red wine vinegar
1 tablespoon ground nutmeg
salt and pepper
1 teaspoon capers, rinsed
12 black olives pitted and roughly chopped
2 tablespoons fresh parsley, chopped

For the dressing:

150ml (¼ pint) olive oil
zest of 1 lemon
2 teaspoons white wine vinegar
6 basil leaves, shredded
freshly milled pepper and salt

3 large ripe avocado pears
175g (6oz) feta cheese, cut into 6 slices

Fresh basil leaves, to garnish

To make the caponata put the aubergine in a colander, sprinkle with salt and set aside for 30 minutes to 1 hour. Press gently to extract as much water as possible, then dry on kitchen paper or a clean tea towel.

Heat 4 tablespoons of olive oil in a heavy-based frying pan. Sauté the celery until brown. Remove using a slotted spoon and set aside. Fry the aubergine in the same oil, until browned and tender, adding a little extra oil if necessary. Set aside to cool.

Add the remaining oil to the pan, and sauté the onion until golden. Add the tomatoes and simmer for 15 minutes until thick, stirring occasionally. Add the sugar, vinegar and nutmeg and cook for a further 10 minutes, until you have a rich sweet and sour sauce, stirring occasionally. Add a little salt and plenty of pepper. Stir in the capers, olives. parsley, aubergine and celery. Taste and adjust the seasoning, then set aside to cool.

To make the dressing, mix all the ingredients together and season.

To finish the dish cut the avocados in half and remove the stones. Brush the flesh with a little dressing to stop discolouration. Carefully fill each hollow with caponata, top with a slice of feta cheese and then pour over the remaining dressing. Garnish with a basil leaf. Serve with couscous salad and crusty bread.

Chalmers and Gray

67 Notting Hill Gate, London W11. Tel: 0171 221 6177

JOHN GRAY SET UP the fishmongers Chalmers and Gray in Notting Hill Gate, 11 years ago. He was a marketing director for Cadburys Schweppes, but saw the need for a good fishmongers in Central London. They have a very good reputation, supplying only the best quality of fish for which their customers are willing to pay. Their fish buyer purchases the fish directly from the major ports, such as Aberdeen, Grimsby, South Shields and Brighton as well as Cornish ports. They always supply fresh fish and never sell frozen. John says that they would rather not sell the variety if it can't be bought fresh – this puts the price at a premium on fish such as sea bass and red snapper, but they will not compromise on the quality. There are many different quality gradings with fish, cod alone having six different levels, and their fish buyer will always buy the top level. The staff at Chambers and Gray are skilled fishmongers – and I have had first hand experience of this as I use the shop to supply me with fish for photography shoots. It's very important for these that the fish should be the freshest I can buy, so it looks good in the shot and also that it is prepared in the correct way.

They boil their own lobsters and crabs in the shop and deliver free daily in central London. Here is John's recipe for turbot.

Fillet of Turbot with Herb Sauce

Serves 2

2 skinned pieces of turbot fillet, between 175g-225g (6-8oz) each
600ml (1 pint) court bouillon
(bayleaves, white wine,
$^1/_2$ teaspoon salt, water)
4 tablespoons lemon juice
$^1/_2$ teaspoon Dijon mustard
1 tablespoon each of chopped fresh dill and chives

Preheat the oven to 200°C/400°F/gas mark 6. Place the turbot fillets in a greased tin and cover with boiling court bouillon. Place in a preheated oven for 8 minutes.

Meanwhile mix the remaining ingredients together, then heat gently in a bowl over a pan of hot water.

Drain the fish and serve the tepid sauce separately.

Mr Christian's

11 Elgin Crescent, London W11 2JA. Tel: 0171 229 0501

THIS IS AN EXCEPTIONALLY busy working delicatessen which overspills onto the outside pavement in front of the shop. With a huge variety of good breads, cheeses and salamis, a 'foodie' simply can't resist being lured inside.

This recipe also appears in Mr Christian's *Portobello Cook Book*, published in 1995 to celebrate 21 years of the delicatessen. All proceeds are going to the London Lighthouse, a local centre for people suffering from HIV or AIDS.

Wild Mushroom and Seaweed Risotto

Serves 4

50g (2oz) unsalted butter
2 tablespoons olive oil
1 onion, finely chopped
2 litres (3½ pints) vegetable stock
350g (12oz) arborio rice
50ml (2fl.oz) white wine
4 tablespoons finely grated fresh Parmesan
250g (9oz) wild mushrooms, sliced
150g (5oz) fresh seaweed, washed
(*laitue de mer*)

Heat 25g (1oz) butter plus the olive oil in a large pan and sauté the onion until soft but not brown (about 10 minutes).

In a separate pan, heat the vegetable stock until boiling. Lower the heat and simmer gently for 15 minutes.

Add the rice to the onion and cook until lightly toasted. Add the stock, one ladleful at a time, to the rice. Cook until the rice has absorbed the stock, then add another ladleful of stock. Repeat this process until all the stock has been used up or the rice is almost cooked (15-20 minutes). Add the wine and grated Parmesan and mix well together.

In a separate pan, melt the remaining butter and sauté the mushrooms for a few minutes. Stir the mushrooms and seaweed into the rice and serve immediately.

Chiaroscuro Townhouse

24 Coptic Street, London WC1A 1NT. Tel: 0171 636 2731

SALLY JAMES at Chiaroscuro has created these two dishes for us. She has earned a reputation for selecting the finest ingredients and transforming them into modern British dishes. A family affair, she and her husband run this elegant, simple restaurant in Bloomsbury. Upstairs in this building is an intimate eating room – ideal for a small private party. All the food is well-prepared, executed and seasoned – a great find in this part of London.

Chicken and Lemon Grass Salad

Serves 4

For the chicken court bouillon:
1.5 litres (2½ pints) water
4 tablespoons lemon juice or white wine vinegar
2 teaspoons salt
1 carrot
½ stick celery
1 onion, sliced
6 parsley stalks
3-4 sprigs fresh tarragon
dill or chervil (optional)
6 black peppercorns

2 chicken breasts
3 lemon grass stalks (top half only)
¼ bunch spring onions
1 red onion
3 small red chillies
½ bunch of fresh chopped mint
½ bunch of fresh chopped coriander

For the dressing mix:
juice of 3 limes
2 dessertspoons fish sauce
2 teaspoons caster sugar
2 dessertspoons sesame oil

Court bouillon: Put all the ingredients, except the peppercorns, into a covered saucepan (not aluminium). Simmer for 45 minutes, then add the peppercorns and simmer for 10 minutes more. Strain the mixture before using. The court bouillon will keep refrigerated for about one week.

Poach the chicken breasts in the court bouillon for approximately 20 minutes. Drain.

Finely slice the chicken while still warm. Finely dice all the vegetables and then mix all the ingredients together. Allow to stand at room temperature for 1 hour. Pour over the dressing mix. Serve with some finely shredded fried savoy cabbage.

Blackened Red Mullet with Caper Relish

Serves 4

For the blackening spice:
1 dessertspoon each of:
ground cumin
cayenne pepper
celery salt
dried thyme
dried ground onion flakes
dark brown sugar
plain flour

4 red mullet, about 175g (6oz)
each, filleted
clarified butter, for frying

For the caper relish:
1 red pepper, seeded
1 yellow pepper, seeded
1 red onion
1 bunch spring onions
1 red chilli, seeded
115g (4oz) jar of capers,
roughly chopped
1 bunch of fresh chopped mint
zest of 1 lemon
1 clove garlic, chopped
3 tablespoons extra virgin olive oil

Mix the ingredients for the blackening spice together and coat the red mullet fillets in spice before frying them in clarified butter, for about 2 minutes on each side. Keep warm.

Caper relish: Finely dice the peppers, onion, spring onions and chilli. Place in a bowl with the remaining ingredients and mix well.

Mound the caper relish in the middle of the plate and top with two fillets of red mullet. Serve immediately.

La Cuisinière Cookshop

81-83 Northcote Road, London SW11 6PJ. Tel: 0171 223 4487

ANNIE PRICE is Cordon-Bleu trained, and a holder with distinction of their Diploma and Advanced Certificate. On completing her training she became cook to the Master of Jesus College, Cambridge for two years before taking off to travel, and subsequently to live and work abroad for several years. Returning to the UK, she co-founded a ski tour operating company (Ski MacG) which she ran for 12 years, including vetting the chalet girls and making sure the standard of food was up to scratch! After selling the company, she spent a year working for an Antarctic expedition before setting up her cookshop, La Cuisinière, in Clapham in 1988.

Chicken in Mango Sauce

Serves 4

For the mango sauce:
1 fresh ripe mango, peeled and stoned (or 1 can mango pieces)
1 finely chopped onion
25g (1oz) butter
$^1/_2$ teaspoon grated lemon zest
1 chicken stock cube
1 tablespoon lemon juice
salt and black pepper
1 stick of celery, finely chopped
2 tablespoons chopped walnuts
60ml (2$^1/_2$fl.oz) sour cream or crème fraîche

1 tablespoon oil
25g (1oz) butter
4 chicken breasts

To prepare the sauce, purée the mango in a food processor or blender. Sweat the onion in butter until soft but not coloured. Add the mango purée, lemon zest and stock cube. Gradually stir in the lemon juice and season with salt and black pepper. Boil rapidly for 10 minutes until the sauce has reduced. The sauce can be set aside at this stage.

To cook the chicken, heat the oil in a frying pan and add the butter. When frothing, fry the chicken breasts for about 20 minutes until cooked. Place in a serving dish and keep warm.

Reheat the sauce slowly and add the celery and walnuts, then stir in the cream or crème fraîche. Do not boil once the cream has been added. Pour a little sauce over the chicken and serve the remainder separately. Serve at once.

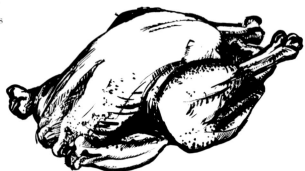

Futures

2 Exchange Square, London EC2A 2EH and at 8 Botoloph Alley, London EC3R 8DR. Tel: 0171 638 6341

FUTURES IS A vegetarian take-away outlet and delivery service in London's Broadgate development in the heart of the City. It also has another branch at its premises near Monument. Their famous porridge is a great breakfast dish (see page 222). Their lunch and supper dishes have a world-wide flavour, placing a strong emphasis upon the Orient. Bowls of spicy Thai noodles, korma, gado-gado and Polynesian spring rolls are a regular feature.

Stir Fry with Shiitake Mushrooms and Sugar Snap Peas, served with Sauté Fresh Fine Noodles and Ginger Tamari Sauce

Serves 4

For the ginger tamari sauce:
125ml (4fl.oz) sunflower oil
2 cloves garlic, crushed
1 dessertspoon finely chopped fresh
root ginger
5 dessertspoons tamari (available
from health food shops)
350g (12oz) fresh fine noodles
(available from Chinese
supermarkets)

For the stir-fry vegetables:
115g (4oz) shiitake mushrooms,
stalks trimmed off and then sliced
2 medium carrots, cut into thick
sticks 3cm (1¼in) long x 1cm (½in)
salt
2 medium courgettes, cut into
sticks as above
300g (10oz) broccoli florets
115g (4oz) baby sweetcorn
175g (6oz) sugar snap peas
300ml (½ pint) vegetable stock
1 heaped dessertspoon cornflour
2 spring onions, cut into thin slices

Heat up a quarter of the oil and add the prepared garlic and ginger. Stir occasionally. When golden brown, remove from the heat. When cool, add the tamari.

Bring a large saucepan of salted water to the boil and add the noodles. Stir, then cook for one minute. Drain and refresh them under running water and leave to drain thoroughly. In a saucepan over a medium heat with a little bit of oil, sauté the noodles for a few minutes, then set aside and keep warm.

In a wok or large saucepan, heat up the remaining oil and when quite hot add the mushrooms and carrots. Stir and cook for one minute. Season with a dash of salt and the ginger tamari sauce. Quickly toss in the courgettes, broccoli, sweetcorn and sugar snap peas, stir and cook for one minute, stirring occasionally. Season with a little salt and add in the remaining ginger tamari sauce and mix well. Add the vegetable stock.

Dissolve the cornflour in a little water and add to the pan. Stir well. Spoon the stir-fried vegetables over the warm noodles and garnish with thinly sliced spring onions. Serve immediately.

Owen Greedy

LWT, The London Television Centre, Upper Ground, London SE1 9LT. Tel: 0171 620 1620

LWT EMPLOYEES seem to be very cost-conscious when it comes to food, and here Owen Greedy explains the typical sort of meal that he finds is popular with the staff. His experience over the last ten years of cooking in London (mainly for T.V. companies) has shown that his biggest menu problem is satisfying a diverse range of customer preferences. He says 'As ever in catering the dicotemy between the cook's interests and abilities, and what his or her customers are willing to accept or try, determines the final product on the plate!' This menu he feels represents the demand he experiences for traditional recipes and the popularity of a more continental-style of eating.

Chicken with Tarragon and Tagliatelle

Serves 4

For the velouté sauce:
25g (1oz) butter
2 tablespoons flour
350ml (12fl oz) warm chicken stock
salt and freshly ground white pepper
few drops lemon juice
1 egg yolk
1 tablespoon single cream

chicken (whole, approx 1.1kg (2½lb)
¼ bottle dry white wine
150ml (¼ pint) chicken stock
1 teaspoon dried tarragon
2 tablespoons fresh tarragon
cooked tagliatelle (white and green)
tomato concassé (made from 2 tomatoes, peeled, seeded and diced)

Velouté sauce: Melt the butter in a heavy-based saucepan and stir in the flour. Stir over a low heat until straw-coloured. Remove from the heat and cool a little, then add the hot stock (see below)and stir until smooth. Return to a medium heat and stir constantly until boiling. Lower the heat, and cook very gently for 15 minutes, stirring frequently. Season with the salt and pepper and lemon juice. Stir the egg yolk into the cream in a small bowl. Stir into this a little of the hot sauce, then stir this mixture back into the sauce. Cook while stirring, until the sauce is glossy and a little thicker, but do not boil.

Cut the chicken into quarters and remove the skin, if preferred. Braise the chicken quarters in the white wine and chicken stock, with the dried tarragon, for about 40 minutes.

Remove the chicken and keep it warm. Reserve the wine/stock braising liquor and use to make the velouté sauce.

Place the cooked chicken quarters on the bed of cooked tagliatelle. Pour over the sauce, and garnish with fresh tarragon and tomato concassé.

Pear and Almond Tart

Serves 4

For the sugar paste/sweet pastry:
300g (10oz) plain flour
115g (4oz) margarine
50g (2oz) caster sugar
1 egg

575g (1¼lb) can of pear halves
225g (8oz) margarine
225g (8oz) caster sugar
5 eggs
175g (6oz) plain flour
115g (4oz) ground almonds
apricot jam
toasted almond flakes
sifted icing sugar

Preheat the oven to 180°C/350°F/gas mark 4.

To make the sweet pastry, process the flour and margarine together to form a texture resembling fine breadcrumbs. Stir in the caster sugar. Add the egg and process until the pastry pulls together in a ball. Wrap and chill for at least 30 minutes, then use it to line a 30cm/12in flan case/pie tin. Place the pear halves, at intervals, over the base of tin.

Make the sponge filling by beating the margarine and sugar until pale in colour. Whisk in the eggs, then beat in the flour and ground almonds until a dropping consistency is reached (if the mixture is too stiff, add a little extra milk).

Spoon the sponge mixture around the pears in the pastry-lined tin. Bake in the preheated oven for about 45 minutes.

When the tart is cooked, brush the top of the tart with apricot jam (heat the jam in a pan until liquid). Sprinkle with toasted flaked almonds and dust with icing sugar. Serve with plenty of crème anglaise.

Steve Hatt

88-90 Essex Road, London N1. Tel: 0171 226 3963

STEVE HATT has 'fish in his blood'; his great-grandfather started the fishmonger business in Essex Road in Islington at the turn of the century. This is very much a local fishmongers and is considered an Islington institution, with a great rapport between staff and customers.

I have often rung Steve up for advice and orders for the perfect fish I need for photography shoots. He is very knowledgeable and always has a happy, smiling face to greet you.

A quick recipe is very much his style and here he gives a tasty monkfish dish.

Marinated Monkfish

Serves 4

450g (1lb) monkfish tail, filleted, skinned and cubed
1 tablespoon olive oil
juice of 1 lemon
2/3 cloves garlic, crushed
freshly ground black pepper and salt, to taste

Marinate the monkfish in the oil, lemon juice, garlic and seasoning for 2 to 3 hours.

Sauté the fish in a hot frying pan with the marinade for 4-5 minutes. Serve with rice and either a quick provençal sauce (made from tomatoes, onion and garlic) or a dill sauce.

The same marinade can be used for stewed monkfish kebabs to cook on the barbecue.

The Imperial Arms

577 King's Road, Fulham, London SW6 2EH. Tel: 0171 736 9179

CORNELIUS O'GRADY cooks good Irish fare, specialising in fresh seafood dishes.

This is a large, family-run pub with Cornelius and his wife working behind the bar. Its location is easy to recognise with a huge wooden cut-out board standing outside the pub. The board has a caricature of Cornelius, with his apron and glasses on, making him instantly recognisable when you walk through the door and see him standing behind the bar.

Potato and Smoked Salmon Gratinée

Serves 4-6

1 kilo (2.2lb) waxy new potatoes
5 shallots
knob of butter
300ml (¹/₂ pint) double cream
black pepper
675g (1¹/₂ lb) smoked
salmon ends
parsley, to garnish

Preheat the oven to 220°C/425°F/gas mark 7.

Peel and boil the potatoes. Cut the potatoes into thickish slices and sauté them lightly with the shallots and the knob of butter until they are just beginning to turn in colour.

Pour in the cream and stir thoroughly. Chop the salmon into bite-sized pieces and stir into the potato and cream mixture.

Place at the top of the hot oven until the mixture is hot and just beginning to brown.

Garnish with parsley and serve immediately with a green salad.

Mary Lowden

Private address.

MARY LOWDEN HAS BEEN COOKING in the city for some years, preparing directors' lunches. Nowadays, the trend is very much towards lighter meals at midday, such as fish or a light snack, but luckily where she cooks today the bankers still enjoy having a dessert. Here she shares three of her favourite recipes that she regularly cooks for her clients.

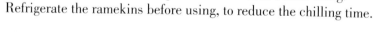

Cream Cheese Mousse with a Raspberry Purée

Serves 6

1 tablespoon powdered gelatine
450g (1lb) cream cheese
1 tablespoon caster sugar
2 eggs, separated
4 tablespoons milk
175g (6oz) frozen raspberries,
defrosted
caster sugar
framboise liqueur
115g (4oz) fresh raspberries
6 fresh mint sprigs

Sprinkle the gelatine over 3 tablespoons of water in a small bowl and leave to soak for 2 minutes. Place the bowl over a pan of simmering water and stir until the gelatine has dissolved.

Place the cream cheese, sugar, egg yolks and milk in a blender or food processor and blend until smooth. Mix in the gelatine. Leave in a cool place for 30 minutes, or until the mixture starts to set.

Whisk the egg whites until they just hold their shape and then fold them into the mousse mixture. Place the mixture in 6 individual ramekins and refrigerate for 2 hours.

Sieve the defrosted raspberries, and add the sugar and framboise to taste.

To serve, place each ramekin in a bowl of hot water for 6 seconds, loosen with a round-bladed knife and turn out on to a plate. Spoon some raspberry purée around each dessert and decorate with fresh raspberries and mint sprigs.

Hints: Use a ladle when sieving raspberries.
Leave the cream at room temperature for 1 hour before using.
Refrigerate the ramekins before using, to reduce the chilling time.

Poached Figs with Apple and Sultana Parcels, served with Cinnamon Ice Cream

Serves 6

For the ice cream:
2 egg yolks
25g (1oz) caster sugar
$1/4$ teaspoon ground cinnamon
300ml ($1/2$ pint) double cream

2 Cox's apples
1 lemon
2 tablespoons sultanas
50g (2oz) unsalted butter
6 sheets of filo pastry
6 figs
125ml (4fl.oz) port

Preheat the oven to 200°C/400°F/gas mark 6.

To make the ice cream: Cream the egg yolks, sugar and cinnamon together. Bring the double cream to the boil and whisk into the egg mixture, then set aside to cool. Once cool, place the mixture in a suitable container and freeze, beating every 30 minutes until firm.

Grease a baking tray. Peel, core and roughly chop the apples. Finely grate the rind and squeeze the juice from the lemon. Mix the chopped apples, lemon rind and juice and sultanas together. Melt the butter. Cut the pastry sheets into 4 squares each. Brush 4 pastry squares with butter and layer into a star. Place a heaped tablespoon of apple mixture into the centre of each star and draw up the sides to make a parcel. Repeat to make 6 parcels. Place on the baking tray and bake in the preheated oven for 10 minutes.

Gently poach the figs in the port for 5 minutes and serve with some syrup and an apple parcel on a plate with a spoonful of cinnamon ice cream.

Pears and Ginger Baked in Puff Pastry

Serves 8

15g ($1/2$oz) unsalted butter
115g (4oz) stem ginger
2 lemons
4 ripe Williams pears
450g (1lb) puff pastry
4 tablespoons apricot jam
300ml ($1/2$ pint) double cream, whipped

Preheat the oven to 200°C/400°F/gas mark 6.

Grease a baking tray with the butter. Chop the stem ginger and squeeze the juice from the lemons. Peel the pears, cut them in half lengthways and core them. Place the pear halves, lemon juice and ginger in a bowl and turn a few times.

Cut 8 thin strips from the rolled pastry and then cut the remaining pastry into 8 squares. Place a pear half on to each square, trim the pastry to leave a narrow border around the pear half. Dampen the pastry edge with water and run one of the pastry strips around the pear. Press down firmly. Spoon over the reserved stem ginger. Bake the pears in the preheated oven for 20 minutes.

Meanwhile, boil the reserved lemon juice, stem ginger syrup and jam in a saucepan until the mixture becomes syrupy in consistency. When the pears are cooked, spoon over the syrup. Serve hot with the double cream.

Hint: Use a melon baller to remove the pear cores.

Milburn's Restaurant

The Victoria and Albert Museum, South Kensington, London SW7 2RL. Tel: 0171 938 8500

MILBURN'S RESTAURANTS LTD. are very close to my heart. It is in their café, in the undercroft at Durham Cathedral, where I first started earning my living by cooking at 16. The food was then, and is still now, freshly prepared daily, to no-nonsense recipes that work. I used to make the quiche lorraines, scones and mayonnaise, the latter forming two of the recipes which Michael Milburn, the company's owner, has given to me. The connection with the Milburn family firm from Sunderland goes back even further with my family. My mother's twenty-first birthday cake was made by Leslie Milburn's bakery (Michael's father) in Sunderland, and my grandmother, clad in her Sunday best ('hat and all') used to meet her sisters on a Saturday morning for coffee in

Scones

Makes about 30 scones

900g (2lb) plain flour
a pinch of salt (or more for cheese scones)
50g (2oz) baking powder
125ml (4fl.oz) oil
50g (2oz) caster sugar (substitute grated cheese if you wish)
approx. 600ml (1 pint) milk, or milk and water mixed
beaten egg or milk, to glaze

Preheat the oven to 200°C, 400°F, gas mark 6.
Sift together the flour, salt and baking powder. Make a well in the flour in the mixing bowl or on the work surface and pour in the oil. Add the sugar or cheese and enough liquid to make a very soft batter. Mix until this is shiny.

Press out to 1cm (½in) thick, on a floured work surface. Cut out shapes with a cutter and brush with egg or milk. If making cheese scones, sprinkle with a good pinch of grated Cheddar cheese.

Bake in the preheated hot oven for approximately 15 minutes.

the high quality café, stocked from the bakery. I can remember going with Nana for coffee there and having these very same scones.

Their company now run the restaurants in the British Museum, Victoria and Albert Museum, Museum of London and the Royal Academy of Art in London. They also run the Pump Rooms in Bath and the café at York Minster.

Michael says: 'This is the scone recipe from our bakery days in Sunderland, although we make it in rather bigger quantities. It carries a very large volume of liquid and is therefore rather difficult to handle. However, a liberal dose of dusting flour on the work surface will assist'. The mayonnaise recipe is one that I used when I first started cooking at Milburn's.

Mayonnaise

Makes about 600ml (1 pint)

2 eggs
juice and zest of half a lemon or
1 tablespoon white wine vinegar
salt and pepper
splash of water
600ml (1 pint) olive oil or mixture of
olive and sunflower oil

Optional extras:
crushed garlic
chopped fresh herbs
curry paste
grain mustard

This system is for those in a hurry, those who have everything on the table ready for lunch and then remember that the mayonnaise was finished at the last meal. It is made with a hand-held blender and a tall plastic jug.

Put the eggs, lemon juice or vinegar, seasoning and a splash of water into a jug. Place a hand-held blender over the eggs, pour a little of the oil in and start blending. Keep the oil pouring in a steady stream until all the oil has been used up. If the mayonnaise is too thick, add some more water. Add the lemon zest and any of the optional extras, taste and adjust the seasoning.

Mohammed al Fayed

Harrods, Knightsbridge, London SW1. Tel: 0171 730 1234

MOHAMMED AL FAYED, chairman of Harrods and L'Hotel Ritz, Paris, shares the secrets of his favourite oyster recipe.

Any meal which begins with oysters tends to be special. I love oysters and so did Londoners in the early years of the century – there were oyster stalls on hundreds of street corners and the shellfish were cheap (see page 216). Over the years they have become more expensive, which is a shame because they are so versatile as an appetiser or as a first course.

While it is one of life's great pleasures to eat an oyster simply, with a dash of lemon juice and perhaps a little Tabasco sauce if you like the heat, they are also a versatile shellfish and may be cooked in many different ways. The recipe below is recommended by Mohammed al Fayed as a delicious way to serve oysters.

Oysters with Herb Garlic Butter

Serves 4

5 tablespoons plus 1 teaspoon butter, softened
1 tablespoon fresh parsley, finely chopped
2 garlic cloves, crushed
juice of 2 limes
4 tablespoons brandy
15 fresh oysters, preferably Belon
225g (8oz) cooked lobster or crabmeat
2 medium tomatoes, peeled, seeded and diced
5 tablespoons plus 1 teaspoon tomato ketchup
5 tablespoons plus 1 teaspoon caviare
6 tablespoons grated fresh Parmesan
rock salt

In a small bowl, combine the butter, parsley and garlic and mix to a smooth paste. Set aside.

In a medium bowl, combine the lime juice and the brandy. Shuck the oysters and place them in the lime/brandy mixture. Discard the top shell and rinse the bottom shell clear of all sand and any other debris.

In each shell, layer the following ingredients in order: one teaspoon of herb butter, one drained oyster, 15g ($^1/_2$oz) cooked lobster or crab meat, a bit of diced tomato, a teaspoon of ketchup and a teaspoon of caviare. Flatten the mound slightly with the back of a spoon and sprinkle with half a tablespoon of Parmesan.

Place the oysters on a bed of rock salt in a double saucepan. Boil for 3-4 minutes. Serve immediately.

Museum of London

London Wall, London EC2Y 5HN. Tel: 0171 600 3699

THE MUSEUM OF LONDON'S CAFÉ is one of the smaller of the Milburn establishments. It serves the usual selection from the Milburn's menu, with freshly-made scones, quiches and chef's 'specials of the day'. Relax over the invigorating taste of high quality teas, and remember to sample one of the best museum-café cups of coffee around.

Pecan Pie

Serves 6

For the pastry:
175g (6oz) plain flour
pinch of salt
75g (3oz) butter
40g (1¹/₂oz) lard or white fat
1 level teaspoon caster sugar
1 egg, beaten
2 tablespoons milk or water

For the filling:
25g (1oz) butter
175g (6oz) soft brown sugar,
light or dark
3 large eggs, beaten
175ml (6fl.oz) maple syrup
1 teaspoon vanilla essence
good pinch of salt
115g (4oz) pecan nuts
syrup or apricot jam, for glazing

Preheat the oven to 190°C/375°F/gas mark 5.

To make the pastry, sift the flour and salt into a bowl. Add the butter and lard and rub them into the flour. Stir in the sugar, then add the beaten egg and enough milk or water to bind. Knead lightly and chill for 30 minutes.

Roll the pastry out and use to line a 20cm (8in) fluted flan ring, tin or dish. Bake blind in the preheated oven.

To make the filling, cream the butter and sugar together, then gradually beat in the eggs, followed by the maple syrup, vanilla essence and salt. Arrange the pecan nuts in the pastry case, flat side down, then carefully pour the filling over the nuts. Return to the oven at 190°C/375°F/gas mark 5 for 35-40 minutes. The filling rises quickly, but will fall again on cooling. Glaze with syrup or warmed apricot jam.

New Quebec Cuisine

13, New Quebec Street, London W1 7DD. Tel: 0171 723 0128

LONDON IS A CITY FULL OF COSMOPOLITAN, sophisticated people who share a love of good food. So when New Quebec Cuisine became an approved caterer at the Royal Festival Hall in February, 1995, it was no mistake.

To quote Sharon Davy, Managing Director of New Quebec Cuisine, 'Show me another pleasure like dinner which comes every day and lasts an hour'. She believes that New Quebec Cuisine's catering reflects the marvellous food available in our capital city. To illustrate this she has selected the following main course which has some strong and distinctive tastes that you will remember.

Boned Breast and Thigh of Guinea Fowl, served with Dried Ceps in a Classic Light Wine Sauce and decorated with Fresh Asparagus Tips

Serves 4

2 guinea fowl
1.2 litres (2 pints) stock, made as instructed in recipe
25g (1oz) ceps (dried wild mushrooms)
300ml ($^1/_2$ pint) red wine
1 tablespoon cornflour
seasoning
8 small asparagus tips

Note: All the preparation needs to be done the day before cooking.

Bone the guinea fowl, keeping the skin on the breast. Bone and skin the thigh. Roll the thigh, place the breast on top and secure with two cocktail sticks (place in the fridge until needed).

Make a strong, brown stock with the carcass and drumsticks. Place the guinea fowl carcass in a large pan, heat until very hot, turning it as it browns. Add 1 bayleaf, 1 quartered onion, 2 celery sticks, 1 chopped carrot and 1.2 litres (2 pints) water. Simmer, uncovered for about 1 hour, then cool and strain. (Make this the day before and leave it in the fridge overnight so that you can take off the excess fat). Soak the ceps overnight, in cold water.

Make a sauce by mixing together the cep liquid, stock and red wine. Bring to the boil, reduce by half and then thicken with cornflour. Simmer gently for 3 minutes, stirring.

To roast the guinea fowl, season the birds well, then roast them in a preheated oven at 230°C/450°F/gas mark 8, for 10-15 minutes, depending on their size.

To serve, pour the sauce on to a plate and place the roasted guinea fowl on top of the sauce with the ceps. Criss-cross two small asparagus tips on top of the ceps to finish.

Serve with potato dauphinoise. To make this, firstly peel and finely slice potatoes, then layer them in a baking dish with Gruyère cheese, thinly sliced onions, salt, pepper and cream. Bake in a preheated oven at 180°C/350°F/gas mark 4, for approximately 45 minutes or until slightly browned.

Paxton & Whitfield Ltd

93 Jermyn Street, London SW1Y 6JE. Tel: 0171 930 0259

THE OWNER OF Paxton & Whitfield, Arthur Cunningham, a high-quality cheesemonger in Jermyn Street, gave me this recipe. The origins of his company are in the eighteenth century.

Arthur says: 'I really like my cheese as a cheese course rather than cooked. It is so wonderful eaten simply by itself – maybe with a little salad – and is certainly preferable to most desserts. I tend not to use cooked cheese dishes, but I do appreciate that others find cheese so very useful, versatile and delicious in cooking.

'I have therefore chosen a dish where the cheese is not overwhelming – cloying and stringy as it can sometimes be when cooked – but rather adds a delicious light extra touch to complete a dish which would otherwise lack something.'

Venison Medallions with Stilton Soufflé

Serves 4

4 x 115g (4oz) medallions of
venison saddle
1 tablespoon olive oil
2 medium-sized leeks
25g (1oz) butter
25g (1oz) plain flour
200ml (7fl.oz) milk
3 eggs, separated
75g (3oz) grated Stilton
salt and pepper

Preheat the oven to 230°C/450°F/gas mark 8. Seal the meat on all sides in a little olive oil in a very hot pan. Put aside to cool.

Cut the leeks in half lengthways, blanch in boiling water for 1 minute, then cool. Tie strips of leek around each medallion, leaving 1cm (½in) above the level of the meat.

Melt the butter in a pan and add the flour. Cook for ½ minute then whisk in the milk. Heat the sauce until it has thickened. Simmer gently for 2 minutes, stirring. Season well, then whisk in the egg yolks and Stilton. Whisk the egg whites until stiff and fold them gently into the mixture.

Divide the mixture into four and fill the cavity left by the leeks on each medallion. Cook on a greased tray in the preheated oven for 12-14 minutes. Serve immediately.

Princess Grace Hospital

42-52 Nottingham Place, London W1M 3FD. Tel: 0171 486 1234

PAUL KIMPSON, executive head chef at the Princess Grace Hospital, has cooked delights for a host of famous patients, including the football star Paul Gascoigne, known as Gazza. Here he shares two of his favourite recipes.

Steaming a fresh lobster quickly is perhaps the best way to appreciate the natural, delicate flavour and texture of lobster meat. It is also the way that Paul likes doing it to tempt his patient's appetites at the Princess Grace Hospital.

Spring Lamb Noisettes Cussy

Serves 4

900g (2lb) trimmed fillet of
spring lamb
175g (6oz) butter
75g (3oz) finely chopped shallots
seasoning
2 slices bread, each halved to
give 4 croûtons
oil for frying
1 small can of tiny artichoke hearts
115g (4oz) puréed chanterelles
50g (2oz) fresh breadcrumbs
4 cooked kidneys
2 tablespoons madeira

Cut the fillets of lamb into medallions or noisettes. Sauté the noisettes in butter, add the shallots and sauté for 3 minutes, then season. Shallow fry the quartered slices of bread on both sides in oil until golden. Arrange the noisettes and shallots on the fried croûtons.

Garnish with little artichoke hearts filled with chanterelle purée and sprinkled with breadcrumbs and cooked chopped kidneys.

Serve with a demi-glace sauce made from the reduced juices diluted with Madeira.

Freshly Steamed Scottish Lobster Salad with a Ginger Soy Sauce

1 x 1.4kg (3lbs) fresh
Scottish lobster
3 tablespoons salt

For the ginger soy sauce:
2 tablespoons light soy sauce
2 tablespoons red wine vinegar
2 tablespoons caster sugar
2 tablespoons grated fresh
root ginger
1 crushed clove garlic, if desired

Place the lobster in a large bowl. Slowly run cold water continuously over it. Add 3 tablespoons of salt and allow to stand for 1 hour to eliminate sediments in the lobster.

Rinse and drain the lobster. Steam quickly over a high heat for 15-17 minutes. While the lobster is steaming, combine the ginger sauce ingredients. Mix well, strain the sauce through a sieve, discard the solids and set aside.

Make up a nice, crispy, assorted leaf salad. To serve, crack open the lobster and remove the meat. Arrange over the salad. Serve with some ginger sauce and thin slices of brown bread and butter.

Note: West coast lobster are normally larger and may take a little longer to steam.

Bon Appetit!

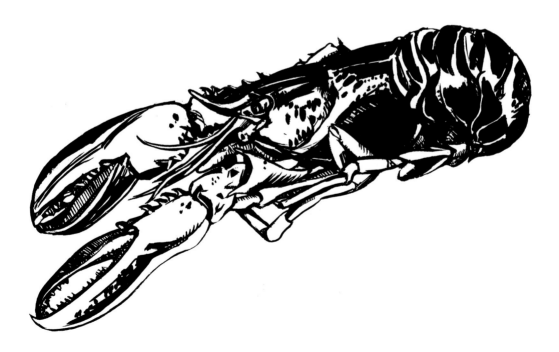

The People's Palace

Royal Festival Hall, South Bank, London SE1 8XX. Tel: 0171928 9999

GARY RHODES first came to public attention when he appeared in *Hot Chefs* on television. He went on to present a highly successful television series, *Rhodes around Britain*. He carried on his successful career while continuing as the head chef of The Greenhouse restaurant. He is now at the newly opened People's Palace at the Royal Festival Hall in the South Bank Centre. A great carnivore friend relished this dish at The People's Palace. Gary says the combination of tastes and textures in this recipe are simple and delicious! The bite from the black pepper and the sweetness of the meat react beautifully with the tang of capers and mayonnaise. There is, quite simply, no better way to enjoy it than on crispy toast with soft-fried eggs!

Open Peppered Beef Sandwich with Fried Eggs

Serves 4-6

700-900g (1½lb-2lb) rib of beef, trimmed and tied
finely crushed black peppercorns
salt and pepper
1 thick slice of wholewheat (or other good quality) bread per portion
olive oil
1 onion
1 open lettuce, picked, washed and seasoned with salt
vinaigrette
mayonnaise
2 eggs (per portion)
75g (3oz) butter
4-6 teaspoons fine capers
chopped parsley, to garnish

Preheat the oven to 200°C/400°F/gas mark 6.
Roll the rib of beef in the crushed black peppercorns until fully covered. Season with salt. Fry the beef in a hot pan or roasting tin on top of the stove turning until it is completely sealed. The beef can now be roasted in the preheated oven for 30-40 minutes (to achieve a medium to medium/well done roast).

The beef should be left to rest for a minimum of 20 minutes before carving. Meat is at its most tender when served just warm.

While the beef is resting, brush the sliced bread with a little olive oil and cook under a preheated hot grill. Slice the onion into rings. Season the onion rings and salad leaves and dress both with vinaigrette or some more olive oil.

Spoon some mayonnaise liberally on to the toast and sit two or three salad leaves on top with a few onion rings. Fry the eggs in a little oil and butter. Place the beef on the top of the onions and cover with the fried eggs. Sprinkle the capers over the eggs and garnish with parsley.

Richoux

Piccadilly, 172 Piccadilly, London W1. Tel: 0171 493 2204

A CLASSIC FAVOURITE of mine, the Richoux tea room and restaurant in Piccadilly is the place to have a snack. Welsh rarebit is one of my favourites and here is the delicious Richoux recipe.

This is a traditional London café offering great tea and coffee, breakfast, lunchtime and supper dishes in the comfortable surroundings of an old fashioned tea room/restaurant. It has a small, separate area for lighter snacks on comfortable chairs, where the daily newspapers are available. It is a very pleasant place to spend a welcome respite from the bustle of Piccadilly.

Welsh Rarebit

Serves 1

25g (1oz) butter
15g (¹/₂oz) plain flour
150ml (¹/₄ pint) milk
115g (4oz) Cheddar cheese, grated
1 egg yolk
1 teaspoon mustard powder
1 teaspoon Worcestershire sauce
pinch of freshly grated nutmeg
pinch of salt and freshly
ground black pepper
toast, to serve

Melt the butter in a pan. Add the flour and mix well. Cook on a gentle heat for a few minutes without colouring. Gradually add the cold milk off the heat and mix to a smooth sauce. Allow to simmer for a few minutes, stirring well. Add the grated cheese off the heat.

Allow the cheese to melt slowly over a gentle heat, stir until smooth. Add the egg yolk to the hot mixture. Remove from heat. Add the other seasonings and allow the mixture to cool slightly before spreading on toast to serve.

Rosslyn Hill Delicatessen

56 Rosslyn Hill, London NW3. Tel: 0171 794 9210

HELEN SHERMAN IS THE VERY ENERGETIC owner of the famous Rosslyn Hill Delicatessen in Hampstead, which is one of North London's best-known secrets.

The place buzzes at the weekend, as local inhabitants of Hampstead, and others from much farther afield, rush to get the freshly baked croissants and the *pains au chocolat* which are the best in town.

Helen can usually be found in the middle of all this fray, chatting away to the regulars who use this as their weekend meeting place, to catch up on their various week's events.

Starting out in her career as a scientist, she changed track and now combines the busy role of a solicitor with the equally (if not more) hectic life of the deli, as well as spending time with her family and one very large dog, Indi.

Food has always been her consuming passion and when the chance came to buy the deli in 1990, she jumped in with both feet – and the

Chicken Roulade Stuffed with Julienne of Vegetables served with a Saffron Sauce

Serves 6

6 boned chicken breasts
fine strips of carrot, courgettes,
Chinese leaves and leek (or any
combination of seasonal vegetables
to give colour)
1 tablespoon sesame oil
1 tablespoon plain flour
1 shallot, finely chopped
1 tablespoon sesame oil
2 tablespoons dry white wine
300 ml ($^1/_2$ pint) chicken stock
2-3 tablespoons double cream
pinch of saffron powder

Place the chicken breasts between two sheets of cling film, and flatten with a rolling pin.

Sauté the strips (known as a julienne) of vegetables in a small amount of sesame oil until 'al dente'.

Season and lightly flour one side of the chicken breasts. Add some of the vegetables lengthwise, roll the chicken breasts into a sausage shape and wrap in clingfilm, tying firmly at both ends. Place the chicken into a saucepan of boiling water and poach for about 10-12 minutes.

Meanwhile, gently sauté the shallots in some sesame oil. Pour in the dry white wine and chicken stock then boil the sauce rapidly until it is reduced by half. Finally add the cream and a pinch of saffron powder.

When the chicken is done, unwrap the clingfilm, cut the roulades into 1cm ($^1/_2$in) slices across and arrange overlapping slices with the sauce on the side. Serve with fluffy white rice.

odd wooden spoon and saucepan – and set about importing delicacies from around the world.

There is a large American section at the deli, and a selection of over 120 cheeses. Pastries, croissants, ready meals and salads are made daily in the busy kitchens.

'It's a busy life, and frequently I find myself at my desk at home at 3am not having the time or inclination to sleep', she says. 'But I wouldn't have it any other way.' Life is definitely a bowl of cherries for Helen – along with any other fruit that can be crammed in!

How she finds time to do any cooking it's hard to say, but both of these recipes have been devised using ingredients from the delicatessen.

Ginger Ice Cream

Serves 6

2 eggs
2 tablespoons caster sugar
150ml (¹/₄ pint) double cream
Relvoir ginger cordial
Rosslyn stem ginger in syrup

Whisk the eggs and sugar together until fluffy and light. Whisk the cream in a separate bowl until fairly stiff, then add to the egg and sugar mixture. Then add the cordial to taste, remembering that freezing will weaken the flavour.

Add some chopped stem ginger for further flavour. Pour the mixture into a shallow, freezer-proof container. Freeze until firm.

Place the ice cream in the fridge for 30 minutes to soften and bring out the flavour prior to serving. Serve with thin sweet biscuits.

Royal Academy of Art Café

Burlington House, Piccadilly, London W1V 0DS. Tel: 0171 439 7438

THIS IS THE LARGEST, in terms of numbers of customers, of the Milburn's Museum cafés. It has a renowned menu, popular with museum visitors, downstairs in the Academy. This café has the atmosphere befitting a learned institution, with its subdued decor. There are always large numbers of people around at the self-service counters, but an efficient staff ensure quick service-time, even when there are the huge numbers generated through the special exhibitions.

Daube of Beef

Serves 6

4lb (1.8kg) braising steak cut into 75g (3oz) cubes
1 litre (1³/₄ pints) Cotes du Rhone
50ml (2fl.oz) red wine vinegar
50ml (2fl.oz) brandy or cognac
1 tablespoon lightly crushed black peppercorns
3 large onions, coarsely chopped
2 celery sticks
5 carrots, cut into slices
1 veal trotter, cut in half lengthways
2 tablespoons dripping
salt and pepper
6 unpeeled garlic cloves
4 large tomatoes, peeled, seeded and chopped
1 bouquet garni
2 wide strips of orange zest
1 tablespoon chopped thyme

Marinate the beef overnight in the red wine, vinegar, brandy or cognac, together with black peppercorns, half the onions, celery and carrots. Cook the veal trotter in boiling water for 10 minutes. Drain the beef, keeping the marinade.

Over a high heat melt 1 tablespoon dripping in a heavy frying pan, then brown the meat on all sides. Add the remaining carrots and salt and pepper.

In a large ovenproof casserole, sweat the remaining onions in 1 tablespoon dripping. Add the beef and carrots, and the unpeeled garlic cloves, and sweat for 5 minutes over a high heat. Add the tomatoes, strain in the marinade, then bring to the boil. Add the trotter, bouquet garni, orange rind, thyme and remaining celery, then cook very gently for 2¹/₂ hours, stirring occasionally.

Take out the trotter and discard any bones, fat or gristle, then cut the meat into cubes and place it back in the daube. Remove the garlic cloves. Taste and adjust the seasoning. Serve with boiled rice or potatoes.

Alternatively, this dish may be refrigerated overnight and eaten cold with a crusty baguette and some beaujolais.

Scotts Restaurant and Oyster Bar

20 Mount Street, London W1. Tel: 0171 629 5248

MARK HOLMES is the head chef at the renowned Scotts Restaurant and Oyster Bar in Mayfair. Synonymous with glamour in the 1930s and 40s, Scotts was referred to in the British film 'The Great Escape'. The prisoners of war it featured had no hesitation in agreeing to rendezvous at Scotts if they made it home. Famous for its soul and wit, Scotts was also known as the favourite London haunt of many film stars and celebrities. These included Marlene Dietrich, Charlie Chaplin, Shirley Temple, Arthur Miller and even Marilyn Monroe.

Today's restaurant has a simpler approach with its reputation for classic seafood and British cuisine – traditional British food with a lighter, modern accent. This delicious recipe reflects this.

Grilled Tiger Prawns with a Bloody Mary Relish

Serves 4

For the relish:
2 beef tomatoes, skinned and seeded
2 shallots, chopped
25ml (1fl.oz) vodka
1 dessertspoon Worcestershire sauce
5 drops of Tabasco sauce
pinch of celery salt
1 dessertspoon lemon juice
black pepper
50ml (2fl.oz) olive oil
50ml (2fl.oz) fresh crushed tomato flesh ('pomi') or passata

For the lemon dressing:
1 medium lemon
good pinch of caster sugar
pinch of salt
dollop of Dijon mustard
50ml (2fl.oz) good olive oil

24 tiger prawns
mixed lettuce leaves
2 shallots, chopped
1 bunch fresh chives, chopped
1 lemon, cut into wedges

First make the relish, combining all the ingredients and mixing them well. Add more of each to taste if required. Prepare the lemon dressing, mixing together the juice and zest of the lemon, caster sugar, salt, Dijon mustard and olive oil. Add more of each to taste if required. (Note that the refrigerated shelf life of both the relish and dressing is no more than 1 month).

Peel the tiger prawns, removing the shell and head but leaving the tail shell on. Cook the prawns over a hot charcoal grill or barbecue until they are cooked through. This will take about 1 minute for each side, depending on the heat of the grill.

Wash the lettuce leaves thoroughly and shred them. Toss the leaves in a little of the dressing. Add the chopped shallots and place a small handful on each plate.

Spoon some Bloody Mary relish over the lettuce and place the cooked prawns on top of the relish. Sprinkle liberally with chives and serve with a wedge of lemon.

Veronica's Restaurant

3 Hereford Road, London W2. Tel: 0171 229 5079/221 1452

VERONICA AND I FIRST MET when we were both sitting as guinea pigs at a waiters' competition in a London hotel, ready to be served with a three-course lunch, during which we had to mark our waiters' service. With plenty of opportunities to talk between courses I found out more about her unique catering company and restaurant.

There has been a restaurant at No.3 Hereford Road, in a Victorian stucco-fronted parade of Grade II listed buildings, since the turn of the century. Before the second World War it was a local restaurant called the 'Green Parrot', frequented by actors, and in the 1950s it was bought by Clement Freud and Robert Morley. Staffed by resting actors, it became known as a restaurant for show business people.

In the early 60s the restaurant was purchased by Franco who changed its name to 'Chez Franco' and introduced the then highly fashionable Italian style of food. In 1971, the ownership switched to Bruno and Carlo, who altered the menu to Franco/Italian food and the restaurant enjoyed popularity from local customers in the area. The food reached a high standard and business flourished until the late 1970s, when film studios moved out of the area and it waned.

Veronica, living in the area since 1963, witnessed and enjoyed the various patronages and menus until 1982, when Bruno and Carlo suggested that she should come into the restaurant as manageress and revitalise the business. In fact she purchased the restaurant a few months later and made renovations to the interior to produce a cosy, warm and flower-filled room decorated in apricot and grey.

Throughout the next year, subtle changes took place within the menu to widen the scope to include some English dishes. Since then the English dishes have gradually overtaken the menu to make it totally English, with themed menu changes taking place monthly. Though Veronica started to experiment with English dishes at a time when English food was not fashionable, the beginning of the 90s saw an increasing interest in British food and a return to our culinary heritage. The regional and historical themes – such as Scottish Food or Edwardian Revival of London Bread Dishes – are presented in a modern and innovative way and for this type of cooking the restaurant has received accolades and awards.

Veronica's Restaurant offers home-made and imaginative interpretations of unusual and classical favourites from early English cookery, such as a medieval Midlands recipe, Pershore Baked Plums with Almonds, or Elizabethan Pork with Fresh and Dried Fruits, or Tudor Salamagundy. It also explores food from the more recent past 'like mother used to make', such as steak and kidney pudding (Victorian style, with oysters) and rhubarb charlotte and from the new style of English cookery, with dishes such as elderflower and strawberry fritters, fillet cooked between seasoned oak or fillets of sea bass in a parcel with fresh peach dressing.

Veronica Shaw, who has endless energy and enthusiasm for her food, formed an outside catering company, initially to provide lunchtime customers with food for dinner parties and food for her husband, a film producer, who wanted meals supplied on location for his film crews. This led to the preparation of special food at Christmas time, catering for 16,000–20,000 visitors a week in the Tudor kitchens at the Royal Palace of Hampton Court – where these were two of the original Elizabethan recipes prepared.

Leche Lumbard Date Slices

800g (1¾lb) stoneless dates
425ml (¾ pint) medium dry white wine
75g (3oz) light soft brown sugar
½ teaspoon cinnamon
½ teaspoon ground ginger
175g (6oz) wholemeal breadcrumbs

Best served as a sweetmeat or petit four after dinner.

Simmer the dates in wine until soft. Whisk briefly all remaining ingredients in a food processor until stiff, like marzipan. Form it into a 5cm (2in) roll, wrap in clingfilm and refrigerate.

Slice and either serve straight or, if liked, with a sweet madeira wine sprinkled over.

A Fine Cake

150g (6oz) butter at room temperature
75g (3oz) sugar
1 egg yolk
200g (8oz) self-raising flour
1 teaspoon mixed spice
½ teaspoon cinnamon
pinch ground saffron (optional)
egg white

Preheat the oven 160°C/325°F/gas 3.

A melt in the mouth shortbread with excellent spicing – good served with a syllabub, whipkull or even zabaglione.

Butter a 23cm (9in) square baking pan. Sieve together the flour and spices into the bowl of a food processor. Add all the remaining ingredients (except the egg white) and whisk together for 10-15 seconds. Whisk the egg white separately until it forms peaks, and fold gently into the mixture. Press the mixture into the pan. Bake for 45 minutes or until the cake feels firm when pressed lightly in the centre. Cut into squares while still hot. Cool on a wire rack.

Makes approximately 25 small cakes.

Sea Bass with Samuel Pepys Spinach and Orange Condiment

8oz/225g fresh spinach, washed and roughly chopped
juice and grated rind of 2 oranges
1 tablespoon/15ml cider or wine vinegar
1oz/25g butter
1 teaspoon (5ml) salt, pepper and nutmeg, combined in equal proportions

fillets of sea bass (1 per person)

This dish, a great success in Veronica's restaurant, is from a 17th century collection of recipes made by Samuel Pepys.

Add to a simply grilled fillet of Sea Bass .

Put the spinach in a pan with the orange juice, rind, butter and vinegar and cook gently for one minute until 'wilted'. Season to taste if required.

Serve this totally delicious condiment warm with a simply grilled fillet of sea bass.

French Cooking

French food has an important effect on Londoners' food, with many areas having their own local French bistro. French pâtisseries and bakeries are very much in evidence and classic French recipes, based on traditional techniques, are served in many fine eating places. The influence of the Roux Brothers has been enormous, and their training of many chefs has brought a high culinary standard to a number of the capital's restaurants, shops, bars and brasseries.

The style of modern French cooking has changed in a similar way to that of Italian food. Much more relaxed, with less emphasis on the complicated presentation of the nouvelle cuisine years, it has developed simpler and more subtle recipes to express the flavour of high quality ingredients.

Café Rouge epitomises French brasseries and cafés; this chain of restaurants appears all over London.

The Carnivores Club

Tel: 0171 405 8638

LAURENCE ISAACSON IS A DIRECTOR of the London Tourist board, vegetarian, a restaurateur, and director of the Chez Gérard group. He is the founding member of the Carnivores Club which was set up to counter-balance the relentless onslaught of tourism and its myths – it celebrates meat as part of a healthy, balanced diet. Anyone with a robust appetite for meat-eating can join the club or can at least cook this recipe at home.

Boeuf Bourguignon

Serves 8

225g (8oz) piece bacon, rinded
1.8kg (4lb) braising steak or topside
50g (2oz) butter
4 tablespoons oil
2 garlic cloves, crushed
4 tablespoons plain flour
salt and freshly ground pepper
bouquet garni
300ml (1/2 pint) beef stock
600ml (1 pint) Burgundy
24 button onions, peeled
350g (12oz) button mushrooms
chopped fresh parsley, to garnish

Dice the bacon. Cut the beef into 4cm (1½ in) pieces. Heat half the butter and oil in a flameproof casserole and fry the bacon for 5 minutes. Drain. Fry the meat in batches for about 8 minutes or until browned.

Return the bacon to the casserole with the garlic. Stir in the flour and add seasoning, bouquet garni, stock and wine, then bring to the boil, stirring. Cover and cook at 170°C/325°F/gas mark 3 for 1½ hours.

Meanwhile, heat the remaining butter and oil in a frying pan and sauté the onions for 10 minutes or until golden brown; remove. Add the mushrooms and fry for 5 minutes. Add the mushrooms and onions to the casserole. Cook for a further 30 minutes or until the meat is tender. Garnish with parsley.

Le Cordon Bleu School

114 Marylebone Lane, London W1M 6HH. Tel: 0171 935 3503

LESLEY GRAY IS THE PRINCIPAL of Le Cordon Bleu school in London. The name Cordon Bleu has symbolized fine gastrononomy for over 400 years. Members of the Order of the Holy Spirit, founded by Henri III of France, were known as Cordon Bleus, whose emblem was a cross on a blue ribbon.

The art of fine cuisine developed naturally in France, and when Madame Distel founded the famous Le Cordon Bleu in Paris at the end of the 19th century, there were many magnificent recipes in existence. Some 30 years later Rosemary Hume – a graduate of Le Cordon Bleu, Paris and pupil of the famous chef Monsieur Henn – together with Paul Pellaprat, founded a school in London of the same name, which became as well known in London as in Paris. In 1991 the name travelled further afield and a Tokyo Cordon Bleu was opened. Here is a recipe taught to pupils in the school today.

Braised Sea Bass with Fennel

Serves 8

1 x 3kg (6-7lb) sea bass, filleted, or
8 x 450-700g/1-1½ lb sea bass,
cleaned and scaled
3-4 large fennel bulbs
115g (4oz) butter
salt and freshly ground pepper
200ml (7fl.oz) white wine
300ml (½ pint) fish stock
300ml(½ pint) chicken stock
16 baby fennel bulbs
1 bunch fennel leaves, chopped
3 tomatoes, skinned, seeded
and diced

Preheat the oven to 180°C/350°F/gas mark 4.

Rinse the fish under cold, running water, and pat dry. If using small individual fish, leave them whole. Cut the fillets of a large sea bass into portion-size pieces.

Trim the stalks from the top of each fennel bulb and reserve. Thinly slice 2 of the fennel bulbs and soften them in a little butter on a low heat in a covered pan. Do not allow to colour. Place a little softened fennel inside the individual fish. Do not use at this stage for the portioned fillets.

Roughly cut the fennel stalks and place in a shallow, ovenproof dish. Lay the fish on top (the fillet portions should be skin side up), and smear with a little softened butter. Sprinkle with salt and a few turns of the peppermill. Half cover with a mixture of white wine, fish and chicken stocks. Cook in the oven for 10-15 minutes.

Drain off 90 per cent of the cooking liquor into a saucepan, bring to the boil, add the remaining 2 fennel bulbs (sliced) and cook, uncovered, to reduce the liquid by half and to soften the fennel well. Blanch the baby fennel in boiling water. Pour the liquid and fennel into a blender and purée; return to a clean pan, adding a little extra butter to this sauce if wished. Keep warm. Serve the whole fish on a warm serving plate. For individual portions, serve on some of the reserved, reheated, softened fennel. Pour the sauce around the fish; garnish with baby fennel, chopped leaf fennel, and diced tomato for colour.

La Cuisinière Cookshop

81-83 Northcote Road, London SW11 6PJ. Tel: 0171 223 4487

ANNE DAVID WAS BORN and brought up in Libourne, which is a little town between Bordeaux and St Emilion where her father is a *vigneron*, producing red wine from their vineyards. Anne came to England in 1987 and has been shop manager at La Cuisinère for the past seven years. The Tourain Blanchi (Garlic Soup) is a traditional recipe from the Périgord region. It was the first thing Anne ever learnt to cook. She used to have it at home at least once a week. Anne now cooks food at home in London to her own taste.

Tourain Blanchi (Garlic Soup)

Serves 8

1 large tablespoon goose fat (or 2 tablespoons vegetable oil)
4 large garlic cloves, finely sliced
2.3 litres (4 pints) chicken stock
salt and freshly ground pepper
4 teaspoons of good red wine vinegar
4 eggs, separated
6 nests of vermicelli (8 nests if you prefer a thicker soup)
salt and pepper

Melt the goose fat in a large saucepan over a low heat. Gently cook the garlic until brown, being careful not to burn it! Add the hot stock, season with salt and pepper and bring to the boil.

Meanwhile mix the vinegar and egg yolks in a small bowl and set aside. At this stage you can 'pause' in the cooking.

Just before serving, bring the soup back to the boil and add the vermicelli, slightly crushed. Stir to create a whirlpool effect and then stop stirring and gently pour in the egg whites. Continue cooking until the vermicelli is cooked (see instructions on the packet).

Remove from the heat. Add the egg yolk and vinegar mixture and stir well. Serve immediately.

NB. The soup should not be reheated once you have added the egg yolk.

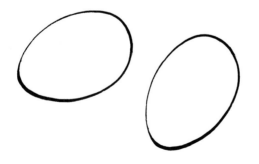

L'Escargot Restaurant and Brasserie

48 Greek Street, London W1. Tel: 0171 437 6828

L'ESCARGOT IS AN INFAMOUS old restaurant in Greek Street, which has now been divided into two defined rooms. The upstairs of the restaurant is the more formal, and downstairs on the ground floor attempts to be more brasserie-like. Called the Ground Floor Restaurant, it has a less expensive menu. In both rooms however, the accent on the food is most definitely French.

Roast Maize Chicken with Morels and Broad Beans

Serves 4

900g (2lb) maize-fed chicken
115g (4oz) fresh morels
450g (1lb) broad beans in their pods
1 bunch of fresh chives
salt and freshly ground pepper
2 tablespoons clarified butter
4 large red potatoes, baked in the oven
600ml (1 pint) veal stock
2 shallots
1 clove of garlic
1 bunch of fresh thyme
4 tablespoons double cream
4 tablespoons white wine

Prehehat the oven to 180°C, 350°F, gas mark 4.
Roast the chicken in the preheated over for 60-75 minutes. While the chicken is cooking clean, wash and trim the morels.
Pick over the broad beans and cook in rapidly boiling salted water for a couple of minutes. Shell the beans, cooland refrigerate. Chop the chives finely.

Take 4 small, deep non-stick dariole moulds, season and add a little clarified butter to each. Now break open the baked potatoes and, using a fork, remove the potato flesh and fill each mould (it should be well packed in). Cook for 20 minutes in the oven.

Remove the chicken from the oven and joint. Chop the chicken carcase up and put into a saucepan. Add the veal stock, shallots, garlic, thyme and any morel trimmings. Simmer for 30 minutes, then strain and return to the heat.

Remove the potato cakes from the oven and place in the centre of a plate. Arrange the chicken around.

Now add to the sauce a little cream, the wine and morels and finally add the beans and chives. Pour the sauce over the chicken.

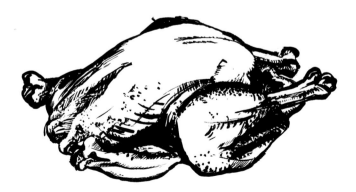

The Four Seasons Restaurant

Four Seasons Hotel, Park Lane, London, W1 Tel: 0171 499 0888

JEAN-CHRISTOPHE NOVELLI'S cooking came to my attention after enjoying a delightful lunch at the Four Seasons Restaurant with my fellow authors from the Guild of Food Writers.

He is a native of Arras, Nord-Pas-de-Calais in France, and Chef de Cuisine at the Four Seasons Restaurant. He began his career at the early age of 14 as an assistant baker and moved on two years later to the Victor Hugo restaurant as apprentice chef.

A few years after joining the team at the Victor Hugo, Jean-Christophe was called to Pau for his military service. In 1980, he worked at the PLM (Paris-London-Marseilles) St Jacques in Paris, but left in 1981 to become private chef to the Rothschild family. He spent two years cooking for them in France and abroad, including Cologne and Corsica, where the family travelled both for holidays and business.

In 1984, Jean-Christophe decided to travel a little further and headed for England, where he started as second commis-chef at the renowned Chewton Glen Hotel in Hampshire. There, he worked through the ranks and, just prior to his departure in 1986, was offered the position of sous-chef at the nearby Parkhill Hotel. In 1987 he became Chef de Cuisine at Geddes in Southampton. There he attracted the attention of the country's most respected food critics and started having good ratings in all the restaurant guides. He was soon voted 'Face of the Future' and his restaurant won the accolade 'Best Restaurant outside London', both by *The Times*.

After a couple of years, Jean-Christophe moved to Falmouth to become Chef de Cuisine at the Nansidwell House Hotel, where the standard of his cuisine earned him entries in all the major guides. A year later he met Keith Floyd, the TV celebrity, and worked with him. When Keith Floyd went to Australia to write about Australian food, Jean-Christophe took over the running of Floyd's Inn, his establishment in Devon. This entailed being in charge of the small hotel and outside barbecue, the picnic boat trips, the gourmet restaurant and bar food.

When Floyd returned, Jean-Christophe was offered an attractive position in New Milton, Hampshire where he had first started his career in the UK. In November 1990, he assisted in both the planning and re-opening of the Gordleton Mill Hotel and Provence Restaurant and in April 1991 took over as Chef Patron. The restaurant soon received national acclaim and the success was crowned in January 1993 with the awarding of its first Michelin star.

In September 1993, Jean-Christophe was appointed Chef de Cuisine at The Four Seasons Restaurant at the Four Seasons Hotel in London. Despite his move, Jean-Christophe managed to retain his Michelin star, being awarded one for the Four Seasons Restaurant only a few month's after his arrival on the London scene. He is now widely recognised as one of this country's rising stars in the restaurant world.

Gâteau of Steamed Baby Carrots, Emmenthal Cheese and Basil, Wrapped in Lettuce Leaves, with Chive Cream

Serves 4

For the gâteau:
350g (12oz) baby carrots
salt and freshly ground pepper
10ml (½fl.oz) olive oil
10ml (½fl.oz) honey
25g (1oz) chopped fresh basil
15g (½oz) chopped garlic
75g (3oz) Emmenthal cheese, grated
75g (3oz) carrot purée (cooked
carrots, blended with a little cream)
3 eggs
50ml (2fl.oz) double cream
2 cos lettuce
25ml (1fl.oz) orange juice
12 baby carrots
12 asparagus spears
15g (½oz) butter
15g (½oz) chopped fresh tarragon

For the sauce
15g (½oz) sliced mushrooms
15g (½oz) sliced shallots
15g (½oz) sliced celery
125ml (4fl.oz) white wine
65ml (2½fl.oz) vegetable stock
2 tablespoons double cream
15g (½oz) unsalted butter
15g (½oz) chopped fresh chives
fresh chervil, to garnish

Dice the 350g (12oz) baby carrots into small pieces (approx. 1cm/½in cubes). Sprinkle with salt and steam for approximately 8 minutes or until cooked *à point*.

Place the olive oil and the honey into a pan. Add the cooked carrots, toss all together and add the basil and garlic. Mix well and cook until the carrots are soft. Set aside to cool.

When the carrot mixture is cool, place in a bowl and add the cheese and carrot purée and season well. Mix the eggs and the cream together and add to the mixture. Adjust the seasoning.

Wash the lettuce leaves and grease 4 moulds or tea cups. Place the middle lettuce leaves around the mould to make a lining, pour in the carrot mixture and cover with clingfilm. Steam for 12-15 minutes or until the mixture has set.

Place the orange juice in a saucepan and boil rapidly until it is reduced by three-quarters and it becomes like a thick gel. Cook the baby carrots and asparagus for 3-4 minutes. Slice the carrots and asparagus into 3 pieces lengthways. Toss in 15g (½oz) butter, add the tarragon and season well.

To make the sauce: Sweat the mushrooms, shallots and celery together. Add the white wine and reduce by half. Add the vegetable stock and reduce by half again. Add the cream, leave to reduce and season. Whisk in the butter, then pass through a fine sieve. Add the chopped chives.

To serve: Place the carrot gâteau in the middle of the plate, place a spoonful of orange gel on the top. Carefully pile up some sliced carrots and asparagus on the top as high as you can. Pour a little of the chive sauce around and garnish with fresh chevril.

Fry's of Chelsea

14 Cale Street, Chelsea, London SW3 3QU. Tel: 0171 589 0342

PAUL FRY IS QUITE USED TO RISING at 4 a.m. to collect messages on his answer machine for orders to be made up. I am a frequent caller, leaving messages because I need products totally out of season, such as soft fruits in the middle of our British winter, for a summer fruit feature. More often than not Paul can rustle them up from someone in Covent Garden market and they're ready for me to pick up 7am. the next morning. I am just one of the happy customers Paul serves daily – this shop is a delight, with a superb display of top quality fruit and vegetables arranged with care and attention by Paul every morning. Here, Paul shares his Roast Ratatouille.

Roast Ratatouille

Serves 4
as an accompaniment

1 of each red, green and yellow peppers, deseeded and cut into large pieces
1 medium aubergine, cut into large pieces
4 medium courgettes, sliced into thin pieces
4 plum tomatoes, each cut into four pieces
8 shallots, peeled and cut in half (or 2-3 onions)
4-5 tablespoons virgin olive oil
2 cloves garlic, finely chopped

Preheat the oven to 220°C/425°F/gas mark 7.
Place all vegetables into a roasting tray or flameproof dish, spoon the olive oil over all the vegetables and sprinkle with the chopped garlic. Place into the top of the preheated oven for 35-40 mins, until all the vegetables have blackened slightly
   Serve immediately with grilled chicken or pork and rice.

Halcyon Hotel

The Room, 129 Holland Park, London W11. Tel: 0171 221 5411

THIS IS A VERY DISCREET HOTEL in Holland Park which appears from the exterior to be just a large town house. Once inside, it is usual to be led downstairs to 'The Room' restaurant. Martin Hadden, the very young head chef, trained with Shaun Hill when he was at Gidleigh Park and also with Nico Landenis.

The hotel itself is often frequented by pop stars so it is always worth looking around the restaurant for well-known faces.

Crème Brulée with Banana

Serves 6

6 egg yolks
75g (3oz) caster sugar
375ml (13fl.oz) double cream
200ml (7fl.oz) evaporated milk
1 vanilla pod
2 bananas
extra caster sugar, for sprinkling

Preheat the oven to 150°C/300°F/gas mark 3.
Whisk together the egg yolks and sugar until pale in colour. Boil the cream, evaporated milk and vanilla pod together and then whisk this into the egg yolk and sugar mixture. Put the mixture into a saucepan and cook gently over a low heat, stirring constantly, for 2 minutes. Remove and discard the vanilla pod, pour the mixture into 6 ramekins and cook in a bain-marie in the preheated oven for 15 minutes until set. When cool, slice the bananas and arrange on top. Sprinkle with caster sugar and place under a preheated grill until caramelised. Allow to cool, then refrigerate for at least 3 hours before serving.

London Hilton

22 Park Lane, London W1Y 4BE. Tel: 0171 493 8000

DAVID CHAMBERS is the executive chef at the London Hilton on Park Lane. Previously he cooked for nine years at London's Le Meridien Hotel where he was well known for the menus he created for the hotel's infamous Oak Room.

David enjoys promoting speciality dishes using British ingredients and has taken our produce abroad to New York, France and Portugal. Away from his large kitchens David enjoys, believe it or not, cooking for dinner parties.

Ragoût de Poissons à la Carte

Serves 4

1 pinch aniseed
900ml (1½ pints) fish stock
10 cloves of garlic (small)
1 pinch of turmeric
salt and freshly ground pepper
50g (2oz) button onions
¼ minature bottle of Pernod
575g (1¼lb) grey mullet
350g (12oz) whiting
2 x 225g (8oz) gurnard
300g (10oz) potato, chopped into
2.5cm (1in) pieces
150g (5oz) fennel, sliced (keep tops)
150g (5oz) green courgettes, sliced
150g (5oz) yellow courgettes, sliced
450g (1lb) beef tomatoes, diced
90g (3½oz) butter

Boil a little of the crushed aniseed in some fish stock, to get the flavour. Pass through a sieve, into the fish stock. Blanch the garlic for 1 minute in some boiling water and refresh in iced water. Season the fish stock with turmeric and salt and pepper, add the peeled button onions and blanched garlic. Then add half the Pernod and simmer for 5 minutes.

While the onions and garlic are cooking, lightly grease the base of another pan with butter and season with salt and pepper. Lay out fish in the base of the pan, placing the whiting in last.

Add the potato to the fish stock and cook for another 4 minutes with the onions and garlic. Add the fennel and cook for a further one minute. Add half the tops from the fennel, the yellow and green courgettes, and half the tomatoes; at this point the liquor will only cover half of the garnish. Simmer for a further 5 minutes.

Gently pour some of the cooking liquor over the fish, leaving the vegetable garnish to warm on the hob. Add the remainder of the tomato dice and half of the remaining fennel tops to the fish. Gently poach with a lid on for a further 1½ minutes.

Carefully remove the whiting, place on a serving dish, and keep warm (as this fish has a soft consistency it takes less cooking). Cook the remaining fish for another minute. Take out the gurnard and keep with the whiting. Carefully remove the grey mullet, which is only just cooked, and place with the other fish on the serving dish – keep warm. Pour the cooking liquor back on to the garnish, simmer, add the remaining Pernod and, slowly, the butter. Season.

Remove the fish from the oven and place in the serving dishes as attractively as possible. Arrange the garnish decoratively. Pour a little liquor over each of the dishes and sprinkle remaining fennel tops over each one to garnish.

Joubère Stock Company

Tel: 0181 933 1700.

ALEC J COUSINS BEGAN PRODUCING fresh stock when he realised that, while all good cook books recommended its use, very few people make their own at home and it was difficult to buy fresh stock of good quality.

Dehydrated stocks are satisfactory, but tend to be salty and often contain artificial ingredients. If someone is entertaining at home and has gone to a lot of bother to buy quality ingredients, it is a shame to spoil that with a sub-standard stock. I have been using these fresh stocks ever since they have been produced and it saves me a lot of time, without sacrificing taste any in my dishes.

Classic French cooking is particularly dependant on good stock, and many recipes would be ruined by using a salty, dehydrated stock cube. The Bouillabaisse below can be served as a starter or a main course. I recently used it when entertaining friends one Sunday. Almost any fish can be used, the quantity depending on the number of guests. Any leftover liquid can be added to a soup or made into a fish sauce the next day.

Bouillabaisse Joubère

Serves 4
½ small onion, chopped finely
½ cleaned white of leek, chopped
150ml (¼ pint) olive oil
350ml (12fl.oz) white wine
600ml (1 pint) Joubère Fish stock
salt and freshly ground pepper
5-7 saffron threads
1 bouquet garni
flesh of 2-3 tomatoes – or purée
2 crushed cloves of garlic
1.5kg (3¼lb) of fish – almost any fish, like sole/turbot/ halibut/sea bass, red mullet/ salmon/trout – as well as shellfish such as prawns/langoustines/ crawfish/ crab claws
1 litre (1¾ pints) of mussels/clams/ cockles. (or a mixture)
chopped fresh parsley
25g (1oz) butter
25g (1oz) plain flour
sliced French baguette – toasted and dried in the oven on a low heat
garlic, whole

Sweat the onion and leek in half the oil, until soft. Add the wine, Joubère fish stock, salt and pepper, saffron, bouquet garni, tomato and garlic and bring to the boil. Simmer for 20 minutes.

Cut the fish into large chunks and place into a clean large pan (7 litre/12 pints capacity). Place the shellfish on top. Add the remaining oil, parsley and fish stock mixture. Bring to the boil and cook rapidly for 15-20 minutes. Remove the bouquet garni and thicken by stirring in beurre manié (combined butter and flour).

Rub the toasted bread lightly with a clove of garlic to 'grate' the garlic into the bread.

To serve: Place the cooking vessel in the centre of the table. Each person needs a largish bowl to eat from and something for the shells. Put the bread in separate communal dish and ladle over some liquid to soak into the bread.

Diners will need spoons and a lot of serviettes.

Maison Blanc

102 Holland Park Avenue, London W11 4VA. Tel: 0171 221 2494

MAISON BLANC WAS SET UP by Raymond Blanc and his wife in 1979, to provide bread for their restaurant in Oxford. With the strong culinary base from Raymond, the company expanded and spread to London. My favourite shop is in Holland Park where, as in all the pâtisserie/boulangerie shops, there is coffee available to enjoy with your pastry. I enjoyed my quick breakfast there, at the French-style table where you can stand to eat your snack, as I was en route to my photographer's studio in Shepherd's Bush, collecting my meat from Lidgates butchers en route. With eight shops in all, Maison Blanc are very particular about the quality of their products and I can confirm first hand that they are very good indeed. High quality food stores such as those of Selfridges, Harrods and Fortnum and Mason stock their products. Below is a delicious recipe for Larieux from the Maison Blanc team.

Larieux

Serves 10

To be made one day in advance and kept refrigerated.

10 eggs, separated
175g (6oz) caster sugar
50g (2oz) plain flour
40g (1½oz) cocoa powder
50g (2oz) ground almonds
50g (2oz) butter melted
150g (5oz) bitter dark chocolate
350g (12oz) whipped double cream
150g (5oz) milk chocolate

Preheat the oven to 200°C/400°F/gas mark 6.

Making the biscuit: Whisk 6 egg yolks with 115g (4oz) sugar, flour, cocoa and almonds until pale in colour. Carefully fold in the whisked egg whites and melted butter. Spread the mixture to a depth of approximately 1cm on greaseproof paper and bake in the preheated oven for 10minutes. Set aside to cool.

Making the dark and milk chocolate mousses: Place the remaining sugar in a heavy-based saucepan and heat gently, without stirring, until the sugar reaches a temperature of 120°C/250°F and forms a syrup. Whisk the remaining 4 egg yolks, add the sugar syrup and beat briskly until cold. Divide the mixture between 2 bowls.

Melt the dark chocolate in a bowl placed over a pan of simmering water. Mix the melted dark chocolate with half the whipped cream and half of the egg yolk mixture. Repeat with the milk chocolate.

Assembling: Cut the biscuit and place inside a stainless steel ring (23 x 4cm/9 x 1in). Cover with the dark chocolate mousse, then the milk chocolate mousse, smoothing with a palette knife. Refrigerate overnight.

Finishing: Remove the ring – warming the ring with a warm damp cloth helps. Cover with dark chocolate glaze (75per cent chocolate and 25 per cent sugar syrup). Decorate with chocolate fans or thin chocolate squares and serve.

The Michel Montignac Boutique

160 Old Brompton Road, London SW5 0BA. Tel: 0171 370 2010

MICHEL MONTIGNAC, author of *Dine Out and Lose Weight* and *Eat Yourself Slim* is very much part of the London food scene, with Montignac Boutique and Café. It is here that the essential elements of his 'method' can be bought and consumed. The Montignac Method is partly based on understanding and recognising 'excellent', 'good' and 'bad' carbohydrates. All the foods available are low-glycaemic foods and many are chosen to be used in conjunction with Michel's other book, *Montignac Recipes and Menus*. Montignac gives the thumbs up to wine, bread, chocolate, fruit and cheese, so within the shop is a treasure trove of fine foods and wines from France. Here Michel shares with us his famous chocolate mousse.

Michel Montignac's Famous Chocolate Mousse

Serves 6-8

400g (14oz) dark chocolate with 10% minimum cocoa solids
4 teaspoons instant coffee
½ glass rum
8 eggs
a pinch of salt

Break the chocolate into pieces and place in a bain-marie. Make half a cup of very strong instant coffee and add to the chocolate, together with the rum.

Melt the chocolate in the bain-marie, stirring with a spatula. Separate the eggs and whisk the whites, with a pinch of salt added, until they form stiff peaks.

Allow the chocolate to cool down a little in a large bowl and add the egg yolks, beating briskly. Gently fold in the whisked egg whites a little at a time, to obtain a smooth mousse. Pour into a serving dish.

Allow to set in the refrigerator for at least 5 hours before serving. The addition of some orange zest will add a delightful flavour to this mousse.

Mohammed Al Fayed

Harrods, Knightsbridge, London SW1. Tel: 0171 730 1234

MOHAMMED AL FAYED, chairman of Harrods and L'Hotel Ritz in Paris, gave me this recipe. L'Hotel Ritz in Paris opened in 1898 and from its beginning was famous for its food, prepared under the direction of the great August Escoffier. As a tribute to his genius, Mohammed Al Fayed established the Escoffier School of Cooking, where present-day disciples of the great chef may study his methods. Here is a recipe inspired by Escoffier's disciples which can be prepared and enjoyed in your own kitchen at home.

Ritzy Beef

Serves 4

4 beef fillet mignons, cut 2.5cm (1in) thick
salt and freshly ground black pepper
4 tablespoons butter
1 shallot, minced
300g (10oz) fresh mushrooms, quartered
125ml (4fl.oz) beef broth
65ml (2½fl.oz) Madeira
chopped parsley to garnish (optional)

Season the beef with salt and pepper to taste. In a medium sauté pan, melt two tablespoons of the butter. When the butter stops foaming, sauté the beef fillets for 6-7 minutes on each side, for a medium-rare steak. Remove the meat from the pan and pour off any fat.

In a small sauté pan, melt the remaining butter. Sauté the shallot for 2 minutes. Add the mushrooms and cook for 3 minutes until lightly browned. Set aside.

In the meat pan, add the broth and boil rapidly, scraping up the browned bits, until two tablespoons remain. Add the Madeira and boil rapidly until the sauce thickens, approximately 2-3 minutes. Add the mushrooms and simmer for a further minute. Serve the steaks with the sauce poured over the top and garnish with parsley, if desired.

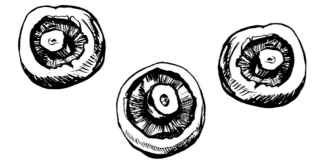

L'Odéon

65 Regent Street, London W1. Tel: 0171 287 1400

BRUNO LOUBET HAS JUST OPENED one of the most exciting restaurants, L'Odéon in Regent Street. Bruno's attitude and passion for food is reflected in his recipes. He's a naturally talented chef who realises his style has probably changed and developed since he first came to cook in London in 1982.

In the introduction to his book *Bistro Bruno – Cooking from L'Odéon Restaurant*, he says: 'Over the years I have made changes and added to my repertoire, sometimes tweaking old classics and sometimes creating my own dishes. I try not to be obsessive, with fussy techniques, because I think this distracts from the original idea, the natural flavours and appearance.'

He continues: 'Even when shopping, use your feelings, go with no preconceived ideas, but let your eyes, nose and imagination – and, of course, your purse – direct your instincts. Be bold and try new ingredients.' Below and on the following page, he shares some of his recipes and ideas.

Scallops and Black Pudding over Mash, Parsley and Garlic Sauce

Serves 4

200ml (7fl oz) chicken stock
200ml (7fl oz) double cream
1 large head of garlic, separated into cloves and peeled
salt and freshly ground pepper
50g (2oz) fresh flat-leaf parsley
500g (1lb 2oz) black pudding (blood sausage), preferably a soft one
vegetable oil
12 large scallops (sea scallops) with coral
lemon juice
mashed potatoes

Preheat the oven to 150°C/300°F/gas mark 2.

Put the chicken stock in a saucepan and bring to the boil. Stir in the cream. Pour half of the mixture into another saucepan.

Simmer the mixture in one pan until reduced to a sauce consistency. Add the garlic cloves to the other pan and leave to simmer until the garlic is very soft. Pour into a blender and blend until smooth. Season with salt and pepper.

Blanch the parsley in boiling, salted water for 30 seconds. Drain well and add to the reduced sauce. Pour into the clean blender and blend until smooth. Keep the two sauces warm.

Cut the black pudding into 12 pieces and put in a baking dish. Bake in the preheated oven for 10 minutes to heat through.

Meanwhile, heat a small amount of oil in a frying pan, add the scallops and cook for about 2 minutes on each side to give a nice colour. Add a squeeze of lemon juice and season with salt and pepper to taste.

Spoon a line of mashed potatoes down the centre of each warmed plate and arrange the scallops and black pudding alternately on top. Spoon over the parsley sauce and then the garlic sauce. Add a grinding of pepper and serve.

L'Odéon

65 Regent Street, London W1. Tel: 0171 287 1400

OF THE RECIPE BELOW, Bruno Loubet says, 'Pot-au-feu is probably the most famous French dish in the world. It should contain at least two kinds of meat, a lean 'muscle' cut and a fatty one.

Cabbage is added in some parts of France. I like to include a stuffed cabbage in my pot-au-feu because it gives it a lot of flavour and also looks very homely.'

Pot-au Feu

Serves 8

800g (1¾lb) beef (short) ribs
800g (1¾lb) shin of beef on the bone
8 pork spare ribs
1 small boiling fowl
coarse sea salt
400g (14oz) carrots
300g (10oz) leeks
300g (10oz) turnips
200g (7oz) celery
300g (10oz) swede
250g/9oz onions
4 garlic cloves, crushed
1 bay leaf
1 sprig of fresh thyme
2 cloves
8 black peppercorns

For the stuffed cabbage:
1 large Savoy cabbage
500g/1lb 2oz minced pork
100g (3½oz) chicken livers, chopped
4 slices of white bread, moistened with milk
2 eggs, beaten
1 teaspoon chopped fresh parsley
salt and freshly ground pepper

Put the beef ribs and shin in a large pot with the spare ribs and boiling fowl. Cover with enough water to come 10cm (4in) above the meats. Add 1 tablespoon of sea salt. Bring to the boil, skimming off the foam.

Clean all the vegetables and cut them into large pieces then add to the pot. Add the garlic, herbs, cloves and peppercorns. Leave to simmer while you prepare the cabbage.

Working from the base, cut the core out of the cabbage. Separate the leaves. Blanch the leaves in a large pan of boiling, salted water for 1 minute, then drain and refresh. Pat dry with a clean cloth. Mix together with the pork, chicken livers, bread, eggs and parsley. Add some salt and pepper.

Starting with the yellow leaves from the heart of the cabbage, put a bit of the pork mixture on each leaf and reshape the cabbage, overlapping the leaves as you go. Wrap the reshaped cabbage in a piece of muslin or cheesecloth or a clean kitchen cloth and tie firmly at the top with string. Plunge the cabbage into the pot-au-feu. Cover the pot and leave to simmer for about 2 hours.

Lift the cabbage out of the pot and unwrap it. Cut it into 8 wedges. With a slotted spoon, remove the meat and vegetables from the pot. Cut into serving pieces and arrange on a large platter with the cabbage wedges and vegetables on one side and meat on the other. Serve with Dijon mustard, coarse sea salt and a sauceboat of salsa verde.

Note: When bringing the liquid to the boil at the beginning of the cooking, it is important to skin off all the impurities that rise to the surface. I often add 1 or 2 tablespoons of dark soy sauce with the vegetables for a more richly coloured bouillon. Traditionally, the bouillon is strained and served separately as a soup. Leftover pot-au-feu makes a great salad, with a balsamic vinegar dressing.

'In French bistros, the choice of desserts is quite limited and they are often boring, due to a lack of attention. I don't have much of a sweet tooth, but I have always thought about the end of a meal as seriously as the start. This is probably due to the influence of one of my first teachers.

'At the age of 13, I decided that it was time to start my culinary training, with experience in the different areas – pastry chef, charcutier, and so on. Libourne, where I was born and brought up, was lucky to have a master pâtissier named Manuel Lopez. His work was so highly respected that people travelled even from Bordeaux, 20 miles away, to purchase his beautiful cakes, chocolates and ice creams. So you can understand that for me the first choice for work experience was with M. Lopez, and I found a place with him during the school holidays.

'M. Lopez has now retired, leaving his son to run his pastry shop, and is enjoying his new hobby, cooking in his beautiful home in Bordeaux. This recipe is one of his favourites.'

Monsieur Lopez's Almond Cake

Serves 6

For the dough:
2 eggs
2 tablespoons rum
2 pinches of salt
200g (7oz) caster sugar
200g (7oz) plain flour
200g (7oz) very soft unsalted butter
100g (3½oz) ground almonds

For the crème pâtissière:
150ml (5fl.oz) milk
3 tablespoons double cream
vanilla pod, split open
2 egg yolks
50g (2oz) caster sugar
1 tablespoon plain flour
bitter almond essence
1 egg yolk beaten with 2 teaspoons water, to glaze

Prepare the dough for the gâteau 48 hours before baking, to give it time to firm up. Put the egg, rum, salt and sugar in a mixing bowl and whisk until the mixture starts to turn white and foamy. Add the remaining dough ingredients, and mix with a wooden spatula to make a smooth dough. Place in the refrigerator.

To make the crème pâtissière, put the milk, cream and vanilla pod in a heavy-based saucepan and bring just to the boil. Meanwhile, mix together the egg yolks and sugar in a bowl, then add the flour. Pour the hot milk over the egg yolk mixture, mixing well. Pour back into the saucepan. Cook on a low heat for 20 minutes, stirring frequently. Pour the crème pâtissière into a shallow dish and leave to cool completely.

When the crème is cold, flavour it with the almond essence, adding just a little – a drop on the end of a knife blade is enough.

When you are ready to bake the gâteau, preheat the oven to 180°C/350°F/gas mark 4. Roll out just over half of the dough to 1cm (½ inch) thick and use to line a 23cm (9in) tart mould. Fill with crème patissière. Roll out the remaining dough thinly and use to cover the top. Seal the edges together. Brush the top of the gâteau with the egg yolk glaze. Bake for 25-30 minutes or until golden brown. The gâteau is best served at room temperature, with raspberry jam.

Pierre Victoire

29/31 Fouberts Place, London W1V 1HE. Tel: 0171 439 2527

PIERRE LEVICKY IS FROM LYON, but he opened his first restaurant (Pierre Victoire) in 1988 in Victoria Street, Edinburgh. It was enormously successful with large queues outside the door within just two months. The hugely successful chain of restuaruants all started there.

The concept could be summed up as cheap and cheerful. The menus are based on a centrally issued cookbook of 500 recipes, changed daily according to the availability of inexpensive produce, which is bought locally by each outlet. The best-selling item on the menu is a char-grilled steak with salad and potatoes. Little is spent on décor, which comprises bare wooden floors, whitewashed walls and second-hand tables and chairs.

This recipe comes from the Pierre Victoire in Fouberts Place.

Roast Monkfish with Red Wine, Cinnamon and Roasted Garlic

Serves 4

4 pieces monkfish tails, approx 150g (5oz) each
25g (1oz) seasoned flour
150g (5oz) unsalted butter
a splash of oil
2 bulbs fresh garlic, peeled
200ml (7fl.oz) red wine
1 stick cinnamon, crushed
½ teaspoon orange juice
1 dessertspoon honey
garlic cloves and sprigs of fresh thyme, to garnish

Preheat the oven to 200°C/400°F/gas mark 6.
Trim the outer membrane off the monkfish and fillet it from bone, then toss it in seasoned flour. Make a fish stock with the fish trimmings covered with water and a generous splash of white wine. Add a small piece of onion, carrot, leek and orange rind, simmer gently for 15 minutes and strain.

Melt 75g (3oz) butter in an ovenproof pan and add a splash of oil to prevent the butter scorching. Quickly seal the monkfish and transfer to a preheated oven with the garlic cloves and bake until the fish is cooked but still firm (approximately 10 minutes)

Deglaze the pan with red wine, add cinnamon, orange juice, honey and 150ml (¼ pint) fish stock and reduce until syrupy. Strain and return to a clean pan. Whisk in almost all the remaining butter, keeping back a small amount to brush over the monkfish when serving.

Serve the monkfish, brush with melted butter and garnish with more crushed cinnamon, a garlic clove and a sprig of fresh thyme and surround with the sauce.

Premier Bar and Grill, Selfridges

Oxford Street, London W1A 1AB. Tel: 0171 629 1234

SELFRIDGES HAS NOW FOLLOWED the success of other ddepartment stores restaurants by opening a restaurant within the store. The Premier Bar Grill is the first in-store restaurant that Terence Conran has designed. The head chef, Paul Calvert, has given this typical dessert recipe, which reflects the type of cuisine he's cooking at the Premier Bar, though the restuarant is still very much in its infancy. It is classic French cooking using healthy, fresh seasonal ingredients and with particular attention paid to colourful presentation.

Chocolate Loaf with Yellow Raspberry Sauce

Serves 8-10

For the loaf:
250g (9oz) dark chocolate
100g (3½oz) caster sugar
175g (6oz) unsalted butter
5 eggs, separated
pinch of salt

For the sauce:
300g (10oz) yellow raspberries
100g (3½oz) icing sugar (sifted)
juice of 1 lime

Serving and garnishing:
50g (2oz) yellow raspberries
cocoa powder, for dusting
8-10 sprigs mint

Place chocolate in a double boiler until melted. Add the sugar and whisk until dissolved. Add the butter, and stir until melted. Add the egg yolks, one at a time, stirring continuously. Remove the top of the double boiler from the heat.

Whisk the egg whites with salt until stiff. Gently fold the whites into the chocolate mixture. Rinse a 1-litre (1¾-pint) loaf tin in cold water. Pour the chocolate mixture into the tin and refrigerate for 10 hours.

Sieve the raspberries and mix with icing sugar. Add lime juice to taste.

To serve dip the loaf tin in boiling water for a few seconds and invert onto a clean cutting board. Slice evenly with a hot, dry knife. Place one slice per portion on the centre of a chilled plate. Surround with the raspberry sauce. Garnish with raspberries dusted with cocoa powder and a sprig of mint.

Note: If yellow raspberries are not available, red raspberries can be substituted.

Les Saveurs

37a Curzon Street, London. W1. Tel: 0171 491 8919

JOEL ATUNES IS A FIRM BELIEVER that in order to produce food of a consistently high standard, the best quality ingredients are necessary. His initial training under chefs such as Troisgros, Maximin and Boaise was in the classic French cuisine. Working in Japan and in the Far East for some time opened his eyes and palate to the importance of spices and seasonings in cooking, and he uses these to give an extra dimension to classic dishes. Atunés gets his spices from the Far East. Always in search of the ultimate ingredients, he ships over game, vegetables, cheeses and wines from different regions of France, Italy, Spain and Morocco.

Veal Sweetbreads with Sweet Peppers and Broad Beans

Serves 4

For the sweetbreads:
700g (1½lb) veal sweetbreads
salt and freshly ground pepper
2 eggs, beaten
200g (8oz) plain flour
200g (8oz) fresh breadcrumbs
200g (8oz) butter

For the sauce:
1 shallot, chopped
1 red pepper, chopped
1 sprig of fresh tarragon
1 teaspoon tomato purée
50ml (2fl oz) vinegar
250ml (8fl oz) crème fraîche

For the broad beans:
500g (1lb 2oz) broad beans
1 sprig of fresh thyme

For the shallots:
160g (5 ½oz) shallots
50g (2oz) castor sugar
300ml (½ pint) red wine
75ml (3fl.oz) vinegar
lemon juice, to season

Leave the veal sweetbreads to soak for 3 hours in cold water, then blanch for 5 minutes in boiling water. Remove the nerves and skin, cut into 1cm (½ inch) thick slices. Season, then coat in the eggs, flour and the breadcrumbs.

To make the sauce, sweat the shallot, red pepper and chopped tarragon in one third of the butter. Add the tomato purée, vinegar and the crème fraîche. Bring to the boil and season to taste.

Boil the broad beans for about 1 minute, remove the shells and pan-fry them lightly in one third of the butter, then add the chopped fresh thyme to give flavour.

Choose large shallots, peel and chop them into round slices. Season with salt, pepper and sugar. Add the red wine and the vinegar. Leave to cook for a few minutes.

Pan-fry the sweetbread escalopes on each side in the remaining butter until brown and slightly crispy. Season each with a drop of lemon juice.

Divide the sauce between the plates, put the escalopes on top, and then arrange the broad beans and shallots attractively around the escalopes.

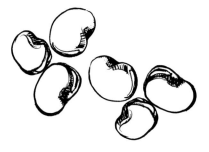

Soho Soho Restaurant and Rôtisserie

11-13 Frith Street, London W1. Tel: 0171 494 3491

LAURENT LEBEAU LEARNED TO COOK in France and came to London about 10 years ago, firstly cooking at Ma Cuisine. He returned to France to do his National Service (in the kitchen of course), but again came back to London to work during his leave at La Maison de Sorbet to learn pastry and ice-cream skills. He re-established himself in London after national service and is now the head chef at Soho Soho. Here he shares a delicious starter dish.

Tartlet of Grilled Scallops Garnished with Thin Slices of Bayonne Ham, Served on a Grilled Courgette Coulis

Serves 2

175g (6oz) scallops
50ml (2fl.oz) extra virgin olive oil
1 clove of garlic, roughly chopped
1 small onion, roughly chopped
300g (10oz) courgettes: keep one aside and roughly chopped the rest
50ml (2fl.oz) white wine
50ml (2fl.oz) fish stock
100ml (3½fl.oz) double cream
seasoning
two pastry tartlet cases
650g (2½oz) Bayonne ham

Cut the scallops in half and set aside.

Heat the olive oil and add the garlic, onion and courgettes. When browned, add the wine and fish stock. Reduce by half and add the cream. Cook slowly for about 15 minutes and then blend in a food processor. Season with salt and pepper to taste.

Cut the remaining courgette into thin strips and pan-fry gently, keeping the courgette crunchy. Garnish the tartlet cases with the sautéed courgette strips.

Grill the scallops for 1 minute each side on a flat-top hot grill and arrange them in the tartlet cases with the slices of Bayonne ham. Serve the tartlets on the courgette coulis.

Les Specialités St. Quentin

243 Brompton Road, Knightsbridge, London SW3 2P. Tel: 0171 589 8005

YVAN CAHOUR IS THE HEAD CHEF at Les Specialités St. Quentin, one of the few truly French-style working pâtisseries in London. All the chefs are French and are trained as pâtissier chefs. Every day the kitchen team start work at 3-4am, in time to bake and prepare the cakes and Vienoisserie for the shop, which officially opens at 9am. Their queue for the sandwich bar often reaches the pavement at lunchtime.

Vienoisserie includes the following (all baked fresh daily): croissants, almond croissants, raspberry croissants, pains aux raisins, petit pains au chocolat, abricotine (puff pastry glazed with two apricots inside), brioche. They also make a selection of cakes, canapés and petit fours, all popular for entertaining, and they produce wedding cakes traditionally too.

Their specially built cheese fridge contains a good selection of cheeses typical of various regions of France – from Roquefort to Reblochon – which is delivered direct from France every Wednesday morning.

The shop is very French, with an ambience to match. All serving staff are French and some of the products sold can only be bought in France

i.e. French biscuits and sweets. The customers are a mixture of French, English, Italian and Arab who all demand a high quality product and service. They deal with the rich and famous on a regular basis, but the base of their custom is the French living in London who want to feel at home on grills which the chef cooks on a large open grill within the establishment.

The St. Quentin group comprises two other restaurants in Knightsbridge, both characterized by a traditional French ambience and style. The other two are: Grill St. Quentin – as the name suggests, the accent here is English or American – and the more typical French Brasserie St. Quentin which was the brainchild of entrepreneur Hugh O'Neill and noted restaurateur, Didier Garmiel. Garmiel was a former trainee of The Connaught, who went on to manage a number of successful restaurants in France and England before returning to London to manage the St. Quentin group. The present site had been for many years the Brompton Grill and the team transformed it into a stylish French restaurant redolent of the traditional brasseries of the Paris in the nineteenth century, with their distinctive French atmosphere.

Chocolate Pavé

1.5 litres (2¼ pints) double cream
1kg (2.2lb) bitter dark chocolate
350g (12oz) chopped orange confit
200g (7oz) pâté à glace

For the brandy snaps:
250g (9oz) butter
500g (1⅛lb) caster sugar
250g (9oz) golden syrup
250g (9oz) plain flour
ground ginger, to taste
orange confit, to serve

Boil the cream and add the chopped chocolate off the heat. Leave to cool and add chopped orange confit.

Line 2 terrine moulds with clingfilm and line with melted pâté à glace. When set add the chocolate ganache to come halfway up the terrine. Leave to set and layer with pâté à glace. When set add another layer of ganache and finish with a layer of pâté à glace.

Slice and serve with a Grand Marnier-flavoured sauce Anglaise, orange confit and two brandy snap curls.

To make the brandy snaps: Preheat the oven to 200°C/400°F/ gas mark 6.

Cream the butter and sugar together. Add the warmed syrup and fold in the flour and ginger. Bake in the hot oven on greaseproof paper until golden brown. While still warm, twist around the handle of a wooden spoon.

Italian Cooking

Italian food in London once meant trattorias and pizzerias serving good basic pizza, lasagne and spaghetti. However, the traditional image of red checked tablecloths and the wine bottle with candle wax dripping down the outside has been transformed. Today's stylish restaurants feature menus moving towards simpler flavours and tastes, offering fresh pasta and herbs with a wide variety of Italian vegetables, breads and delicious olive oils.

Italian-inspired bars and trattorias are now fashionable across London and these respond to the demand for simpler dishes of ciabatta bread, fresh rocket and Parmesan cheese, roasted peppers, sun-dried tomatoes and mozzarella. Italian ingredients have become a staple of home cooking, and authentic imported produce is widely available.

Fratelli Camisa in Soho is one of the most authentic and atmospheric Italian delicatessens in London.

Betsy's Kitchen

3 St. James Gardens, London W11 4RB. Tel: 0171 603 39079

BETSY IS AN AMERICAN-BORN Cordon Bleu trained cook who has been teaching cooking in her own home since 1982. Originally a teacher of English literature with a master's degree from Columbia University, she changed subject matter after years of personal study with such inspiring teachers as Marcella Hazan in Bologna and Simone Bech in Provence. A holiday home in Tuscany and a husband with a love of food and fine restaurants were other major influences in her culinary development. Close associations with cookery writers and chefs of all nationalities in London, many of whom have been guest teachers in her kitchen, round out Betsy's broad international approach to cooking. All these influences have been woven into the fabric of a teaching kitchen, where delicious food and useful techniques produce a complete learning experience. Betsy gave me this recipe which she feels reflects the type of food she likes to cook.

Fresh Egg Pasta with Italian Sausage and Cream

Serves 4

For the egg pasta:
400g (14oz) plain flour
2 pinches salt
2 tablespoons extra virgin oliveoil
1 whole egg
4 egg yolks
pinch of saffron powder
water

For the Italian sausage cream:
4 sausages bought at any good Italian delicatessen
extra virgin olive oil
300ml (½pt) double cream
Parmesan cheese, freshly grated
freshly milled black pepper

For serving the pasta:
25g (1oz) unsalted butter
hot water
flaked fresh Parmesan cheese
freshly chopped parsley

To make the egg pasta, put all the ingredients except the water in a food processor and process for about 30 seconds. Add a small amount of water until a ball is formed. Knead the dough until completely smooth. Wrap in clingfilm and put in the fridge for at least 1 hour. Divide the pasta into 8 equal pieces, flour the work top and roll out as thinly as possible. Cut into 6cm (2½in) squares and place on a lightly dusted tray. Cover with clingfilm to prevent the pasta from drying out.

Remove the sausages from their skins, separate into small pieces and gently fry in a small amount of oil for 5 minutes. Pour in the double cream and reduce slightly. Add some Parmesan cheese and black pepper and set aside. Salt need not be added, as the sausages will already be well seasoned.

To cook the pasta, place 2.8 litres (5 pints) of slightly salted water in a large saucepan and bring to a fast boil. Poach the pasta for 2 minutes, then lift from the saucepan using a slotted spoon and place into a pan holding the butter melted with the hot water. **To serve:** Using large plates, build layers of the pasta, the Italian sausage cream and more grated Parmesan cheese. Top with flaked Parmesan and freshly chopped parsley.

Maxine Clark

Private Address

MAXINE CLARK IS A SCOTTISH COOK, home economist and cookery teacher, who has a fine arts degree. She started her professional cooking career in London at Leith's School of Food and Wine. She now tries to spend as much time as possible in Italy and France. In Italy she is usually teaching as part of 'Tasting Italy' cookery schools. This delicious recipe is a variation on a classic Italian dish in which, normally, a whole piece of beef is marinated in hearty Barolo wine, then slowly braised and served sliced with the puréed sauce. In this version, the wine is reduced before cooking to concentrate the flavour and the meat is cut into large chunks. The sauce is dark and luxurious after the long, slow cooking. This is a very good dish for a crowd. Serve with mashed potatoes and a green vegetable.

Beef Braised in Barolo

Serves 6-8

2 bottles good quality Barolo
1.4kg (3lb) stewing beef such as shin, chuck or skirt
2 onions, skinned and roughly chopped
2 carrots, peeled and chopped
1 stick of celery, trimmed and chopped
2 bay leaves
2 large sprigs fresh thyme
5 black peppercorns
2 allspice berries
3 tablespoons oil
2 tablespoons tomato purée or sun-dried tomato purée
beef stock
salt and pepper
chopped fresh parsley, to garnish

Pour the wine into a large saucepan or saute pan and bring to the boil. Boil hard until reduced by half (750ml /1¼ pints). Cool.

Trim the meat of any fat or gristle and cut into 6cm (2½in) pieces. Place in a large polythene bag with the onions, carrots, celery, bay leaves, thyme, peppercorns and crushed allspice berries. Pour in the cooled wine. Shake the bag to mix then seal and place in the fridge to marinate overnight.

Open the bag and pour the contents into a colander or sieve placed over a bowl. Remove the meat from the vegetables and pat dry with kitchen paper. Reserve the wine.

Heat the oil in a large flameproof casserole and brown the meat well in batches. Return the meat to the casserole and stir in the vegetables, herbs and spices.

Pour on the reserved marinade and wine and stir in the tomato purée. Add enough stock to cover the meat and vegetables. Bring to the boil, turn down the heat, cover and simmer gently for 2-3 hours or until the meat is very tender, stirring occasionally. Or cook in the oven at 170°C/325°F/gas mark 3 for 2-3 hours. Top up the liquid with extra stock if it evaporates too quickly.

Lift the meat out of the casserole with a slotted spoon and place in a bowl. Remove the bay leaves from the sauce. Pour the sauce into a liquidiser or food processor and blend until smooth. The sauce will look pale, but will darken when reheated. Taste and season. The sauce should be quite thick, if not, boil to reduce it. Stir the meat into the sauce, reheat until piping hot and serve.

Café Bertorelli

19-23 Charlotte Street, London W1. Tel: 0171 636 4174

THIS IS THE PREMISES WHERE, IN 1913, with only four marble-top tables, Davide Bertorelli laid the foundations of the family business. With the help of his brothers Guiseppe, Celestino and Ludorico, Bertorelli Brothers soon became the most celebrated Italian restaurant in London, serving what they unashamedly boasted to be 'the best minestrone in the world'.

After selling this particular site in the 1980s, the restaurant moved to Floral Street in Covent Garden.But the Bertorelli name is now back in its home on Charlotte Street in the form of Café Bertorelli, with the grandson of Guiseppe, Adrian Bertorelli, ensuring that the standards of both Bertorelli restaurants will remain as high as they have always been.

Café Bertorelli is the latest venture for chef Maddalena Bonino, who has created several dishes for the new café from Italian origins. She still also produces the menu for the main Bertorelli restaurant in Floral Street. This Carbonara recipe is classic in its simplicity.

Spaghetti alla Carbonara

Serves 6

450g (1lb) spaghetti, fettucine spaghetti or penne
1 tablespoon olive oil
175g (6oz) hot-smoked pancetta or smoked bacon
300ml (½ pint) double cream
300ml (½ pint) single cream
6 eggs yolks
150g (5oz) grated fresh Parmesan
salt and freshly ground black pepper
2 tablespoons chopped flat-leaf parsley

Bring a large pan of water to the boil and cook the pasta for 10-12 minutes. While the pasta is cooking, heat the oil in a frying pan, add the pancetta or bacon and fry until crisp. In a warm bowl large enoughto serve the pasta, mix the two creams with the egg yolks and grated Parmesan.

When the pasta is ready, drain and add to the sauce with the hot pancetta and parsley. Toss well and serve immediately after adjusting the seasoning.

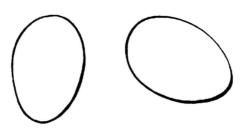

Carluccio's

28a Neal Street, Covent Garden, London WC2. Tel: 0171 240 1407

CARLUCCIO'S IS THE ITALIAN FOOD SHOP in London's Covent Garden, specialising in Italy's finest regional food and funghi.

Antonio and Priscilla travel extensively through the nineteen regions of Italy, personally tasting and selecting every product. Their philosophy is to seek out small manufacturers who still maintain the traditional recipes and methods of working in their region, to produce the authentic taste of Italy.

All the staples of the Italian larder are available here, as well as more specialised products. The range includes the best risotto rice, polenta, the most exotic truffle and mushroom products, a comprehensive selection of oils and vinegars and a wonderful array of antipasto. A well-designed system of labelling and packaging informs the customer about regional origins and product uses.

There is always a selection of the best fresh produce at Carluccio's. Near the door stand baskets of exotic fruits and vegetables and seasonal wild food such as garlic, dandelions and of course a selection of the latest crop of wild funghi. Opposite is an array of freshly baked bread and rolls. There are Italian classics such as ciabatta and focaccia, regional specialities such as Pugliese bread and more unusual varieties of chocolate, apricot and walnut breads.

Antonio Carluccio's best-selling books, *An Invitation to Italian Cooking*, *A Passion for Mushrooms* and *A Passion for Pasta* are all sold here. Along with numerous television appearances, he has generated an enormous public following which brings many visitors to Covent Garden to dine at his Neal Street Restaurant located next door to Carluccio's. To satisfy a nation-wide demand for Carluccio's products, a wholesale business was established in 1994 and Carluccio's branded product range is now supplied to 25 selected retailers of quality food around the United Kingdom.

Antonio is well-known for his knowledge of mushrooms and he makes regular forays to find them, in this country as well as abroad. The quiche overleaf can be made with a variety of mushrooms, depending on the season. During the spring fresh morels and oyster mushrooms are available and during the autumn ceps and chanterelles are plentiful. The tarts can also be made at any time of the year with cultivated button mushrooms and dried ceps.

Carluccio's

28a Neal Street, Covent Garden, London WC2. Tel: 0171 240 1407

Mini-Quiches with Seasonal Mushrooms

4 small flan tins (8cm/3in
in diameter)

For the pastry:
100g (3½oz) plain white flour
pinch of salt
65g (2½oz) butter
3 tablespoons water

For the filling:
(1) 16 medium-sized morels and
150g (5oz) oyster mushrooms *or*
(2) 25g (1oz) dried ceps and
200g (7oz) button mushrooms *or*
(3) 200g (7oz) fresh ceps and 150g
(5oz) chanterelles
1 large onion
25g (1oz) butter
1 tablespoon chopped fresh parsley
3 eggs
600ml (1 pint) full fat milk
25g (1oz) grated Parmesan cheese
salt and pepper to taste

Preheat the oven to 200°C/400°F/gas mark 6.

To make the pastry, sieve the flour and salt in a mixing bowl. Rub in the butter until it forms breadcrumbs. Gradually add the water to make a smooth dough. Knead very gently into a ball, wrap in clingfilm and refrigerate for about 30 minutes.

Grease the flan tins. Roll out the pastry to a thickness of 0.5cm (¼in) and line the tins. Bake blind for about 10 minutes or until the pastry turns a golden brown.

If using option (1), clean the morels and oyster mushrooms by using a cloth. Do not wash them in water unless the morels are very sandy. Remove the lower stems of the morels and leave whole. If the oyster mushrooms are large, cut in half, otherwise leave whole. If using option (2), put the dried ceps in a small bowl of lukewarm water for about 20 minutes so that they rehydrate. Clean and cut the button mushrooms in half. If using option (3), clean the fresh ceps and chanterelles. Do not wash. Keep the ceps whole, but chop the chanterelles in half if they are large.

For all options, chop the onion finely. Heat the butter in a pan and sauté the onion. Add the mushrooms then the parsley and sauté for 5 minutes. Take the pan off the heat and cool. When cool, divide the mushrooms between the four pastry cases.

In a bowl beat the eggs and add the milk and grated Parmesan. Season with salt and pepper and mix together. Pour the mixture equally into the four pastry cases and bake in the oven for about 12 minutes.

This is delicious served hot or cold with a crunchy French bean salad made from lightly cooked green French beans, dressed with virgin olive oil, fresh mint leaves and salt.

Pasteria di Grano (Wheat Tart)

Serves 10 or more

For the flavoured grain:
200g (7oz) whole wheat, to be soaked, *or* a 440g (15oz) can of cooked wheat called Gran Pasteria, made by Chirico and obtainable from Italian delicatessens
600ml (1 pint) milk (if you are soaking your own whole wheat)
zest of ½ a lemon
pinch of ground cinnamon
(1 teaspoon
1 small sachet of vanilla sugar
(2 teaspoons)
zest of ½ an orange

For the pastry:
150g (5oz) caster sugar
150g (5oz) butter
3 large egg yolks
300g (10oz) plain flour

For the filling:
300g (10oz) ricotta cheese
4 large eggs, separated
1 small wine glass orange water
150g (5oz) candied peel, chooped
225g (8oz) caster sugar
icing sugar, for dusting

In Naples, Easter isn't Easter without this wonderful tart. It has ancient origins and it symbolizes wealth. Grain and ricotta cheese are the most basic of foods, and if you do not have them, it means you are very poor. Whatever Neapolitans may think of this, the tart is still a remarkable sweet. The important ingredient for it is whole wheat grain, which can even be bought in cans precisely for this purpose. I would suggest, though, that you buy the real thing anddd allow plenty of time for preparation. The grain should be soaked for 24 hours in several changes of water and needs to be cooked the day before the tart is made.

Simmer the grain in the milk with the lemon zest for 3-4 hours on a very low heat. When cooked, add the ground cinnamon, vanilla sugar and the orange zest. Cool and keep until the next day. Alternatively, use the canned ready-cooked grain, and add to it the ground cinnamon, vanilla sugar and the lemon and orange zest. Mix them together well.

Make the pastry by working together the sugar, butter and egg until smooth, add the flour and make a smooth pastry. Put aside in a cool place for at least 1 hour. Preheat the oven to 190°C/375°F/gas mark 5.

To make the filling, beat the ricotta with the egg yolks and the orange water. Cut the candied peel into tiny pieces, then add them and the flavoured grain to the ricotta mixture. Whisk the egg whites with the sugar and fold them very gently into the ricotta. Grease a large flan tin 35cm (14in) in diameter. Press two-thirds of the pastry into the flan tin, covering the bottom and sides with an equal thickness. Pour in the filling. Roll out the remaining pastry and cut into long strips to form a lattice top to the tart. Bake in the oven for about 45 minutes. Allow to cool and dust with sifted icing sugar. The Neapolitans drink the locally produced wine, Lacrima Christi, along with this delicious tart.

Lina Stores

18 Brewer Street, Soho, London W1. Tel: 0171 437 6482

LINA STORES IN THE HEART OF SOHO is the eptiome of Italian delicatessens. The aromas of fresh Parmesan, fresh basil plants and the authentic atmosphere of a shop in Italy create a feeling of being transported onto the continent and makes one want to speak in Italian to the people behind the marble counter.

Lina Stores has been trading since just after the war, when the original Lina used to make pasta on the counter in full view of the customers. The Stores have been owned by Mr and Mrs Saccomani since 1978 but they are now semi-retired and their daughter and son-in-law, Mr and Mrs Fillipi, run the business, carrying on the family concern. Their specialities include various filled pastas, which are still made daily on the premises. The recipe below uses agnolotti, a type of pasta 'parcel'.

Fresh Sage Pasta

Serves 4

450g (1lb) agnolotti
(a type of pasta)
salt and freshly ground
black pepper
115g (4oz) butter
fresh sage leaves
freshly grated Parmesan

Place the agnolotti in plenty of boiling water with a pinch of salt added. Simmer gently for 5-6minutes or until *al dente*. Meanwhile, melt the butter and add the sage leaves. Season to taste. Drain the pasta and pour the sage butter over it. Sprinkle with Parmesan cheese and serve immediately.

Pizza Express: The Original

30 Coptic Street, Bloomsbury, London WC1A 1NS. Tel: 0171 636 3232

PETER BOIZOT IS THE FOUNDER of Pizza Express which started in London in 1965, in premises which used to be a restaurant called The Romanella. He claims that Pizza Express have achieved success because they have always striven to be authentically Italian, using Italian ingredients and equipment, always looking mainly to Italy for their inspiration.

My favourite pizza is Giardiniera, so here is the recipe for the basic tomato sauce and for two different toppings for you to make at home. The recipe for pizza dough is on the next page.

Pizza Tomato Sauce

For 4 pizzas

1 large onion
1 clove garlic
2 tablespoons olive oil
450g (1lb) can Italian plum tomatoes
2 tablespoons tomato paste
salt and freshly ground pepper
1 bayleaf, crushed
dried oregano

Finely chop the onion and garlic. Cook for about 10 minutes in the oil – just let the vegetables soften, not brown or fry. Add the canned tomatoes, the tomato paste, some salt, a generous grinding of black pepper, the bay leaf and a sprinkling of oregano. Stir well to dissolve and disperse the paste, then leave to simmer and reduce until you have a thickish sauce.

To add variety to the sauce you can add any of the following, all finely chopped, to the onion and garlic: celery, peppers (green or red), leeks, parsley, Italian fennel, carrots.

The sauce keeps well in a screw top jar in the refrigerator and has many other uses.

Two Pizza Toppings

For the Margherita topping:
tomato sauce
olive oil
50g (2oz) Mozzarella
salt and freshly ground pepper
2 or 3 basil leaves

For the Giardiniera topping:
tomato sauce
oregano
small quantity of mixed vegetables, to include onions, peas, spinach
40g (1½oz) Mozzarella
1 dessertspoon grated Parmesan
1 artichoke heart and 1 olive
fresh chopped chives

Preheat the oven to 230°C/450°F/gas mark 8.

To make Pizza Margherita: This is the foundation for almost any pizza. After spreading the dough in a lightly greased pizza pan, cover with tomato sauce almost to the edge. Sprinkle with oil and distribute the Mozzarella over the tomato. Season and place in the hot oven for 20 minutes or until the dough has cooked through. Decorate with fresh basil leaves.

To make Pizza Giardiniera: Cover the dough with tomato sauce, almost to the edge. Sprinkle with oregano. Spread a thin layer of the vegetables over the tomato. Add Mozzarella and sprinkle with Parmesan. Season, then put the artichoke heart and olive in the centre of the pizza. Cook in the hot oven 20 minutes. Scatter a few chives over the pizza before serving.

Pizza Express: The Original

30 Coptic Street, Bloomsbury, London WC1A 1NS. Tel: 0171 636 3232

Pizza Dough

Makes 2 standard pizzas

150ml (¼ pint) water
1 level teaspoon sugar
15g (½oz) fresh yeast or 2 level
teaspoons dried yeast
225g (8oz) plain flour
1½ level teaspoons salt
olive oil

Measure the tepid water (about 27°C/80°F) into a bowl. Add the sugar. Squeeze the fresh yeast in the liquid with both fingers and swirl the liquid until sugar and yeast are dissolved. If using dried yeast, sprinkle it over the surface of the water and whisk it into the liquid with a fork until the yeast and sugar are dissolved. Stand for 10-15 minutes in a warm place until froth develops.

Sift the flour and salt into a large mixing bowl. Pour in the yeast liquid. Lightly oil or flour your hands. Work the flour and liquid together until it becomes a coherent mass. Sprinkle your work surface generously with flour. Tip the dough on to the work surface and scrape out any which is sticking to the bowl.

Begin kneading. You may already have an established method of kneading dough and certainly you will develop your individual technique. If you have never done this before I suggest you pull the far edge of the dough towards the centre with one hand and push it down and away from you with the heel of the other hand, developing a rythmical rolling motion as you do so. The kneading process mixes the flour and liquid and strengthens and develops the gluten which holds the gas bubbles generated by the yeast.

Continue kneading for about 5 minutes, until the doughball becomes smooth and silky. It should not be sticking to your fingers or to the work surface by this stage. If the dough is still wet and sticky after a few minutes of kneading, flour the work surface again so that more flour is worked into the doughball. If the dough is too stiff and dry, add a little tepid water, no more than ½ teaspoon at a time. The hummidity in the atmosphere and the type of flour you are using can make these adjustments necessary. True pizzarilos can sniff the air on waking up and know by instinct just how much water to put in the dough! It is sometimes quite tricky to get the consistency right, but practice makes perfect.

When the dough has become a soft and supple ball, rinse the mixing bowl with cold water to remove any last remnants of flour, dry it, sprinkle in a touch of olive oil over the surface and place doughball in it. Cover with a damp cloth and allow to stand somewhere warm for approximately 1 hour. Place the bowl clear of draughts but not in direct heat.

An airing cupboard works well but, more often than not, it is just as satisfactory to leave the bowl on your work surface. If you do not wish to make the pizza for several hours, the dough can be placed at the bottom of your refrigerator. Yeast does not work at temperatures below 4.5°C/40°F but providing your refrigerator is not that cold the dough will start to rise very slowly. When you take it out of the fridge, put it in a warm place and leave it until it is approximately twice its original size. If you are short of time the dough will rise faster if you use slightly warmer water – about 38°C/100°F. Hot water must not be used. It is frequently recommended that the dough be placed in an oiled polythene bag, sufficiently large to allow it to expand. Try it if you like, but I find it more trouble that way.

Contain your impatience for at least 45 minutes by relaxing with a drink. You can be gently preparing your ingredients at this stage.

After about 1 hour the dough should have expanded considerably and be roughly twice its original size. Rub a little oil or flour on your fingers and reach down underneath the dough by running your fingers down the side of the bowl. Gently lift the dough up and punch it down again. This is known by bakers as knocking back the dough and releases large air bubbles which otherwise make the pizza uneven. It is very important to do this.

Divide the dough into 2 equal sections by pinching it in the middle with your thumb and forefinger. You should now have 2 lumps of dough, each weighing approximately 200g (7oz.) Roll each piece into a ball on the palm of your hand until it is sealed underneath; if you cannot seal it, nip the cracks together. Place the two balls on the lightly floured surface, cover them with an upturned mixing bowl, a damp cloth, or silver foil and allow them to rest for 10-20 minutes.

Preheat the oven to 230-240°C/450-475°F/gas mark 8-9. Discovering the temperature at which your oven best cooks pizza might be a matter of trial and error. First try it at 230°C/450°F/gas mark 8. Never put the pizza in the oven until it has reached its full heat. When the doughballs have rested for the additional 10-20 minutes and are soft to the touch but not too springy, they are ready to be stretched and spread on to the lightly greased trays.

Sol e Luna

22 Shorts Gardens, Thomas Neal Centre, London WC2H 9AN. Tel: 0171 379 3336

MARK EMBERTON IS 28 YEARS OLD. The first six years of his career were spent gaining experience in Michelin star restaurants including The Savoy and The Dorchester.

After a year and a half as senior sous-chef at Rue St Jacques, Mark was appointed head chef of The Belvedere, where he was able to develop and put into practice his own style of cooking. Mark received substantial critical acclaim, including nominations in Time Out magazine for Newcomer of the Year Award 1993, Best Sunday Brunch 1993 and 3 stars in the *AA Guide* 1993. He hosted Fay Maschler's 20th Anniversary Dinner with Antony Worrall Thompson, Alistair Little and Beth Coventry.

His next appointment was as second chef at Quaglino's where he was heavily involved with menu planning and kitchen design in order to

Grilled Pumpkin and Roquette Salad

Serves 4

For the dressing:

rosemary, basil, mint
sun-dried tomatoes
balsamic vinegar
olive oil
1 small pumpkin, peeled, seeded
200g (7oz) sliced pancetta
300g (10oz) washed roquette

To make the dressing, shred all the herbs, chop the tomatoes finely and mix all the ingredients together.

Peel and seed the pumpkin and cut into 1cm (½ in) thick slices. Chargrill 8 nice-looking pieces of the pumpkin until slightly soft, plus 8 pieces of pancetta. Divide the roquette between 4 plates, place the hot pancetta and pumpkin on top and spoon some dressing over. Serve immediately.

Cep Risotto with Parsley and Garlic

Serves 4

For the mushroom stock:

4 teaspoons soy sauce
vegetable bouillon
1 head of garlic
parsley stalks
1 shallot, roughly chopped

250g (9oz) Arborio rice
40g (1½oz) butter, softened
65g (2½oz) fresh Parmesan, grated
200g (7oz) fresh ceps, sliced
2 tablespoons virgin olive oil
2 teaspoons crushed garlic
2 tablespoons chopped fresh parsley

Place all the stock ingredients in a pan with 1.2 litres (2 pints) mineral water. Bring to the boil and simmer for 1 hour. Strain and keep hot.

To make the risotto, place the rice in a pan with a small amount of stock. Cook gently, stirring occasionally until the liquid has been absorbed. Gradually add the more stock and continue cooking gently, adding the stock gradually and stirring occasionally, for about 20 minutes or until the rice is tender and all the liquid has been absorbed.

Mix together the butter and Parmesan and toss the ceps with the hot olive oil, garlic, parsley and pepper.

Serve the risotto on plates with the Parmesan and cep mixture spooned over the top. Sprinkle with Parmesan cheese.

Sol e Stella

43 Blanford Street, London W1H 3AE. Tel: 0171 487 3336

cope with 95 staff producing food from three outlets for up to 1200 covers a day.

In April 1993, Mark became head chef at Antony Worrall Thompson's dell'Ugo, implementing a complete back of house redevelopment which resulted in substantial cost savings and increased food margins. He was also heavily involved in establishing new units and expanding existing ones and was responsible for the design of the new kitchens at Café dell'Ugo, 190 Queens Gate and The Atrium. Mark also trained and promoted two of his sous-chefs to take over at 190 Queens Gate and Palio in Westbourne Grove.

As executive chef of Sol e Luna and Sol e Stella, Mark is responsible for the creation and implementation of a modern Italian menu, using the finest ingredients, for people to enjoy at reasonable prices.

Panino of Chargrilled Vegetables, Mozzarella and Pesto

Serves 4

1 large bloomer-type loaf
1 clove garlic, peeled and halved
125ml (4 fl oz) olive oil
4 tablespoons tapenade
150g (5oz) aubergine, sliced lengthways and chargrilled
150g (5oz) courgette, sliced lengthways and chargrilled
1 red and 1 yellow pepper, chargrilled, seeded and skinned
30 large basil leaves
150g (5oz) sun-dried tomatoes
4 tablespoons pesto
700g (14oz) buffalo Mozzarella, thinly sliced
115g (4oz) stoned black olives
50g (2oz) red onion, peeled and thinly sliced
50g (2oz) rocket leaves
50g (2oz) spinach leaves
salt and freshly ground black pepper

Cut a lid off the top of the loaf and hollow out the bread, leaving a crust of about 1cm (½in) all the way round. Rub the cut surface of the loaf with garlic and then drizzle with olive oil. Spread the tapenade on the bottom of the loaf and then layer the remaining ingredients, using about two layers of everything. Season between each layer with salt and pepper.

Replace the lid and wrap the loaf in clingfilm. Place in the refrigerator and leave pressed under a heavy weight overnight. Serve with char-grilled Italian bread and a little extra virgin olive oil and freshly ground black pepper over the whole dish.

Antony Worrall Thompson

dell 'Ugo, 56 Frith Street, Soho, London W1 V 5TA. Tel: 0171 734 8300

ANTONY WORRALL THOMPSON IS A CHEF who has had a tremendous influence on the food scene in London, creating here a café-society type of restaurant long before anyone else thought of it.

He has been heavily influenced by the Italian way of cooking but admits, as he says in the introduction to his book *Modern Bistrot Cookery*, that his regular travels around the globe have all given him snippets of inspiration which he adapts in his own way to 'create' dishes. The

Roast Pumpkin

1kg (2.2 lb) pumpkin with skin on, cut into 8cm (3in) cubes
salt and freshly ground black pepper
2 tablespoons soft brown sugar

Preheat the oven to 220°C/425°F/gas mark 7.
Roast the pumpkin pieces with a little olive oil in the hot oven for approximately 45 minutes. Season with salt and black pepper. Allow to cool, remove the skin and cook in a saucepan with the brown sugar and seasoning until the pumpkin starts to caramelize and break down. Stir to prevent it from burning. Serve with a main course.

Salad of Spinach and Chicory

Serves 8

For the dressing:
25ml (1fl.oz) balsamic vinegar
125ml (4fl.oz) extra virgin olive oil
1 garlic clove, crushed
salt and freshly ground black pepper

115g (4oz) baby spinach leaves
3 heads of chicory

Make a dressing by mixing together the vinegar, oil, garlic and seasoning. Allow to stand for a couple of hours.

Wash and dry the spinach leaves. Core and rip up the leaves of the heads of chicory. The general rule is not to use a knife when preparing salads as the cut ends of the leaves can go brown. However, if you feel more at home using a knife, do so, but only at the last moment.

Toss the leaves in a little of the

chapter entitled 'Autumn in Italy' includes these two recipes for cooking at home. I think they are very representative of Antony's ideas, not only for cooking in his restaurants, but as devised for people cooking at home. On these pages we give recipes for his Roast Pumpkin, Salad of Spinach and Chicory and Mustard Fruits. You can serve a spoonful of roast pumpkin with a main course or use it in the Pumpkin Gnocchi recipe on the following page.

Mustard Fruits

Serves 8

1.4kg (3lb) white seedless grapes
3 tablespoons mustard seeds
450g (1lb) hard pears
450g (1lb) Granny Smith apples
1 bay leaf
1 sprig of fresh thyme
pinch of ground cinnamon
pinch of ground nutmeg
1 tablespoon caster sugar
2 cloves
a glass of dessert wine or
Amontillado sherry
lemon juice

Mash the seedless grapes in a mortar and pestle and place the resulting pulp in a bowl. Cover and refrigerate for 2 days.
After 2 days, strain the pulp through a jelly bag into a non-reactive saucepan. Add the mustard seeds, bring to the boil, then reduce by half.

Meanwhile, peel, core and dice the pears and apples. Cook the fruit until tender, with the bay leaf, thyme, cinnamon, nutmeg, sugar, cloves and wine or sherry. When the fruit is softish and the liquor evaporated, add the hot grape pulp. Add a good squeeze of lemon juice and allow to cool. Refrigerate before serving.

Mustard fruits can now be bought in upmarket delis, but there's a certain satisfaction about making them yourself.

Antony Worrall Thompson

dell 'Ugo, 56 Frith Street, Soho, London W1V 5TA. Tel: 0171 734 8300

Melted Taleggio Over New Potatoes and Grilled Leek with Prosciutto

Serves 8

For the Taleggio cream:
75g (3oz) unsalted butter
150ml (¼ pint) double cream
150g (5oz) Taleggio cheese, diced
salt and freshly ground
black pepper

700g (1½lb) leeks, preferably baby,
washed thoroughly
extra virgin olive oil

For the potato salad:
450g (1lb) new potatoes, preferably
Jersey mids, scraped but not peeled
225g (8oz) streaky bacon, cut into
lardons from a thick piece
2 shallots, finely diced
1 tablespoon red wine vinegar
4 tablespoons extra virgin olive oil
1 dessertspoon grain mustard
1 tablespoon finely chopped
flat-leaf parsley

To serve:
50g (2oz) rocket leaves
extra virgin olive oil
fresh lemon juice
350g (12oz) thinly sliced prosciutto
(Parma ham)

To make the Taleggio cream, melt the butter in a pan, add the cream and Taleggio cheese. Simmer gently, stirring constantly, until the mixture is blended together. Season to taste with salt and pepper. Allow to cool, and store until ready to use. (May be prepared ahead to this point.)

If the leeks are small, dip them in olive oil, season with salt and black pepper and chargrill, pan-fry or grill for approximately 3 minutes each side. Set aside. If using larger leeks, blanch them for 3 minutes in boiling, salted water, then drain, cool and dry. Split each leek in 2 vertically and chargrill as for small leeks. (May be prepared ahead to this point.)

Make the potato salad well in advance. Boil the potatoes in salted water until tender. Drain and keep warm. Fry the bacon pieces in a non-stick pan until crisp, then add the shallots and sweat until soft but not brown.

Deglaze the pan with vinegar, add the olive oil and mustard, and toss the potatoes in this dressing. Sprinkle with parsley and season to taste with Salt and black pepper. Always toss the potatoes in the dressing while they are still warm as they absorb the flavours more successfully.

Final preparation and presentation: If you wish to serve this starter on individual plates, mix the leeks and potato salad together and position in the centre of heatproof plates. Spread each salad combination with 1oz (25g) of the Taleggio cream and flash under a preheated hot grill so that the salad warms through and the cheese begins to bubble and melt. Scatter the plates with rocket leaves dressed in extra virgin olive oil, a squeeze of lemon juice, salt and ground black pepper. Arrange some slices of prosciutto on each plate just before serving.

Alternatively, serve the potato salad and leek mix, the rocket and the prosciutto in separate bowls and allow your guests to serve themselves. Serve the Taleggio cream separately.

Gnocchi

Serves 8

900g (2lb) roast pumpkin (see
recipe on previous page)
225g (8oz) dry mashed potato
75g (3oz) dry goat's cheese, mashed
2 eggs
250g (9oz) plain flour
50g (2oz) roasted hazelnuts, finely
chopped
freshly grated nutmeg
salt and freshly ground
black pepper

To serve:
24 sage leaves
hot oil for deep frying

175g (6oz) unsalted butter
2 tablespoons finely chopped sage
juice of 1 lemon
175g (6oz) mustard fruits (bought or
made – see recipe on previous
page), finely chopped
Parmesan cheese shavings

In a food processor, blend together briefly the caramelised roast pumpkin and the mashed potato until combined; do not overwork. Add the goat's cheese and combine with the eggs. With the processor running, add the flour until you have produced a well-mashed, smooth paste. Turn the mixture into a bowl and fold in the chopped hazelnuts, nutmeg and salt and pepper to taste.

Put the paste into a piping bag with a wide plain nozzle. Pipe the mixture onto a floured tray, cutting into 2cm (¾in) pieces. Press the shortened lengths with the prongs of a fork. Alternatively, roll the paste into small balls between finger and thumb and, as before, indent each ball with the prongs of a fork.

Bring a large pan of salted water to the boil and cook the gnocchi in small quantities. The gnocchi will float to the surface after about 2-3 minutes. Continue to simmer for a further 5-6 minutes. Remove from the water, drain and keep warm in a buttered tray covered with a damp cloth, while cooking the remaining gnocchi.

Note: If gnocchi is one of those dishes you panic about – don't. The trick is to balance the amount of flour you add to the mixture: too little and the gnocchi will fall apart; too much and it will end up being too doughy. If in doubt, poach a piece on its own to test it. It should retain its shape and yet not be heavy in the mouth.

Final preparation and presentation: Deep-fry the sage leaves in the hot oil until the sizzling stops – moments only. Drain well on absorbent paper. They will crisp up as they wait. When all the gnocchi are cooked, heat a frying pan and drop in the butter with the chopped sage. Swirl the butter around until it is melted, then allow to cook until it froths and there are just hints of nutty aroma and the butter turns pale brown. Add the lemon juice.

Arrange the gnocchi on a large serving dish or on 8 plates. Scatter with the chopped mustard fruits and top with the nut brown butter which you pass through a fine sieve. Top with deep fried sage leaves and Parmesan shavings.

As a contrast to the sweetness of this dish, serve it with a bitter salad of baby spinach and chicory or Belgian endive.

Mediterranean Cooking

Countries around the Mediterranean, in particular Spain, Portugal, Greece and Cyprus, the southern part of Italy and Sicily have had a considerable influence on London food in recent years. Extra virgin olive oils, attractive fish and meat dishes, fresh herbs and vegetables and delicious local breads are key ingredients of these very different cuisines that capture the flavours of their respective regions. The structure of a 'Mediterranean style' meal can be adapted to suit appetite or pocket; two starters, one course only or a starter and light dessert are all quite acceptable and make this the perfect type of food to eat at any time.

A Mediterranean style of eating has also become very popular in London and many eating places have a relaxed, continental atmosphere. Middle Eastern influences in Egyptian, Israeli and Lebanese also feature in this chapter.

Shops in some areas of London strongly reflect the ethnic make-up of their inhabitants. This shop offers Turkish specialities in the North-east of London.

Adamou & Sons

124-126 High Road, Chiswick, London W4. Tel: 0181 994 0752

ADAMOU & SONS IS A SUPERB SHOP packed with fresh produce from all over the world but they supply mostly Greek and Cypriot foodstuffs, especially good Greek olive oils and olives. The olives come in all types of marinades, dressings and 'au naturel'.Other products include various herbs and spices as well as couscous, matzos and different kinds of nuts.

Taua

Serves 6

1.4kg (3lb) Cyprus potatoes, cut
into large pieces
1.4kg (3lb) boned leg of lamb, cut
into large pieces
1 large onion, chopped
450g (1lb) diced tomatoes
approx 50g (2oz) cumin seeds
2 tablespoons tomato purée
3 bay leaves
salt and freshly ground
black pepper

Preheat the oven to 200°C/400°F/gas mark 6.
Mix together the potatoes, lamb, onion, tomatoes and cumin seeds and place in a deep baking dish.

Make a stock using the tomato purée and add just enough stock to cover the meat and vegetables in the baking dish. Add the bay leaves and seasoning.

Cover the dish with foil and bake in the preheated oven for 2 hours. Uncover and serve hot.

Albero & Grana

Chelsea Cloisters, 89 Sloane Avenue, London SW3 3DW. Tel: 0171 225 1048

THIS IS THE BEST FORMAL-TYPE Spanish restaurant in London, as recommended by Maria José Sevilla Taylor, author of *Spain on a Plate*, from BBC Books. It uses great authentic ingredients and recipes. Sylvia Ligonie from Albero & Grana gives this unusual recipe for suckling pig. Their supply of suckling pigs comes from outside London, from:
Pugh's Piglets, Bowgreave House Farm, Bowgreave, Garstang, Preston PR3 1YE
tel: 01995 602 571
fax: 01995 600 126.

Cochinillo à la Sergoviana

Serves 6

½ suckling pig weighing 2kg
(4lb 4oz)
1 lemon
coarse sea salt

Preheat the oven to 200°C/400°F/gas mark 6.
Cut the suckling pig lengthways and place it in a large baking tray. Add 5cm (2in) of water and the juice from the lemon and sprinkle some salt over the pig. Bake in the preheated oven for 1½ hours, basting every 20 minutes. Then turn the oven up and bake for a further 1½ hours at 220°C/425°F/gas mark 7 but do not baste during the last 30 minutes – this helps to form a crispy skin.

Serve with the juices from the tray – these juices may have reduced during the cooking time, if so add more water.

To garnish, boil some new potatoes in a mixture of chicken fat and water, until just cooked. Drain and mix with a bunch of chopped fresh mint. Sauté the potatoes and mint in mixture of butter and olive oil and cook for 20 minutes until crisp and golden.

Aroma Cafés

Greenland Place, 115-123 Bayham Street, London NW1 0AG. Tel: 0171 482 6666

ROBERT ANCIL, OPERATIONS MANAGER of the highly successful Aroma Café, is one of the ideas men behind the development of Aroma's menus. Aroma's are renowned for their gourmet sandwiches as well as their fabulous coffee. Aware of their creative local customers, such as the staff of MTV, Warner Brothers and Carlton TV, Robert's experience as a freelance chef and food consultant gives him the practical knowledge needed to create visually appealing, tasty sandwiches. Robert shares his particular favourite with us and has listed two special coffees to accompany his sandwiches. A menu from which to enjoy Aroma Cafés' specialities is to be found in 'Books etc' on Charing Cross Road, where you can browse, eat and drink to your heart's content.

Roasted Red Pepper, Courgette and Fresh Mozzarella Sunset Manoucher Bread Sandwich

Serves 4

1 red pepper
1 large courgette
olive oil
a pinch of salt
freshly ground black pepper
1 fresh whole Mozzarella
1 round Manoucher bread (can be found at most large supermarkets)
fresh basil leaves

Wash the red pepper and courgette. Slice courgette and cut the pepper into 4 slices, discarding all the pips. Put 2 teaspoons of olive oil into a frying pan and heat gently. Once hot, add the 4 pepper quarters, a pinch of salt and some ground black pepper and cook until brown. Take out of the pan and leave to cool.

Flash the sliced courgette in the same pan and heat for 45-60 seconds. Slice the Mozzarella into 6 thin slices.

Cut the Manoucher bread horizontally, in order to separate the top and bottom.

Lay out the cooked peppers, courgettes and sliced mozzarella onto the bread base, and add 4 or 5 basil leaves. Splash a small amount of olive oil onto the filling, with a light sprinkling of salt and black pepper on top. Close the sandwich with the crown of the bread and cut into 4 wedges, to serve.

Café Amandine

Serves 1

1 shot of espresso
1 measure of almond extract
frothed milk
ground cinnamon
caramelised almonds, to serve

This is flavoured *caffe latte*. Extract one shot of espresso into a tall (heat-resistant) glass. Make sure you produce a thick, dense espresso and ensure that it has a thick, creamy surface (*crema*). If the surface is black, or has only intermittent *crema* floating on top of it, it is not an acceptable beverage. You achieve the correct effect by densely packing the finely ground coffee in the filter basket, and 'expressing the espresso' under high pressure.

Add a measure of almond extract. If possible, try to obtain real almond extract rather than a syrup. Experiment with the precise quantity to your taste, although less than 25g (1oz) may produce too weak, and more than 75g (3oz) too intense, a taste.

Add frothed milk. Froth the milk slowly and near the surface. The milk needs to start off cold and be frothed in a metal container. Pour the milk and froth in equal parts into the espresso. The froth needs to be dense and creamy, and poured slowly. Sprinkle cinammon lightly over the top. Serve with several caramelised almonds.

Aroma Cacaocino

Serves 1

2 scoops chocolate ice cream
300ml (½ pint) warm milk
with 25g (1oz) good dark chocolate
melted in it
double espresso
2 tablespoons double cream,
whipped
cocoa powder

This is a coffee to be served in the spring or summer, making a warm, long drink.

Place the chocolate ice cream in the base of a tall glass. Pour over the warm milk and double espresso. Top with whipped cream and a sprinkling of cocoa powder.

Bertorelli's

44A Floral Street, Covent Garden, London WC2E 9DA. Tel: 0171 836 3969

MADDALENA BONINO CREATED this warm salad for me one evening when I popped into her flat to see her and her son Matteo, who watched intently as his mother quickly rustled up this recipe. She has been head chef at Bertorelli's for the past few years. With a busy pizza basement restaurant, this ideally situated restaurant caters brilliantly for pre-theatre and post-theatre diners. The upstairs restaurant is light and airy and serves tasty, well-prepared dishes. These dishes reflect the philosophy of the food and recipes Maddalena cooks at Café Bertorelli (see page 72), using good fresh ingredients, strong flavours and authentic Italian roots.

Mad's Warm Salad

Serves 4
This salad is ideal for lunch or a light supper.

200g (7oz) trimmed asparagus spears
250g (9oz) washed mixed salad leaves
4 plum tomatoes, washed and cut into chunks
2 stalks celery, sliced
8 spring onions, washed, trimmed and cut into long thin ribbons
1 tablespoon sunflower oil
2 medium red onions, peeled and thinly sliced
225g (8oz) smoked rindless streaky bacon, diced
2 large flat field mushrooms, cleaned and sliced
4 tablespoons ketjap manis (Indonesian soy sauce)
2 tablespoons rice vinegar
4 tablespoons extra virgin olive oil
freshly ground black pepper
salt
4 free range eggs

Bring a pan of salted water to the boil and blanch the asparagus for about a minute, then drain and refresh in cold, running water. Divide the salad leaves, asparagus, tomato chunks, celery slices, spring onion ribbons and avocado pieces between 4 serving bowls.

In a frying pan heat the sunflower oil, add the red onion and bacon and fry for a couple of minutes, then add the sliced mushrooms and keep frying until the bacon is fairly crisp; finally deglaze the pan with balsamic vinegar and remove from the the heat.

While the bacon and mushrooms cook, dress the salads by drizzling over them the ketjap manis, a little rice vinegar and the extra virgin olive oil with a generous grinding of black pepper and some salt.

Bring a pan of water to the boil and add the remaining rice vinegar. Reduce the heat and crack one egg at a time into the pan and poach for a couple of minutes or to the desired firmness.

While the eggs cook, divide the bacon and mushroom mixture between the four salads, then top each with a well-drained poached egg, one last grind of black pepper and serve with warm baguettes or toasted ciabatta bread. Yum!

Aubergine and Ricotta 'Lasagne' with Black Olives and Tomato Sauce

Serves 4

2 large aubergines
salt and freshly ground pepper
450g (1lb) ricotta
1 small clove garlic
1 teaspoon dried oregano
6 tablespoons chopped fresh flat-leaf parsley
225ml (8fl.oz) extra virgin olive oil
2 tablespoons grated Parmesan
2 large ripe beef tomatoes, cut into small dice
100g (3½oz) black olives, pitted and chopped

Preheat the oven to 220°C/425°F/gas mark 7.

Slice the aubergines diagonally about 1cm (½in) thick. Place in a colander and sprinkle with salt. Leave to 'weep' for 20 minutes.

Meanwhile blend in a food processor the ricotta with the garlic, oregano, 4 tablespoons of chopped parsley, 4 tablespoons of the oil and seasoning.

Heat a grill pan until very hot. Wash the aubergine slices very well, pat dry, then grill for a couple of minutes on both sides. When cooked, place them in a mixing bowl and generously sprinkle with oil while still hot. When all the slices have been grilled place some slices over the base of a lasagne dish or tray and spread with the ricotta mix. Top with more slices and continue the layering until all the aubergine slices are used up and are equally distributed, finishing with a thin ricotta layer.

Sprinkle with the Parmesan and bake in the oven for about 15-20 minutes.

Make the sauce by heating together over a low heat 4 tablespoons of oil, the diced tomato and the chopped olives for 5 minutes. Check the seasoning and add the remaining parsley. Keep warm.

When the lasagne is ready, serve with a little of the sauce and one last drizzle of oil. Serve with toasted ciabatta or sun-dried tomato bread.

Brindisa

Tel: 0171 403 0282

MONIKA LAVERY OWNS BRINDISA, a company importing wonderful Spanish products into the UK. Monika has given me recipes for her favourite snacks or quick supper dishes that she would prepare after a hard day at the office, all with a distinctive Spanish flavour. She also describes some authentic Spanish ingredients.

A favourite rice pudding (see opposite) from my birthplace, Asturias, is a recipe from Rudi, who works with Monika at Brindisa.

Empanada Bonito

Serves 4-6

1 onion, chopped
2 tablespoons olive oil
a few saffron strands
450g (1lb) puff pastry, rolled out
300g (10oz) can tuna, drained and flaked
150ml (¼ pint) tomato passata
8 piquillo pepppers, chopped

Preheat the oven to 220°C/425°F/gas mark 7.
Sauté the onion in the olive oil. Infuse the saffron strands in some warm water. Bake half the rolled out pastry in the oven for 10 minutes until puffed and golden. Remove from the oven and set aside.

Add the tuna, tomato passata, peppers and saffron to the onions, and sauté gently for a few minutes. Cover the cooked pastry with the filling

Place the remaining rolled out pastry over the filling, tucking the pastry edges underneath the cooked base. Bake in the oven for 20 minutes. Serve hot.

Calasparra Rice with Langoustines

Serves 4-6

1 medium onion, skinned and finely chopped
2 medium fresh squid, finely chopped
3 tablespoon olive oil
2 tablespoons chopped fresh tomatoes
300g (10oz) Calasparra white rice
750ml (1¼ pints) water
16 small fresh langoustines (Dublin Bay prawns)
8 fresh prawns
salt
a few saffron strands

In a large, flameproof casserole gently fry the onion and squid in the oil, adding the fresh tomatoes for the last few minutes.

Stir the rice around in this mixture for a minute or two. (You can prepare the dish ahead up to this point.) Pour the water over the rice and add the shellfish, salt and a few strands of saffron. Keep the heat high enough that the water remains at a gentle boil and cook until the rice is nearly done; it should retain some liquid even after standing away from the heat. Serve hot.

Asturian Creamed Rice

Serves 4-6

250g (9oz) Calasparra white rice
1.2 litres (2 pints) milk
1.2 litres (2 pints) water
1 cinnamon stick
1 vanilla pod, or a strip of thinly pared lemon rind
8 tablespoons sugar
100g (3½oz) unsalted butter (optional)
sugar, for caramelising

This dish is the product of long, slow cooking which will leave the rice grains almost disintegrated and the milk thickened into a thick cream. The cooled rice can be simply sprinkled with cinnamon, but the burnt sugar is characteristically Asturian and makes a big difference.

Put the rice in a saucepan with 250ml (9floz) of the milk and all the water. Bring to the boil and cook at a fast simmer for 3-4 minutes, to open the grain.

Lower the heat, add the cinnamon and vanilla or lemon rind, and continue cooking at a very slow simmer, adding the remaining milk – gradually – as it is absorbed and stirring with a spoon all the time: this is essential, even if the rice is not sticking. This may take 1-1½ hours, by which time the rice will be fully swollen and almost breaking up.

Add the sugar and, if you like, the butter, stirring until the sugar is dissolved. Place into individual bowls. Sprinkle some sugar over the top and grill or singe with a salamander to produce a caramelised top.

The Blue Print Café

The Design Museum, Shad Thames, London SE1 2YD. Tel: 0171 378 7031

DANIEL LEBERMAN, THE HEAD CHEF at the Blue Print Café, shares with us one of his truly Mediterranean dishes. Part of the Design Museum complex at Terence Conran's Butler's Wharf, this restaurant has a light, airy feel and is close to Tower Bridge and the Thames, where you can take a pleasant walk after you have enjoyed your meal.

Grilled Sea Bass Fillets with Roast Leeks, Vine-Tomato Salsa and Black Olive Dressing

Serves 6

4 x 115-175g (4-6oz) sea bass fillets
(ask the fishmonger to
scale and fillet them)
450g (1lb) small leeks
450g (1lb) vine tomatoes (firm
but ripe)
1 hot red chilli
2 cloves garlic
1 red onion
juice of 1 lime
115g (4oz) pitted black provençale
marinated olives
3 tablespoons olive oil
1 tablespoon balsamic vinegar
salt and freshly ground black
pepper
1 bunch flat-leaf parsley

Preheat the oven to 200°C/400°F/gas mark 7.

Keep the fillets of sea bass in the fridge until you are ready to cook them. Prepare the leeks first. Cut off the tops and bottoms, then slice them diagonally into lengths of about 1cm (½in). Rinse by placing in a bucket of cool water.

For the salsa, score the tomatoes and remove the stem, then blanch them in boiling water for 10 seconds. Remove and refresh in ice-cold water. Peel, cut into quarters and deseed, then cut into strips and put to one side. Cut the chilli in half, deseed and slice very finely. Chop the garlic and red onion. Juice the lime. Mix all these ingredients together and season with a little salt and pepper.

Chop the olives roughly, mix with the olive oil, balsamic vinegar, salt and pepper and roughly chopped parsley leaves. Set aside.

Blanch the leeks in boiling water for 2-3 minutes, then drain and place in a very hot pan or roasting tray and place in the oven for 5-8 minutes (depending on their size).

Brush the fillets of sea bass with olive oil, season and place under the grill for 5-8 minutes turning once. Keep warm. Remove the leeks from the oven.

Place a dessertspoon of salsa on the side of a warmed plate, arrange the roasted leeks next to it and then the grilled fillet of sea bass. Spoon the black olive dressing over the top.

Note: If sea bass is not available, you could use trout, bream or arctic char.

Penny Charalanbons

Cyprus Trade Centre, 3rd Floor, 29 Princes Street, London W1R 7RG. Tel: 0171 629 6288

PENNY CHARALANBONS IS AN enthusiastic cook living in London who shares with us two of her native Cypriot dishes. This cuisine is closely related to the Greek, but has some distinctive flavours and ingredients. The quantities of vegetables and lamb in the recipe for the casserole can easily be varied according to how many people you want to serve.

Home-made Raviolis

Serves 4-6

For the pasta:
450g (1lb) plain flour
125ml (4fl.oz) vegetable oil
pinch of salt
water to mix

For the filling:
1 large haloumi cheese, grated
2 tablespoons crushed dried mint
3 large eggs

Mix the pasta ingredients together and allow the pasta to rest while you mix all the filling ingredients together. Cut balls of pasta to the size of tennis balls and roll out into thin sheets.

Place spoonfuls of the filling mixture in rows and cover with another sheet of pasta. Cut around the mixture to make ravioli parcels, either with a cutter or use a small round glass.

Boil a saucepan of water with a drop of oil and a pinch of salt. Place the raviolis in the boiling water until cooked and tender (about 8-10 minutes). Serve with plenty of extra grated haloumi cheese and crushed dried mint.

Greek-Cypriot Vegetable and Lamb Casserole

Serves 6

3 artichokes, quartered
4 courgettes, sliced
8 potatoes, peeled and sliced
4 tablespoons vegetable oil
1 teaspoon salt
6 lamb chops
salt and pepper to taste
½ teaspoon ground cinnamon

Clean and wash the artichokes, courgettes and potatoes. Cut them in long, thin slices. Lightly brown them in a little vegetable oil, removing from the pan and allowing the oil to drain away, either on kitchen paper towel or in a colander.

Wash and lightly salt the lamb chops and also brown them lightly in some oil. Do not remove from the pan but add approximately 475ml (16fl.oz) of water and leave to cook for about 15 minutes.

On top of the meat place the potatoes first, then the artichokes, then the courgettes. Add 225ml (8fl.oz) of water, a pinch of salt and pepper and the cinnamon. Allow to simmer and cook slowly for 1½ hours.

Note: By leaving out the meat, this can also be a vegetarian dish.

Merces Carqueïjerio–Gibson

The Portuguese Embassy, 11 Belgrave Square, London SW1. Tel: 0171 235 5331

MERCES CARQUEIJERIO-GIBSON remembers her childhood in Portugal: 'The smell of orange peel cooking pervaded the house and was a sign that Christmas was near. I remember the smell from both my grandparents' and my parents' homes and having this pudding every Christmas when I was a child. I have now carried on the tradition and every Christmas I cook this sweet for my own children.' Born in Setubal in Portugal, she received her higher education in Lisbon, where she also worked as a teacher. She married an Englishman in 1984 and now lives in England with her two sons, and works in the Cultural Department of the Portuguese Embassy.'

Pudim de Laranja (Orange Pudding)

Serves 4

peel of 12 oranges
450g (1lb) caster sugar
6 whole eggs
6 egg yolks
1 tablespoon butter, melted
ground cinnamon

Preheat the oven to 180°C/350°F/gas mark 4.

Peel the oranges with a potato peeler to produce thin peel, and cook the peel with enough water to cover for about 20-30 minutes, until it is very soft. Blend the orange peel in a blender until you get a rough mash. It is nice to feel some little bits of orange peel.

Put the sugar and the eggs (6 whole eggs and 6 egg yolks) in a big bowl and beat the ingredients together by hand with a wooden spoon until they are well mixed. Add the mashed orange peel and the melted butter and mix everything carefully together.

Place the mixture in a well-buttered pudding ring mould, 18-20cm (7-8in) in diameter, with a hole in the middle, and sprinkle cinnamon powder very generously over the top.

Cook the pudding in the oven for 45 minutes to 1 hour or until the pudding is set and the mixture is just firm throughout. Remove the pudding from the tin while it is still warm and serve it cold.

Konaki

5 Coptic Street, Bloomsbury, London WC1A 1NH. Tel: 0171 580 9730

TELOY COMMATAS OF THE GREEK RESTAURANT Konaki shares with us his most popular dish, Kleftico. This dish originates from the time of the revolution in 1821 when the Greeks were being chased by the Turks and the Greeks needed to have a dish that would cook while they were away fighting, so the long cooking time for the lamb of up to 5 hours was ideal.

Kleftico

Serves 4

4 lamb shanks on the bone
50g (2oz) butter
1 teaspoon dried oregano
1 bay leaf
2 cloves crushed garlic
1 onion, finely chopped
150ml (¼ pint) white wine
4 tablespoons Greek olive oil
2 tablespoons lemon juice
salt and freshly ground
black pepper

Preheat the oven to 150°C/300°F/gas mark 2.

Steam the lamb shanks in a large roasting pan of water in the oven for about 5 hours, topping up the water when necessary during the cooking period.

Remove the lamb from the oven and keep it warm. Add the butter and the remaining ingredients to the pan and increase the oven temperature to 240°C/475°F/gas mark 9. Cook the sauce for 10-15 minutes in the oven before serving. Pour the sauce over the lamb and serve with roast potatoes and broccoli or cauliflower.

Lisboa Delicatessen

54 Golbourne Road, London W10. Tel: 0181 969 1052

EDITE VIEIRAPHILLIPS shares her views on Portuguese shopping in London.

Lisboa Delicatessen sells all the foodstuffs necessary for Portuguese dishes, including salted cod, excellent olive oil, smoked garlic sausages (chourico) and even salted pork meat, for typical dishes like bean stew. Table wines, ports and firewaters are all there, too. It also stocks Spanish chorizos and other Spanish goods – because, says Sr. Gomes, the owner, he has many Spanish customers (notably from Galicia) and so he has to satisfy them as well.

Edite Vieira Phillips was born in Portugal but spent her teenage years in Mozambique, where she started a career in radio. Since then, journalism and broadcasting have been her main occupations, not only in the ex-Portuguese colony but also Madrid, Lisbon and London. For many years now she has worked for the BBC. She has also contributed to Portuguese TV and was London correspondent for several Lisbon magazines. Her book *The Taste of Portugal* is published by Grub Street.

Here she shares a recipe which is made with salt cod. It is very much in fashion at the moment. She says people are intrigued by it, wishing to try but without knowing how. Salt cod needs preparation; it is not cheap but it goes a long way, because it more than doubles in volume after soaking and is very nourishing.

Weigh the salt cod dry for the amount the recipe states. Soak in clean, cold water for at least 12 hours, changing the water two or three times. If the slices are thick, a 24-hour or at least an 18 hour soak is advised. The salt cod will then be ready to scale, bone and prepare as necessary. The cooking times, and whether the flesh should be flaked or not, are indicated in the particular recipes.

Salt cod is an accquired taste and people from outside Latin or Mediterranean countries may take a little while to become accustomed to its characteristic flavour. Once familiarized, however, it is generally a taste for life. When you first start to use it in cooking, you must stop seasoning with salt for obvious reasons.

The Portuguese give the name of *acorda* to a dish made mainly with bread but including strong seasonings and, in many instances, fish, shellfish and other ingredients as well. There is a great variety of acordas and each region specialises inits own. Acorda Alentejana is much more of a soup than other acordas and generally eaten as such, although it can also be a main meal in itself if accompanied by fried fish, for instance. Contrary to most other acordas, this one is not cooked. The bread is served swimming in a lovely fresh broth prepared with coriander, garlic and olive oil. But in order to have a very good acorda (of whatever type) you must use what the Portuguese call 'peasant bread' which is a cross between French bread and ciabatta, baked generally as a large loaf. If in London, it is possible to buy this at the Lisboa Delicatessen (freshly baked daily). Otherwise you could try Italian or Greek bread as reliable alternatives as each of these has, a close texture.

Salted Cod in the Oven

Serves 4

350g (12oz) salted cod
1 medium onion, finely sliced
2 cloves garlic, finely sliced
1 tablespoon olive oil
250g (9oz) ripe tomatoes, peeled,
seeded and chopped
paprika
1 tablespoon chopped parsley
450g (1lb) potatoes, boiled and cut
into thick slices
dry breadcrumbs, for sprinkling

Preheat the oven to 200°C/400°F/gas mark 6.

Have the salted cod well soaked from the previous day, as explained in the introduction. Skin it and discard the bones. Cut the cod into smallish pieces or flake it. Set aside.

Fry the onion and garlic gently in half the oil until translucent. Add the tomato, cook for another 5 minutes or so, until soft, and season very lightly with a sprinkling of paprika. Mix in the parsley. At this stage add the cod, and cook for about 6 minutes, over a low heat.

Meanwhile grease an ovenproof dish with a spoonful of oil and spread about one third of the potatoes over the base. Cover with the cod mixture and place the remaining potatoes on top, smearing with the rest of the oil.

Sprinkle with some dry breadcrumbs and place in the middle of the preheated oven for about 15 minutes or until it is golden and crisp. Serve with a side salad and black olives.

Note: When boiling the potatoes, season with only the slightest amount of salt. Dishes containing salted cod do not, as a rule, need salt added to them, despite the previous soaking.

Acorda Alentejana (Coriander Bread Soup)

Serves 4

3 cloves garlic
8-10 good sprigs fresh coriander
900ml (1½ pints) boiling water
salt
4 tablespoons olive oil
450g (1lb) day-old bread
4 eggs, poached

Process the garlic and coriander together (or crush with some salt in a pestle and mortar) and place this pulp in a large serving bowl or tureen. Add the boiling water, salt to taste and the oil. Break the bread into small chunks and add to the water. Soak it well.

Divide the soup between 4 soup bowls and place a poached egg on each. Serve at once.

This acorda is meant as a soup and it should not be excessively dry. It all depends on the kind of bread used, but you may need to add a little more boiling, salted water in order to have some liquid with the bread. It can be served with a side dish of fried or grilled fish and olives.

La Mancha

Putney High Street, London SW15. Tel: 0171 780 1022

TONI SKELTON IS CHEF AT LA MANCHA, which has a great informal Tapas bar on the ground floor and a more formal restaurant upstairs. The Patas Bravas and Chorizo Rosario are dishes from the extensive tapas menu. Other favourites include tortilla. Choose about 1½ dishes per person – sharing several dishes is the best way to enjoy them. Beware – one tends to over order!

Patas Bravas

Serves 4

For the tomato sauce:
2 onions, finely chopped
450g (1lb) ripe tomatoes, skinned and chopped
1 dried chilli
1 small glass of white wine
1 bay leaf
1 teaspoon dried basil
salt and freshly ground black pepper
1 teaspoon sugar

For the potatoes:
900g (2lb) old potatoes, peeled and cut into cubes
oil, for frying

Cook all the ingredients for the sauce in a large pan for 10 minutes. Meanwhile fry the potatoes in the oil and then mix the two together to serve.

Chorizo Rosario

Serves 4

chorizo sausage
red wine
red pepper, deseeded and sliced
salt and pepper

Slice some chorizo sausage into 1cm (½in) slices and simmer it in a little red wine and with some sliced red peppers, for about 15 minutes. Season well and serve warm.

The chorizo at La Mancha comes from Spain and can be bought at Products from Spain Ltd, 89 Charlotte Street, London W1P 1LB. tel: 0171 965 7274.

Paella Valencia

Serves 4

2 tablespoons olive oil
1 large onion, finely chopped
1 red pepper, deseeded
and chopped
1 green pepper, deseeded
and chopped
115g (4oz) pork, roughly chopped
1 chicken breast, roughly chopped
115g (4oz) squid, cleaned and
roughly chopped into rings
115g (4oz) monkfish, roughly
chopped
800g (1¾lb) round paella rice
1.7 litres (3 pints)good fish stock
pinch of saffron strands
salt and freshly ground
black pepper
225g (8oz) mussels, cleaned
75g (3oz) frozen peas
4 large mediterranean prawns
115g (4oz) peeled prawns

Paella Valencia is served in the upstairs part of the restaurant and is served from the pan in true Spanish style.

Heat the oil and fry the onion, peppers, pork and chicken until golden brown. Add the squid, monkfish and rice and mix well.

Add the fish stock, a pinch of saffron strands, salt and freshly ground black pepper and cook gently for 20 minutes or until all the liquid has evaporated. At this stage put the mussels, peas and all the prawns into the paella, cooking for another 12 minutes.

Cover the dish and leave to rest for 5 minutes until the mussels open. Serve hot.

Monkfish with Pistachios

Serves 4

1 onion, finely chopped
150g (5oz) pistachios nuts
115g (4oz) butter
900g (2lb) monkfish
450g (1lb) baby clams
300ml (½ pint) white wine
300ml (½ pint) fish stock
150ml (¼ pint) double cream

Sauté the onion and pistachio nuts in the butter until the onion is softened but not browned. Add the monkfish and clams. Pour over the wine and fish stock. Cook for 5 minutes then add the cream. Arrange the fish on a plate, reduce the sauce by half and pour over the fish. Serve immediately.

Mortimer and Bennett

33 Turnham Green Terrace, London W4 1RG. Tel: 0181 995 4145

DAN MORTIMER, PARTNER in his busy delicatessen on a very villagey road in Turnham Green, likes introducing new products. Spanish beans are one of his favourites. He describes the beans available and gives his favourite recipe.

The bean varieties

Planchada – long white haricots.
Ludion – large butter beans.
Canela – long cinnamon haricots.
Arrocina – tiny round white haricots.
Morada larga – large crimson haricots.
Morada redonda – round deep crimson haricots.
Garbanzo Pedroillano – small chickpeas.
Salamancan lentils – green lentils.

Suggested dishes

Pork or lamb stew – lentils, coloured beans.
Shellfish or smoked fish – white beans.
Soups and to thicken soups – white beans.
Chicken casseroles – white or canela beans.
Vegetarian main dish – all types.
Cold or warm salads – all types.

Cook the beans in a good vegetable stock before using them in any dish.

Tormesina beans from El Barco de Avila

Avila is a Spanish province situated between Madrid and Portugal, where the famous mountains, Sierra de Gredos, dominate the landscape. The Avila region is famous for producing the best pulses in Spain.

Tourmesina beans are cultivated in optimum climate and conditions: the high altitude, the purity of the Gredos water, the mineral wealth in the soil, and finally the cold winters and dry summers. The harvesting is done by hand, even pod by pod, to ensure ripeness. Not only does the rate of the pods drying differ between varieties of bean, but it can also vary by as much as 20 days between beans on the same plant. Tormesina beans are always graded and selected from the newest harvest. Packaging and sealing at source ensures that the beans reach the customer in excellent conditions

The beans themselves are rich and creamy and they absorb flavours beautifully. They have very thin and tender skins and are rich in protein, minerals, vitamins and fibre. They cook up to become two to three times their dry weight: 250g (9oz) of dry beans is a good quantity for four to five people.

Tips

Cooking the beans

First wash the beans under running water, place in a bowl and cover well with cold water, allowing considerable room for the beans to swell. Drain after 12 hours, place in a deep cooking pot and cover with fresh, cold water. The beans are now ready for cooking.

The beans turn out more tender if you bring them to the boil, drain, and start the cooking them again with cold water. Otherwise, you can add a splash of cold water when the pot comes to the boil. (Never do this with chickpeas, however, since if cooking stops, they will toughen.)

Seafarer's Beans with Clams

Serves 4

575g (1¼lb) judion butter beans,
soaked overnight
1 onion, peeled
1 green pepper, whole
1 head of garlic
1 farcellet sausage
3 tablespoon olive oil
1 tablespoon chopped parsley
1 glass dry white wine
1litre (1¾ pints) fish stock
24 clams in their shells
salt and pepper

Place the beans in a large pan with the onion, green pepper, half the garlic head and the farcellet. Cover with water and simmer for 1½ to 2 hours or until tender. Add salt, stir and drain, reserving the beans.

Finely chop 3 garlic cloves and lightly fry them in olive oil in a deep saucepan until golden. Add the chopped parsley, white wine, fish stock, clams and a sprinkling of pepper. Cover and wait for the clams to open, shaking the pan vigorously from time to time to ensure even cooking. Add the rinsed beans and bring the mixture to the boil, simmering gently for 5-10 minutes. (If the dish is too dry, add some of the reserved broth.) Serve hot.

Chrystalla Papaleontiom

Cyprus Trade Centre, 3rd Floor, 29 Princes Street, London W1R 7RG. Tel: 0171 629 6288

CHRYSTALLA PAPALEONTIOM WORKS at the Cyprus High Commission Trade Centre and enjoys cooking authentic Cypriot dishes. Here she shares her favourite ones with us. Classic Cypriot ingredients include bulgur wheat, a cracked wheat now available in most supermarkets or good health food shops. Tahini is also a classic Cypriot recipe – tahini is a paste made from sesame seeds.

Rabbit Stifado

Serves 4

1kg (2lb 2oz) very small onions
1 rabbit, cut into portions
oil for frying
125ml (4fl.oz) vinegar
225ml (8fl.oz) dry red wine
2-3 bay leaves
2 sticks cinnamon
salt and freshly ground black
pepper, to taste

For the bulgur pilau:
1 small onion, chopped
2 tablespoons olive oil
1 roll of vermicelli
200g (7oz) bulgur crushed wheat
1 stock cube (chicken or vegetable)
225ml (8fl.oz) water
1 ripe tomato, skinned and chopped

Peel the onions and wash and dry the rabbit. Fry the rabbit and onions gently in hot oil. Transfer to a dish and fry the onions gently until light brown. When the onions are cooked transfer them to another plate and put the rabbit back in the pan with the vinegar, wine, bay leaves and cinnamon. Let it simmer for 10 minutes then add the onions, salt and pepper and enough water just to cover. Simmer gently, stirring occasionally, for about 45 minutes, until the rabbit is tender and the sauce thickens,

Serve with bulgur pilau. To make this, gently fry the onion in the oil, add the crushed vermicelli and stir a couple of times. Then add the bulgur wheat (it doesn't need to cook, it will just absorb the water and be ready to serve), stock cube, water and tomatoes. Stir a few times and cook until the bulgur wheat absorbs all the water.

Remove from the heat, cover with a clean towel and put the lid on top so that all the moisture is absorbed. It will be ready to serve in 10 minutes.

Tahini Dip

Serves 4

1 jar (240g) tahini
Half 125ml (4fl.oz) luke warm water
1 level teaspoon salt
juice of 4-5 lemons
3 tablespoons olive oil
2 cloves garlic, crushed
finely chopped parsley

Place the tahini in a blender, add the water, then the salt and blend together. Gradually add the lemon juice and the olive oil. Taste and add more lemon juice or salt if required. Stop the blender and add the garlic and parsley. Mix with a wire whisk. Serve with hot pitta bread.

You can prepare this dip the night before. It is ideal to accompany roast or barbecued meats.

Paris & Rios Delicatessen

93 Columbia Road, London EC2 7RC. Tel: 0171 729 1147

I FIRST CAME ACROSS THIS FABULOUS delicatessen when working at a photographic studio on a food shoot just around the corner. Here Isabel Rios shares her wonderful fabada recipe. (Incidentally, this is one of my favourite dishes of all time as it originates from Asturias in the north-eastern region of Spain and my birthplace.) They sell hot dishes every day and I have sampled one of their white bean soups which was delicious. I highly recommend Isabel's recipe. For a vegetarian version of this dish, they suggest simply omitting the chorizo and serrano ham.

Fabada de Paris & Rios

Serves 6

450g (1lb) Spanish white beans
450g (14oz) can tomatoes
1 medium onion, diced
3 chorizos (Spanish cooking
sausage), chopped
115g (4oz) serrano ham, chopped
50ml (2floz) olive oil
2 cloves garlic, chopped
1 level tablespoon sweet
Spanish paprika
salt

Soak the beans overnight in water.

Put 3 litres (5¼ pints) of water into a large pot with the soaked beans. Add the tin of tomatoes with half of the diced onion. Bring to the boil on a high heat. Once boiling, reduce the heat to a simmer. After ½ hour of simmering, add the chopped chorizo and chopped serrano ham. Continue to simmer gently.

Depending on the size and quality of the beans, they should turn to a soft consistency after 1 hour.

When the beans are soft, remove the pan from the heat and set aside. In a frying pan, cook the remaining onion in the olive oil with the chopped garlic. When the onion is soft, remove the frying pan from the heat. Add the sweet Spanish paprika and 225ml (8fl.oz) of water, taken from the beans.

Add this mixture to the beans and bring to the boil again slowly. Simmer for 5-10 minutes, season, then serve.

The Place Below at St. Mary-le-Bow

Cheapside, London EC2V 6AU. Tel: 0171 329 0789

BILL SENDL STARTED COOKING while studying history at Trinity College, Cambridge. He was a vegetarian and at that time the so-called vegetarian 'options' available were so horrible that he began to cook for himself. He then found that he enjoyed cooking more than he enjoyed studying his subject, history.

On leaving Cambridge he got a job as a skivvy/cook at a vegetarian café in Westminster. He stayed there for a couple of years, then went off to train as an accountant, which he did not enjoy, but during that time he helped research a guide to London's vegetarian restaurants and spent time during the holidays cooking in them. He returned properly to working in the kitchen with a brief stint at Launceston Place before opening 'The Place Below' in the Norman crypt of St. Mary-le-Bow church (of Bow bells fame) in Cheapside, the heart of the City, in 1989. The food is enjoyed mostly by pin-striped non-vegetarians. The restaurant has won the 'Time Out' Vegetarian Meal of the Year Award and I have to agree, as a non-vegetarian, that I too enjoy the food there.

Here Bill shares one of his Greek-inspired dishes, a variation on the classic Greek salad. It is part hot, part cold and for maximum deliciousness needs to be served as soon as the hot ingredients are tossed in with the cold. In its unpretentious combination of fresh and simply treated ingredients, it is typical of the food served every day at The Place Below.

Roast Pepper, Broccoli and Feta Cheese Salad

Serves 4

3 red peppers, sliced lengthways
into eight pieces
75ml (3floz) olive oil
salt and freshly ground
black pepper
450g (1lb) broccoli florets
½ bunch fresh mint, leaves picked
off the stems and roughly chopped
1 small clove garlic, crushed
juice of ½ lemon
225g (8oz) very ripe tomatoes (e.g.
Marmande), chopped
175g (6oz) baby spinach
175g (6oz) feta cheese, crumbled or
in small cubes

Preheat the oven to 220°C/425°F/gas mark 7.
Toss the peppers in one third of the olive oil and season well with salt and pepper. Spread them out on a roasting tray and put in the oven for about 20 minutes until they are just colouring at the edges and feel squidgy rather than crisp to the touch.

Put a large pan of salted water on to boil. Five minutes before the peppers are ready, put the broccoli florets in the boiling water and boil for about 3-4 minutes, until barely cooked. Drain and toss immediately together with the mint, garlic, lemon juice, tomatoes, the rest of the olive oil, the peppers and the baby spinach which will wilt slightly. Season to taste with salt and pepper and arrange the feta cheese on top. Serve with foccacia bread to mop up the juices.

Shepherds

Marsham Court, Marsham Street, London SW1 4LA. Tel: 0171 834 9552

JAMES RICE IS HEAD CHEF at Shepherds, which is co-owned by Richard Shepherd and Michael Caine. His experience of cooking at Shepherd in Quinta do Lago in Portugal has introduced a Portuguese flavour to his cooking and has illustrated his ideas in this smoked haddock dish, which is traditionally English. The atmosphere here is also traditional – relaxed and comfortable.

Smoked Haddock with Leeks, Coriander and a Coddled Egg

Serves 4

1lb (450g) natural smoked haddock fillets
1 oz (25g) butter
400g (14oz) leeks, white and light parts only
1 bunch of fresh coriander
4 large cloves garlic
salt and fresh milled black pepper
300ml (½ pint) double cream
4 eggs, at room temperature

Preheat the oven to 180°C/325°F/gas mark 5.

Place the fillets of haddock, skin side up, on a buttered baking tray. Bake in the moderately hot oven for 10-12 minutes, depending on their thickness, until the skin is easily removed. When slightly cooled, remove and discard the skin and bones from the haddock. Put the flesh aside and keep warm.

Finely slice the leeks, wash and drain them thoroughly, then remove the leaves of the coriander and roughly chop them. Skin the garlic cloves and chop them finely. Place the cream and garlic in a pan, and slowly bring to the boil. Add the leeks and simmer until almost cooked, then season with pepper. Add the coriander and flaked smoked haddock and keep hot.

Place the eggs in boiling water and slowly simmer them for 4 minutes. Refresh in iced water and, when cool, carefully shell them. Return the eggs to hot water and warm through gently with a little added salt.

Pour the haddock and leek mixture onto warm plates, place the eggs gently on the top and season with pepper. Serve immediately.

This recipe can be doubled if desired and used as a main course.

Pâtisserie Valerie

44 Old Compton Street, Soho, London W1V SPB. Tel: 0171 437 3466

THE ORIGINAL PATISSERIE VALERIE was set up by Madame Valerie, a Belgian lady, in Frith Street, Soho in 1926 to feed starving artisans. In 1987, three Scalzo brothers took it over and, through their hard work and dedication, enhanced its reputation and success. It serves continental breakfasts, light lunches and, of course, tea and coffee. Their head chef, Ugo Amato, is Sicilian, and has great respect even from the best French pâtisseries.

The fashionable, cosmopolitan ski resort of Cortina d'Ampezzo in Italy was the inspiration

Cortina Cake

This quantity is sufficient for one 20cm (8in) round tier

125g (4½oz) plain flour
25g (1oz) cocoa powder
8 large eggs
150g (5oz) caster sugar
150ml (¼ pint) rum
25g (1oz) unsalted butter

For the filling:
(Crème chantilly)
Around 2½ times this quantity should be sufficient filling for all 3 tiers
600ml (1 pint) single cream, well chilled
100g (3½oz) icing sugar, sifted
1 teaspoon vanilla essence
a bottle of rum syrup

For the decoration:
3 cake boards of 20, 25 and 30cm (8, 10 and 12in)
6 white pillars
1.6kg (3½lb) white chocolate icing sugar

Preheat the oven to 180°C/350°F/gas mark 4.

Making the sponge: Coat the inside of an 20cm (8in) cake tin with oil and line the base and sides with greaseproof paper. Sift the flour and cocoa powder together twice to remove any lumps. Place the eggs and sugar in a heatproof mixing bowl and place it over a pan of simmering water. Beat thoroughly until thick and pale. Continue to whisk the mixture off the heat until it has cooled slightly and leaves a thick trail on the surface when the whisk is removed.

Lightly sprinkle half the sifted flour and cocoa over the mixture and carefully fold in by hand, using a metal spoon. Fold in the rum. Next, gently melt the butter in a pan and using another metal spoon, carefully fold the mixture in until all the ingredients are blended. Pour the mixture into the cake tin, smoothing with the end of a spatula and bake for 15-20 minutes or until the sponge is golden brown.

To check if it is cooked, look to see if it has shrunk slightly away from the sides of the tin and that it springs back when touched. Cool in the tin for 5 minutes before loosening the edges with a palette knife and turning it out onto a wire rack. Turn up the right way and leave to cool.

Making the crème chantilly filling: Place the cream, icing sugar and vanilla essence into a large mixing bowl and beating until the mixture forms stiff peaks and then chill. Lightly brush the sponge with rum syrup, spread the creme chantilly on to one sponge and sandwich together with another same size sponge.

Decorating the cake: Melt half the white chocolate in a heatproof bowl over a pan of simmering water and spread over the cake to cover the colour of the dark chocolate beneath.

for this stunning cake. Introduced by Ugo Amato over 14 years ago, the snowflake of white chocolate disguises a wickedly rich chocolate and rum Genoese sponge cake.

(Note: The design of this cake design is one that has taken Pâtisserie Valerie years to perfect, and requires a good deal of skill. Therefore the recipe which follows is a simplified version for the home cook to follow. The ingredients are enough for an 20cm (8in) round cake and you will need two rounds sandwiched together to form each tier.

Make a chocolate collar by spreading some melted chocolate onto a strip of greaseproof paper approximately 1cm (½in) deeper than the cake. Make sure it is deep enough to cover each tier and long enough to go around its outside. Cut the edges of the chocolate with a pastry cutter to get the serrated edge effect.

Wrap the chocolate collar around the sides of the cake. Shape the chocolate to the required shape and chill for 5 or 10 minutes or until it has set.

When firm, carefully peel back the paper. The top tier has a collar that is made in the same way but winds from the inside of the tier outwards to form a rose-like effect on the top. Do not wind too tightly as it is difficult to remove the paper once the chocolate has set.

The chocolate curls on top of the tiers can be made by pouring melted white chocolate onto a marble slab or cold worktop. Using a palette knife, spread the chocolate thinly over the surface. Before the chocolate sets, hold the knife at a 45 degree angle to the slab and pull gently at the surface until the chocolate lifts and curls. This can be done using a potato peeler directly on the chocolate block but tends to make smaller curls. Sift some icing sugar over all 3 layers.

Placing the tiers on top of one another is the most delicate part of the process. Make sure the pillars are evenly spread to achieve the correct weight distribution. To support the pillars, put a strip of dowelling through the tier underneath each pillar to take the weight. Or, use taller pillars glued one on top of another and cut the width of each pillar in each of the tiers and insert the tall pillars so that just the top one shows.

Mid-European Cooking

A distinctive food tradition, very different in character from the countries in the south around the Mediterranean, permeates Central Europe. With the collapse of communist regimes, countries such as the Czech Republic, Poland and Russia can re-discover the similarities and differences of their culinary heritage with Austria, Switzerland, Belgium, Germany and even Denmark. In London, their cooking is spread largely through the expatriate community, often initially secrets learned in the kitchens of their national social clubs and embassies. In recent years this knowledge has been expanded into several good new restaurants and delicatessens which stock authentic ingredients for home cooking.

Hot and cold vodkas, along with other spirits, often helped to create the atmosphere of these establishments in the past, but the quality of food now served ensures success by itself. With once-luxury products like caviar becoming more recognisable and affordable, the enthusiasm for mid-European cuisine is growing fast.

Wodka was once a dairy, but now is an excellent restaurant serving authentic Polish food.

Zuzaka Audest

Private Address

Zuzaka Audest was born in the former Czechoslovakia, but for the past 20 years she has lived in England. She has raised her family here, and with two teenage sons, you can imagine that she has done a fair amount of cooking .

For many years Zuzaka has worked for the BBC World Service and, after a hard day at work, she finds cooking quite a nice way to relax and unwind. This recipe is one of her family's favourites.

Prague Pork Fillets with Apricots

Serves 4-6

4 tablespoons oil
50g (2oz) butter
2 large onions, chopped
2 cloves garlic
900g (2lb) lean pork fillets
salt and freshly ground pepper
1 teaspoon ground ginger
25g (1oz) fresh root ginger, grated
1 tablespoon Worcestershire sauce
1 tablespoon soy sauce
1 large tin (450g /1lb) of apricots, drained (reserving the juice)
150ml (¼ pint) orange juice
1 teaspoon brown sugar
2 tablespoons plain flour

Preheat the oven to 190°C/375°F/gas mark 5.

Heat the oil and butter together in a large pan. Add the onions and garlic and sauté for 5 minutes. Sprinkle the pork fillets with salt, pepper and ground ginger on one side and spread fresh grated ginger on the other. Transfer the onions to a casserole dish.

Add a little oil to the pan and fry the pork fillets for 3 minutes on each side until golden brown. Add to the onions in the casserole dish, sprinkle with Worcestershire sauce and soy sauce, then pour the juice from the apricots and the orange juice over the meat. Sprinkle with the brown sugar.

Cover and let it gently simmer for about 10 minutes over a low heat, if necessary adding about 150ml (¼ pint) of water. Cover and transfer to the preheated oven and cook for about 40 minutes. Mix the flour with water and add to the juices to thicken. Finally, add the apricots. Serve with rice, green salad and a smile.

Renate Brautigam

Austrian Embassy, 18 Belgrave Mews West, London SW1 9AB. Tel: 0171 235 3731

RENATE BRAUTIGAM works as the press secretary to the Austrian Embassy. She loves food and feels strongly that in London too few people complain about the standards of food in restaurants. Her experience of eating out in France and Italy have shown her that if standards of food are not up to scratch there, customers are very ready to make vociferous complaints. She feels the result is that in London standards sometimes do not improve, as valid complaints may not be followed up, listened to or acted upon.

Something Renate misses in London is the widespread availability of good, freshly baked bread. She misses the wonderful family-run Austrian bakeries, who bake their bread daily.

Renate shares with us several typical Austrian dishes. Her secret addition to the Stuffed Green Peppers below is a good dash of hot pepper sauce to the tomato sauce, to give it a bit of a kick. If you can make the dish the day before, the flavours will develop and improve on standing, then it can simply be heated up the next day.

Stuffed Green Peppers

Serves 4

For the tomato sauce:
450g (1lb) tomatoes
1 small onion
1 tablespoon fat
salt and freshly ground pepper
sugar
25g (1oz) flour
a little lemon juice

4 large green peppers
1 dessertspoon fat
1 small onion, chopped
50g (2oz) rice
225g (8oz) lean mince (preferably beef and pork mixed)
chopped fresh parsley
salt and pepper

Preheat the oven to 170°C/325°F/gas mark 3.

To make the tomato sauce: Slice or quarter the tomatoes, chop the onion, then melt the fat in a theavy-based saucepan, add onions and brown them lightly. Add the tomatoes, salt, pepper and a little sugar to taste. Fry for a few minutes, then add the flour and mix well. Cover with water, add a little lemon juice and simmer until the tomatoes are pulpy, stirring occasionally.

Cut the tops off the peppers, remove the inside parts and pour hot water over the peppers. Leave for 5 minutes, then drain off the water. Melt the fat, fry the chopped onion lightly, then add the rice and fry until the rice is transparent.

Add 175ml (6fl.oz) of water and simmer until all the water has been absorbed. The rice should then be half cooked. Add the mince, parsley, salt and pepper. Mix everything together and fill the peppers. Replace the pepper tops and stand the peppers in a deep casserole dish.

Pass the tomatoes sauce mixture. through a sieve and pour over the peppers in the casserole (the tomato sauce should be fairly thin). Cover the casserole with a lid and either bake in the preheated oven or cook on top of the stove over a very low heat for 25 minutes, until the meat and peppers are cooked.

Serve with rice or plain boiled potatoes.

Renate Brautigam

AUSTRIA'S CUISINE is derived from a process of the intermingling of people and cultures which at one time or another belonged to the Austro-Hungarian Empire, which had existed for more than 600 years. Within this time the cosmopolitan Hapsburg rule extended to Switzerland, Alsace, Burgundy, Spain, Holland, Bohemia, Moravia, Slovakia, Poland, Hungary, Croatia, Slovenia, Italy and even Mexico.

The famous Apfel Strudel actually is the Austrian version of something the Turks concocted when they were not busy laying siege to

Leberknödelsuppe (Liver Dumpling Soup)

Serves 6

25g (1oz) butter
1 small onion, chopped
1 tablespoon chopped fresh parsley
150g (5oz) finely minced liver
salt and freshly ground pepper
2 moist bread rolls
1 egg, beaten
breadcrumbs
marjoram
garlic
beef broth, to serve
chopped chives, to garnish

Melt the butter and brown the chopped onion, then mix in the parsley, liver and seasoning. Add the broken up rolls, the egg, marjoram and garlic and work into a smooth dough. After allowing the mixture to stand for 10 minutes, mix with enough breadcrumbs to allow you to form little dumplings.

Simmer the dumplings in a pan of boiling, salted water for 10 minutes. Drain and serve the dumplings in the beef broth. Sprinkle with chopped chives.

Tafelspitz (Boiled Beef)

Serves 6

1 carrot, sliced
2 celery stalks, sliced
1 leek, sliced
salt
1.4 litres (2½ pints) water
½ bunch of fresh parsley
1 bay leaf
700g (1½lb) lean fine-grained beef, diced

Put the cleaned and prepared vegetables in salted water and bring to the boil; add the meat and allow to cook until tender, making sure that the meat is always covered with liquid.

Serve either with hot vegetables, such as spinach or cabbage. The traditional way to serve it is with hot or cold chive sauce and/or horseradish with grated apples (mix together 2 tablespoons horseradish, 1 peeled, grated apple, 2 tablespoon warm broth, salt and a little sugar to taste).

Vienna. The Turks too are the instigators of Vienna's café society, by introducing the roasted coffee beans around the city.

Austrian cooking is therefore mostly the cuisine of Vienna, which was itself a culinary melting pot. There are, of course, dishes typical of the other regions, but they are not often exported, being of only local importance or peasant dishes. Traditional influences include the roasts and sausages from southern Germany and the pastries from Bohemia. Renate Brautigam offers some more of her traditional Austrian dishes.

Wiener Schnitzel

Serves 4

4 veal fillets, 115-150g (4-5oz) each
4 tablespoons flour
salt
2 eggs, beaten
about 6 tablespoons breadcrumbs
cooking fat

Pound the veal fillets, flour them, dip them in beaten, salted egg, then in breadcrumbs. Coat them evenly on both sides, then fry them in hot, deep fat until golden brown. Serve with a slice of lemon, lettuce and boiled potatoes sprinkled with parsley.

Sachertorte (Chocolate Gâteau)

Serves 8-12

150g (5oz) butter
150g (5oz) good dark chocolate, melted
100g (3½oz) caster sugar
8 eggs, separated
50g (2oz) caster sugar
150g (5oz) plain flour
hot apricot jam

For the chcoclate icing:
20g (7oz) sugar
200ml (7fl.oz) water
175g (6oz) good dark chocolate

Preheat the oven to 170°C/325°F/gas mark 3.
Beat the butter, chocolate and 100g (3oz) sugar together until fluffy, then beat in the egg yolks one by one. Whisk the egg whites. Add the remaining sugar then fold carefully into the butter mixture, adding the flour as you go along. Grease a 30cm (12in) cake tin. Sprinkle with flour, spoon in the cake mixture and bake slowly for 1½ hours. Turn out on to a cake rack and allowthe cake to cool. Glaze the top of the cake with hot apricot jam and cover with the chocolate icing
For the icing: Bring the sugar and water to the boil and boil until the mixture candies. Add the chocolate and boil until the mixture is thick but fluid. Spread this with a wet knife over the cake. Serve in slices.

Muriel Brouckert

Belgian Embassy, 103 Eaton Square, London SW1 9AB. Tel: 0171 235 5422

MURIEL BROUCKERT is Flemish and this is her father's recipe – he was the cook in her family's household. He inherited the recipe from his mother. Unfortunately she doesn't know the full history behind the recipe, but remembers her father cooking it for minor special occasions such as a birthday. It is usually served with Belgian fries or croquettes. Muriel also serves some good dark Belgian beer with the meal, to make it even more traditionally Belgian.

Lapin à la Flamande

Serves 4

115g (4oz) bacon
115g (4oz) butter
3 onions, finely chopped
1 rabbit
mustard
1 teaspoon salt per 1kg (2lb 2oz) of meat
freshly ground black pepper
nutmeg
3 bay leaves
thyme
garlic
1 glass red wine or 1 bottle dark beer
2 tablespoons wine vinegar
half a glass of water
2 tablespoons sugar
½ tablespoon potato flour
2teaspoon cornflour
prunes and raisins, to serve

Cut the bacon into squares and fry it with 25g (1oz) butter in a frying pan. Add the finely chopped onions after 15 minutes and let it simmer. Cut the rabbit into pieces and reserve the liver. Rub some mustard on the meat, and then fry it in the rest of the butter until golden brown. Add the bacon, onion, salt, pepper, nutmeg, bay, thyme, garlic, wine or beer, vinegar, water, sugar and liver to the rabbit. Cover well and let it simmer for 2 hours.

Take the meat from the pan, let the sauce cool down and remove the fat. Thicken the sauce by adding the potato flour and cornflour. Add the meat, heat through until piping hot and serve with prunes and raisins or apple compote.

Note: It is nice to serve this meal in the evenings with bread. I have changed a few things to the recipe. I fry the rabbit in olive oil, but still tend to use butter with the bacon and onion to keep the taste. I also put the prunes and raisins in milk overnight and put them in with the rabbit to cook together for 2 hours. I generally cook the rabbit with beer and wine vinegar because, together with the sugar, it adds a nice sweet and sour taste to the dish.

Jan Gasparfki

Jan Gasparfki is Polish and is working in London for a major food manufacturer. He enjoys cooking and prepares this traditional Polish dish to remind him of home.

Cooking in Poland has a characteristic mid-European style. Sausage and other meats, as well as pickled vegetables, dumplings and other forms of suet, provide sustaining winter meals.

Bigos

Serves 4

450g (1lb) sauerkraut
250g (9oz) spicy continental sausage, roughly chopped
115g (4oz) mushrooms, roughly chopped
1 teaspoon cumin seeds
300ml (½ pint) red wine
1 x 400g (14oz) can chopped tomatoes
salt and freshly ground black pepper

Place all the ingredients in a large pan, mix well and bring to the boil. Cover and simmer for 2 hours. Allow to cool, pour into a non-metallic container and leave for 1-2 days in the fridge before eating (this will allow the flavours to develop fully).

Serve cold with white continental bread.

Anna Glowka

ANNA GLOWKA is a final year Economics student at the London School of Economics and Political Science. She enjoys cooking and preparing various interesting dishes and finds it very relaxing (as well as tasty afterwards!). She especially likes to experiment with new recipes and is always on the lookout for novel ideas, as well as new tastes and textures.

Here she shares one of her family's favourite dishes, Carp in Mushroom Sauce. Carp is the traditional food to serve on Christmas Eve in Poland, as meat is not normally eaten on that day. The Christmas Eve dinner is full of traditions, and usually the whole family gathers together to enjoy the feast. This delicious fish can, of course, be enjoyed equally well on any other day of the year too.

Anna wishes you 'Smaeznego!' which, loosely translated, means 'Enjoy your meal' but it is actually closer to the French 'Bon appetit!'

Carp in Mushroom Sauce

Serves 4

Carp weighing about 1.5kg (3¼ lb)
lemon juice
salt and freshly ground pepper
flour
oil for frying
500g (1lb 2oz) small wild
mushrooms
300ml (½ pint) soured cream
about 2 tablespoons melted butter

Preheat the oven to 180°C/350°F/gas mark 4.

Prepare the fish and sprinkle it with lemon juice and salt and pepper to taste. Coat the fish in flour and fry in hot oil for 1-2 minutes on each side. Transfer the fish into a baking dish.

Use the oil left from frying the fish to fry the mushrooms (if using larger mushrooms, cut them into smaller pieces first). Cover the fish with fried mushrooms, soured cream and melted butter. Bake in the preheated oven for about 10-12 minutes per pound. Serve immediately with Polish-style bread or crusty white rolls and mixed salad leaves.

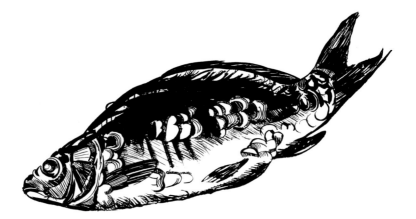

Andrew Grad

ANDREW GRAD, property entrepreneur, shares this favourite recipe, translated from his Hungarian mother's cookbook. A keen bee keeper in Putney, he produces his own honey while his wife Sally looks after the hens (kept for eggs, not for this recipe!) Andrew has a great knowledge and interest in food and enjoys exploring good bakeries, especially in the Golders Green area.

Hungarian Chicken and Potato Casserole

Serves 4

2 small tender chickens
450g (1lb) potatoes
1 teaspoon salt
300ml (½ pint) soured cream
75g (3oz) butter, melted
50g (2oz) grated cheese
50g (2oz) sliced mushrooms
1 tablespoon chopped fresh parsley
300ml (½ pint) chicken stock
black pepper to taste

Preheat the oven to 180°C/350°F/gasmark 4.

Cut each chicken into four pieces and then cut the potatoes into 2.5cm (1in) cubes. Grease a large casserole, put a layer of potato cubes in the bottom, and sprinkle with salt. Arrange the chicken pieces neatly over the bed of potatoes, spoon over 150ml (¼ pint) of soured cream and some of the melted butter. Sprinkle with salt, some grated cheese and the sliced mushrooms, then add the remaining potatoes mixed with parsley. Mix the remaining soured cream, melted butter, chicken stock and grated cheese and pepper together and pour this sauce over the potatoes.

Cover and cook in the preheated oven for about 1 hour. Take the lid off after 45 minutes and leave in the oven for a further 15-20 minutes to brown nicely. Serve with a green salad.

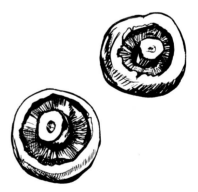

W. Hillie

Embassy of the Federal Republic of Germay, 23, Belgrave Square, London SW1X 8SD Tel: 0171 235 5033

W. HILLIE FROM THE CULTURAL DEPARTMENT of the Embassy of the Federal Republic of Germany shares two of his homeland recipes. Marinated Beef is traditionally served with Potato Dumplings and Apple Sauce (Sauerbraten mit Kartoffeldoessen and Apfelmus). Sauerbraten is a traditional German dish which has become popular abroad. It is claimed by several German regions as their own, but the recipe that follows is from the Rhineland.

Rheinischer Sauerbraten

Serves 6

1.5 kg (3¼lb) rolled brisket, topside
or silverside of beef
1 tablespoon salt
½ teaspoon pepper
2 onions, sliced
1 carrot, sliced
1 stalk celery, chopped
4 cloves
4 peppercorns
2 tablespoons red wine vinegar
2 bay leaves
2 tablespoons kidney fat or dripping
6 tablespoons butter
5 tablespoons flour
1 tablespoon sugar
115g (4oz) sultanas (optional)
8-10 gingersnaps, crushed (or 1 teaspoon cornstarch or arrowroot)

Wipe the beef with a damp cloth then season with salt and pepper. Place in an earthenware bowl. Combine the onions, carrot, celery, cloves, peppercorns, vinegar and bay leaves and pour over meat. Cover and marinate in the refrigerator for 4 days.

On the fifth day, remove from the refrigerator and drain the meat. Sauté the meat in the kidney fat or dripping and 1 tablespoon butter in an enamelware or earthenware pot, until seared on all sides. Add the marinade liquid, bring to the boil, then lower the heat and simmer for about 3 hours.

Melt the remaining 5 tablespoons butter in a pan. Stir the flour smoothly into it. Add the sugar, blend together and let it brown to a nice dark colour. Stir the roux into the liquid in the pot and add the sultanas, if using. Cover and continue to simmer until the meat is tender, about 1 hour longer.

Remove the meat to a warm serving platter. Stir the crushed gingersnaps or the starch into the pot juices and cook until thickened. Pour over the meat. Serve with potato dumplings (see below) and apple sauce. Red cabbage is a good accompaniment.

Potato Dumplings

Serves 6

6 medium-sized potatoes
(about 1kg/2lb 2oz)
3 eggs
6 teaspoons flour
melted brown butter and
breadcrumbs, to serve

Boil the potatoes, drain and allow them to stand for a few hours or overnight, still in their jackets. Peel the potatoes and mash them or put them through a mincer. Add the eggs and the flour and roll the mixture into little balls. Chill in the refrigerator for about 1 hour before cooking.

Cook in a pan of lightly salted water that is just under boiling point. When the dumplings are cooked, they will rise to the top.

Serve hot with a mixture of melted brown butter and breadcrumbs.

Serge Moes

Embassy of Luxembourg, 27 Wilton Crescent, London SW1X 8SD. Tel: 0171 235 8961

SERGE MOES IS A KEEN Luxembourg cook who has lived in London for 15 years. In that time has seen the variety of ingredients available increase dramatically. He still feels, however, that eating out in London costs far more than it does in Luxembourg, even though he willingly acknowledges that the variety and choice to be found in London is astounding.

Trout in Riesling Sauce

Serves 4

4 trout weighing 225g/8oz each
salt and freshly ground pepper
flour
50g (2oz) unsalted butter
3 shallots, chopped
parsley
pinch of chevril
sprig of tarragon
chives
200ml (7fl.oz) dry Reisling
paprika
300ml (½ pint) fresh double cream
50g (2oz) unsalted butter

Preheat the oven to 180°C/350°F/gas mark 4.

Clean, wash and dry the trout with a cloth. Sprinkle them with salt, pepper and flour. Melt the butter in a pan and fry the trout gently for 2 to 3 minutes on each side. Meanwhile grease an ovenproof dish and place the trout in it. Fry the shallots and finely chopped herbs in the frying pan, add the Riesling and pour this mixture over the trout. Season to taste with pepper, salt and a pinch of paprika and place the dish into the preheated oven. Cook for 15-20 minutes, basting the trout occasionally.

Take the trout out and put them on a hot plate. Add the fresh cream and butter to the sauce as you boil it and whisk until it is thick. Cover the trout with the sauce and serve with boiled potatoes and a side salad.

Drinks to accompany this dish: A top notch Riesling, or a Pinot Gris, both very dry. Instead of Riesling wine, my tip is to use some Luxembourg Elbling, which is really crisp and dry.

Nikitas

65 Ifield Road, London SW10 9AU. Tel: 0171 352 6326

THIS IS A VERY COSY RESTAURANT, full of private alcoves with a friendly and relaxed atmosphere. It is the best place to enjoy a wide variety of different types of vodka.

Sylvain Borsi, the owner and chef of Nikitas, gives us his favourite recipe from the restaurant. This is very simple to make, using plain ingredients but producing a very delicious result!

Pozharsky Cutlets

Serves 4

4 slices white bread
300ml (½ pint) milk
4 chicken breasts
150ml (¼ pint) double cream
salt and freshly ground
black pepper
75g (3oz) breadcrumbs for coating
50g (2oz) butter for frying
1 tablespoon chopped fresh
coriander

Soak the bread in the milk and drain away the excess liquid. Place the chicken breasts and soaked bread in a blender and blend until smooth. Add the double cream and seasoning and mix well. With damp hands, form the mixture into 4 cutlet shapes and coat with the breadcrumbs on both sides. Melt the butter and fry the cutlets slowly until nice and golden brown.

Serve the cutlets hot, sprinkled with chopped coriander.

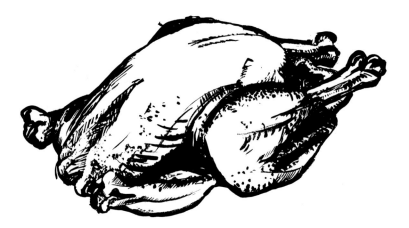

Nils

NILS WAS BORN IN YORKSHIRE to a Danish mother and English father who met in Denmark while he was playing cricket for Oxford University.

In London, he is now pursuing a career in wildlife photography, but still enjoys cooking traditional Danish dishes. This dish is a Jutland favourite; like most Danish food, it is simple, with distinctly separate flavours, and it is made with the freshest of ingredients. Sest Frikadeller is a variation of this recipe, it also contains herbs and spices, which have been developed by generations of experimentation.

Frikadeller (Danish Meat Dumplings)

Serves 4

2 tablespoons fine dry breadcrumbs
125ml (4fl.oz) single cream (or top of the milk)
225g (8oz) minced veal
225g (8oz) minced pork
2 egg yolks
½ teaspoon salt
¼ teaspoon black pepper
300ml (½ pint) water
2 beef stock cubes

Soak the breadcrumbs in the milk and mix these together thoroughly with the veal, pork, egg yolks and seasonings. Using 2 teaspoons, shape the mixture into small balls.

Heat the water in a large pan, add the stock cubes and stir until these have dissolved. Reduce the heat until the stock is just simmering. Add the meatballs, a few at a time, and cook for approximately 5 minutes. Remove carefully, drain on kitchen paper and keep warm.

Serve with boiled or mashed potatoes.

Note: Ask your butcher to mince the meat finely – this makes the end result less like a hamburger.

Mrs R. Rojcevic

Embassy of Yugoslavia, 5 Lexham Gardens, London W8 SJU. Tel: 0171 370 6105

THIS RECIPE HAS BEEN SUPPLIED by Mrs. R. Rojcevic from the Yugoslavian Embassy. She used to live in the former Yugoslavia, but she now lives in London and enjoys cooking her favourite dish from home. The ingredients for this dish are readily available, and is very simply made. It is a popular dish among the former Yugoslavs who are now residing in London.

Meat Pie

Serves 4

175g (6oz) onion, chopped
350ml (12fl.oz) oil
700g (1½lb) of beef, ground
25g (1oz) fresh parsley, chopped
1 tablespoon salt
½ teaspoon pepper
450g (1lb) strudel pastry sheets
6 eggs
350ml (12fl.oz) plain yogurt
350ml (12fl.oz) mineral water

Preheat the oven to 180°C/350°F/gas mark 4.
Fry the onion in the oil until it is light brown. Add the meat and cook it gently until the moisture evaporates. Add the parsley, salt and pepper and remove from the heat.

Put 3 pastry sheets on the bottom of an oiled casserole (save 3 pastry sheets for the top). Make layers of the prepared meat and the pastry sheets. On the top put the 3 pastry sheets, cut into pieces of a desired size.

Beat the eggs well. Add the yogurt and mineral water and beat well. Cover the pie with this mixture. Set aside for 2 hours then bake it in the preheated oven for 45 minutes.

Serve immediately, cut into slices.

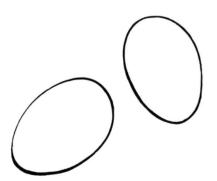

Christopher Roscyki

Private Address

CHRISTOPHER ROSCYKI was born in Poland and graduated from the Lodz School of Theatre and Film. He came to England in 1978 speaking very little English, and had a number of jobs including working in a Polish sausage factory and briefly as an ice cream seller. Of the Polish sausage factory Christopher says, 'After three days I smelled like bacon – it was terrible'.

Recently, Christopher has been playing Edonard de Pomiane, one of the great French cookery writers of this century, in a programme screened on BBC TV and entitled 'French Cooking in Ten Minutes'.

However, when he's not acting, it's back to Polish food – in a commercial sense. As the breaks between contracts can sometimes be long, he uses the time to make Pirogis, which he supplies to local delicatessens. Here Christopher shares his recipe for Pirogis, a Polish delicacy which is stuffed with three kinds of filling: meat (pork or beef) with spices, sauerkraut and mushroom, or potato with cheese.

Pirogis

Serves 4

For the dough:
1kg (2lb 2oz) plain flour
300ml (½ pint) warm water
2 large eggs
2 tablespoons oil

For the fillings:
1 teaspoon of meat filling
(½ quantity pork to beef)
crushed garlic
1 chopped and fried onion

sauerkraut and mushrooms

mashed potato, curd cheese and dill
salt and pepper

oil for deep-frying

Mix the ingredients for the dough together, then roll out as thinly as possible. Cut with a round cutter (about 4cm/1½in diameter) and fill each pastry with one of the fillings.

Fold the pastry circle in half and seal well to form a half moon shape. Cook in a pan of boiling water for 5 minutes. Drain the meat-filled Pirogis and serve hot with melted butter and a salad, or with fried bacon.

Pat dry the boiled sauerkraut and potato Pirogis (not the meat-filled ones) and briefly deep fry until crisp. Serve hot.

Stravinsky's Russian Tea House

6 Fulham High Street, London SW6 .Tel: 0171 371 0001

DAVID FANILOV, ORIGINALLY FROM AZERBAIJAN, is the proprietor of Stravinsky's Russian Tea House. This is a relaxed café where you can enjoy traditional Russian delicacies. There are lots of sweet dishes displayed in the window and at the counter and inside there are a large number of teas to sample. With a traditional dark wood interior, it is an interesting place to sit and spend some time.

Stravinsky's Borscht

Serves 6-8

1 large raw beetroot
1 tablespoon vinegar
25g (1oz) bacon fat
2 teaspoons sugar
2 tomatoes, chopped
2 onions
1 carrot
1 parsley root or ½ parsnip
25g (1oz) slightly salted butter
½ large cabbage
450g (1lb) potatoes
1.7 litres (3 pints) good beef stock
5-6 peppercorns
3 allspice berries
3 bay leaves
1 head of garlic, peeled
fresh chopped parsley
150g (5oz) sour cream

Put the chopped raw beetroot, vinegar, a little bacon fat, sugar, and chopped tomatoes in a pan and cook gently with the lid on for a few minutes. Chop the onions, carrot, and parsley root finely and braise in the butter.

Chop the cabbage and cut the potatoes into little chunks then simmer in the stock for 15 minutes. Add the beetroot mixture, the braised vegetables, the peppercorns, allspice and bay leaves and cook for 10 minutes. Add the minced garlic, the remainder of the bacon fat and the chopped parsley. Let the Borscht cook and mature very slowly over a low heat for 4½ hours. Allow it to stand for 12-18 hours to cool.

Reheat gently before serving and add a teaspoon of sour cream per serving. Serve with some dark rye bread.

Sibilla Whitehead

Private Address

THIS IS A TRADITIONAL SWEDISH family recipe from Sibilla Whitehead's mother's side of the family, who come from Götenberg. Sibilla did a 1-year diploma at Leith's Cookery School, and has worked freelance for five years. She is now studying film at the University of Westminster. She enjoys cooking at home, where she delights her friends with her Swedish delicacies.

Swedish Meatballs

Serves 4 – 6

For the meatballs:
115g (4oz) breadcrumbs
150ml (¼ pint) hot water
1 red onion, finely chopped
butter, for frying
225g (8oz) lean minced beef
225g (8oz) minced pork
1 teaspoon ground allspice
salt and pepper
1 tablespoon chopped chives
1 egg yolk

For the sauce:
25g (1oz) plain flour
300ml (½ pint) meat stock
300ml (½ pint) double cream
salt and freshly ground pepper

Soak the breadcrunbs in the hot water. Fry the onion in a little butter until soft and translucent; set aside to cool.

In a large bowl, mix all the meatball ingredients together until well mixed. Check the seasoning. Shape the mixture into small meatballs and fry in batches of 8-10 in a skillet or heavy frying pan. Shake the skillet occasionally so the meatballs don't stick and they remain round. Keep warm.

Stir the flour into the skillet or frying pan, mix with fat and brown a little, scraping all the sediment from the bottom of the pan. Gradually add the meat stock and whisk until smooth. Add the cream, then cook uncovered, for about 10 minutes, stirring occasionally. Season to taste. Serve the meatballs with the sauce.

This dish is yummy served with mashed potatoes and lingonberry (or cranberry) sauce.

Asian Cooking

Asia embraces many different food traditions and cooking techniques, and most of these can be found somewhere in London. Indian cuisine is extremely well developed in the capital, reflecting Britain's long-standing historical links with the sub-contintent. Certain areas of London represent different aspects of Indian food, which is very regional in character. Brick Lane in the East End, for example, is a Bengali area; Wembley a Gujarati area; Southall in west London predominantly Punjabi and Sikh.

South-east Asian cooking has also made a huge impact on the London food world. Thai restaurants are one of the capital's most popular recent developments, and specialist supermarkets provide authentic ingredients for home cooking, such as leaves of the banana or the kaffir lime, home-made Thai pastes and different types of chillies. Chinese cooking has become popular through take-aways and regional restaurants and shops are widespread. The Japanese culinary tradition is a relative newcomer, but is proving very successful, with several excellent restaurants, supermarkets catering for the Japanese style of cooking.

Excellent Chinese supermarkets in Gerrard Street supply most of Soho's Chinatown.

Bayee Village Chinese Restaurant

24 High Street London SW19 5DX. Tel: 0181 947 3533

CHINESE FOOD HAS A well-established presence in London. The Bayee Village Chinese Restaurant in Wimbledon is one of my local haunts, and the food is deliciously fresh tasting.

Seafood dishes are a house speciality, with the Sichuan and Beijing cuisines dominating. One particularly unusual dish is the marron duck, stuffed with chestnuts.

Sour and Hot Soup

Serves 6

25g (1oz) Chinese mushrooms
15g (½oz) dried fungi
cucumber
50g (2oz) bamboo shoots
25g (1oz) boneless chicken breasts
1.4 litres (2½ pints) chicken stock
1 tablespoon dark soy sauce
salt and white pepper
1 tablespoon cornflour
4 tablespoons vinegar
1 egg, well beaten
1 teaspoon sesame oil

Soak the mushrooms and fungi in warm water for 2 hours. Shred the cucumber, bamboo shoots, Chinese mushrooms and chicken.

Bring the stock to the boil, add the cucumber, bamboo shoots, mushrooms, soy sauce and salt. Blend the cornflour and cold water together and add to the stock, stirring. Cook for approximately 10 minutes. Add the shredded chicken to the soup, cook for 20 minutes then add the vinegar and white pepper.

Away from the heat, pour the beaten egg into the soup, stirring very gently. Add a few drops of sesame oil and serve immediately.

Steamed Sea Bass with Spring Onions and Ginger

Serves 6

1kg (2lb 2oz) sea bass
2 spring onions
2 tablespoons shredded ginger
3 tablespoons cooking oil
2 tablespoons light soy sauce
salt and pepper

Scale and gill the fish. Wash and wipe dry.

Section the spring onion bulbs, arrange them on the centre of a plate and place the fish on top (this is to prevent the fish sticking to the plate and to facilitate steam circulation in cooking). Shred the spring onion tops and set aside. Sprinkle the ginger shreds over the fish and steam for 7 minutes over a pan of simmering water. Drain off the surplus liquid from the plate.

Place the shredded spring onion tops over the fish. Heat the oil and pour it over the shredded spring onions, then pour the soy sauce around both sides of the fish (avoid pouring the sauce directly over the fish as its taste may be distorted by seasoning). Season and serve immediately.

Lobster Cooked with Ginger and Spring Onions

Serves 6

900g (2lb) fresh lobster
3 tablespoons cornflour
1.2 litres (2 pints) cooking oil
4 spring onions, chopped
½ onion, chopped
50g (2oz) root ginger, sliced
300ml (½ pint) stock
2 tablespoons oyster sauce
1 tablespoon soy sauce
1 tablespoon sugar
1 tablespoon white wine

Wash and clean the lobster. Pierce and skewer or push chopsticks into the tail of the lobster and drain the liquids (lobster moisture). Chop the lobster between the neck and the main body.

Cut the lobster into small pieces, trim the legs and use the back of your knife (chopper) to crack the claws. Take away the killer. Sprinkle cornflour over every piece of lobster.

Bring the cooking oil to a very hot temperature or until a piece of dry bread browns in 30 seconds. Put in the lobster pieces and fry for about 20 seconds. Remove from the oil and drain well.

Heat 3 tablespoons of oil in a wok and lightly brown the spring onions, onion and ginger slices. Add the lobster to the wok, stir and mix well. Add the stock or water, then season with oyster sauce, soy sauce and sugar. Put the lid on, cook for approximately 7 minutes to reduce the sauce, then add the wine.
Serve immediately.

Mridula Baljekar

Private Address

MRIDULA BALJEKAR is the Indian food consultant to Tesco, a post that was created for her after she and her family had eaten one of the existing Tesco Indian ready meals and thought it inedible, so recommended a recipe from her own book, *The Complete Indian Cookbook*. She teaches at the Tante Marie School in Woking and frequently travels back to her homeland.

This recipe from Goa for mixed meat curry combines the East–West blend of influences in Indian cooking. Indian cuisine is well known for its regional variations and this recipe from Goa on the west coast offers an amazing variety of flavours, with a very distinctive style. Goan food is a perfect example of the harmonious blend of the three predominant religions, Hindu, Muslim and Christian. Goan cuisine has been also shaped to its unique style by the Portuguese.

Goan Mixed-Meat Curry

Serves 6

175g (6oz) trimmed lean stewing beef
175g (6oz) boned and trimmed lean pork (shoulder or leg)
175g (6oz) skinned and boned chicken thighs
175g (6oz) any fresh spicy sausages
50 ml (2fl.oz) sunflower oil
1 large onion, finely sliced
4 large cloves garlic
4cm (1½in) piece of fresh root ginger, peeled and grated
1 teaspoon ground turmeric
1 chicken stock cube
1 beef stock cube
450ml (¾ pint) warm water
6 whole cloves
2 x 5cm (2 inch) pieces cassia bark or cinnamon sticks, halved
175g (6oz) potatoes, peeled and cut into 2.5cm (1 inch) cubes
1 teaspoon ground cumin
150ml (¼ pint) single cream
½ teaspoon salt or to taste
½-1 teaspoon black pepper

Cut the beef, pork and chicken into 2.5cm (1in) cubes. Grill the sausages until well browned. When cool, cut each sausage into 3-4 pieces.

Put the beef in a saucepan and add 125ml (4fl.oz) water. Bring to the boil over a high heat. Reduce the heat to medium, cover the pan and cook for 15-20 minutes or until the beef is completely dry. Remove from the heat and set aside.

Heat the oil over a medium heat in a heavy-based saucepan and fry the onions until they are soft but not brown. Add the boiled beef, the pork, garlic, ginger and turmeric. Stir and fry for 3-4 minutes. Add the stock cubes blended with the warm water and the cloves and cassia or cinnamon. Bring to the boil, cover the pan and simmer for another 20 minutes, stirring occasionally. Add the chicken and bring back to the boil. Cover and simmer for 10 minutes.*

Add the potatoes, sausages and cumin. Cover and simmer for 20-25 minutes or until the potatoes are tender.

Add the cream, salt and pepper, stir and mix well. Simmer, uncovered, for 5-6 minutes, then remove from the heat. Serve with plain boiled basmati rice and steamed broccoli tossed in a little garlic butter.

*Cook's note: If you want to freeze this dish, then do so at the point indicated.. Thaw and complete rest of recipe.

Bengal Clipper

11-12 Cardamom Building, Shad Thames, Butler's Wharf, London SE1. Tel: 0171 357 9001

RUF UDDIN, HEAD CHEF from The Bengal Clipper restaurant in China Wharf, in East London, shares one of the restaurant's popular lamb dishes. This fairly hot curry is made to a recipe which originates from the central regions of India. It features a special sauce made with whole coriander seeds and bulb chillies, which gives it its unique flavour.

Lamb Curry

Serves 4

For the lamb curry:
225ml (8fl.oz) vegetable oil
900g (2lb) boneless lean lamb, cut into large, bite-sized pieces
3 medium onions, peeled and finely chopped
2 medium tomatoes, chopped
3 cinnamon sticks
3 green cardamom pods
4 bay leaves
4 cloves
5 curry leaves
2.5cm (1in) peeled root ginger
½ teaspoon ground turmeric
1 teaspoon ground cumin
1 teaspoon ground coriander
4 garlic cloves

For the kadi massala:
15 bulb chillies
2 tablespoons whole coriander seeds
1 tablespoon whole cumin seeds
4 whole cloves
4 green cardamom seeds
3 javentri (mace)

To serve:
225ml (8fl.oz) plain yogurt
salt, to taste
3 tablespoons chopped fresh coriander

To prepare the lamb curry: Heat half the oil in a large, heavy-based saucepan over a high heat. When hot, add the lamb in batches to avoid crowding and cook, stirring frequently, for about 5-7 minutes, until it is browned on all sides. Remove the lamb from the pan using a slotted spoon, then put to one side.

Reduce the heat to medium, add the remaining oil, the onion, tomatoes, cinnamon, cardamon pods, bay leaves, cloves and curry leaves and brown them. Add the ginger and garlic, stirring frequently to prevent burning, and cook for 7-8 minutes,

Return the lamb to the pan with the turmeric, cumin and ground coriander and add hot water as necessary to prevent the mixture from burning. Simmer for 5-7 minutes. When the lamb is tender, strain the broth but retain the juices. Return the lamb mixture to the pan.

To prepare the kadi massala: Mix all the kadi massala ingredients in a heavy-based saucepan for a few minutes over a medium heat, then grind to a rough texture in a blender. Add the kadi massala to the lamb mixture and simmer for 10 minutes, adding only a sufficient quantity of the strained broth to prevent the meat from sticking. Add the yogurt and salt and simmer gently for a further 3 minutes. Add the fresh coriander and cook for a further 3 minutes. Serve with saffron pilau rice or chapati.

Chutney Mary

535 King's Road, London SW10 0SZ. Tel: 0171 351 3113

THIS EXCELLENT ANGLO-INDIAN RESTAURANT caters very much for the British palate. Indications on the menu as to the heat of the dishes are indicated by the symbol of a chilli. Wines are also matched specifically to guide your choice. Here, Namita from Chutney Mary shares a favourite recipe.

Masala Roast Lamb

Serves 4

¼ teaspoon white jeera
¼ teaspoon caraway seeds
2 tablespoons poppy seeds
2 tablespoons sesame seeds
¾ teaspoon fennel seeds
4 black peppercorns
1 black cardamom pod
½ teaspoon green cardamom seeds
½ stick cinnamon
1½ tablespoon roasted Bengal gram
2 cloves
5 cashew nuts
1 teaspoon turmeric
½ teaspoon coriander seeds
salt
4 lamb shanks
4 peppercorns
4 bay leaves
2.5cm (1in) piece fresh root ginger, crushed
8 cloves garlic, crushed
2 tablespoons oil
1 large onion, finely chopped
1½ teaspoons red chilli powder
4 tablespoons tomato purée
4 large potatoes
50g (2oz) full fat yogurt, whipped to a creamy consistency
1 tablespoon tamarind juice or lemon juice

Preheat the oven to 150°C/300°F/gas mark 2.
Lightly dry roast the first 14 ingredients listed for 30 seconds and grind, using some water, if necessary, to make a finely ground masala paste.

Put the lamb shanks to boil in a small pot with 900ml (1½ pints) water, salt, peppercorns, 2 bay leaves, half the crushed ginger and 4 crushed garlic cloves. When half-cooked, after about 1 hour, remove the lamb from water, strain and keep the stock. Set aside.

Heat the oil in a pan and add the onion and the remaining bay leaves. Cook until brown, then add the remaining crushed ginger and garlic cloves, chilli powder, all the ground masala paste and continue to sauté until the oil leaves the sides of the masala.

Add the tomato purée, salt to taste, lamb shanks and potatoes. Cook over a low heat for 10 minutes, adding 475ml (16 fl.oz) reserved lamb stock and the yogurt. Add the tamarind juice or lemon juice, then place the meat with the potatoes and gravy onto a roasting tray.

Roast in the preheated oven for 1½ hours, until the meat is tender. Serve hot, with rice if desired.

Confuscius

271-273 The Broadway, London SW19 1SD. Tel: 0181 542 4272

CONFUSCIUS IS ONE OF MY favourite Chinese restaurants situated near me in South London. It has a tasteful airy interior and the quality of the cooking is very good. The Chinese food here has clean, fresh tastes and the modern atmosphere reflects this. It is a great place to enjoy a more leisurely Chinese experience. The head chef has shared his Confuscius Har Lok recipe, which is a dish of prawns cooked in a light tomato sauce with ginger and garlic.

King Prawns Stir-Fried in Tomato Sauce with Ginger and Garlic

Serves 8

8 large prawns
475ml (16fl.oz) boiling water
2 slices of fresh root ginger
2 spring onions
2 garlic cloves
2 tablespoons corn oil
½ tablespoon wine
50ml (2fl.oz) stock
3 tablespoons tomato ketchup
salt and pepper
1 teaspoon vinegar
1 teaspoon cornflour
1 tablespoon water
1 teaspoon sesame oil
115g (4oz) lettuce

Trim and de-vein the prawns neatly. Wash and divide each prawn into head and body. Discard the heads. Put the prawns in a strainer and scald with boiling hot water. Drain.

Shred the ginger and slice the spring onions. Peel and slice the garlic. Heat a wok and bring the oil to the boil. Sauté the ginger, spring onions and garlic until aromatic. Add the wine, pour in the stock and bring to the boil. Add the ketchup, salt and vinegar and mix well. Season to taste, then add the prawns and simmer for 3 minutes.

Mix the cornflour with the water, then slowly pour it into the sauce to thicken, stirring continuously. Sprinkle in the sesame oil and pepper to taste and toss well.

Wash and arrange the lettuce on a platter. Place the hot prawn mixture in the centre and serve immediately.

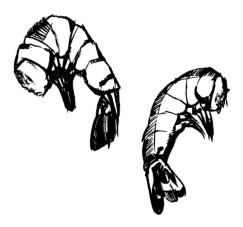

Aaron Hung

Singapore Tourist Promotion Board, Carrington House, 126-130 Regent Street, London W1R. Tel: 0171 437 0033

NONYA OR PERANAKAN FOOD is the closest Singapore has to local cuisine, combining Chinese and Malay food. Typically Chinese ingredients such as pork, Chinese mushrooms and beanshoots are combined with spices, chilli and coconut cream.

Nonyas are also renowned for their sweet cakes and desserts. The Indian element of Singaporean cuisine derives from Southern India, where coconut milk is used instead of yogurt. Dishes are hotter, using chillies and pungent spices.

Aaron Hung, UK regional director of the Singapore Tourist Promotion Board, provides us with a taste of his native country in the two delicious following recipes.

Singapore Chicken Curry

Serves 6

900g (2lb) chicken breasts
3 large potatoes
1 medium onion
4 tablespoons curry powder
4 tablespoons oil
1 teaspoon ground ginger
300ml (½ pint) coconut milk
300ml (½ pint) water
2 teaspoons salt
1 tablespoon lime juice

Cut chicken into 1cm (½in) slices. Peel the potatoes and quarter them. Finely mince the onion. Mix the curry powder with 3 tablespoons water until it becomes a moist paste.

Heat the oil in a heavy-based saucepan or wok and fry the onions until light brown. Add the ginger and curry paste and fry over a low heat for 3 minutes. Add the chicken pieces and mix well. Add the coconut milk, water, salt, lime juice and potatoes.

Cover and simmer for 20 minutes stirring occasionally. Adjust the seasoning and serve with plain boiled rice or bread.

Note: If you like a more or less liquid curry, simply reduce or increase the amount of coconut milk and water accordingly.

Hokkien Mee (Singapore Noodles)

Serves 6

325g (11oz) prawns
vegetable oil for frying
475ml (16fl.oz) water
1 teaspoon salt
2 teaspoons monosodium glutamate
(optional)
325g (11oz) squid, sliced into rings
325g (11oz) pork belly, cut into 1cm
(½ inch) cubes
2 tablespoons lard
4 eggs, beaten
575g (1¼lb) bean sprouts
575g (1¼lb) fresh yellow noodles
6 teaspoons crushed garlic
2 tablespoons light soy sauce
50g (2oz) fresh chives, cut into 3cm
(1¼ inch) lengths
4 red chillies, sliced thinly
4 limes, halved

Making the stock: Remove the prawn heads and wash and drain them. Fry the heads in 1 tablespoon vegetable oil for 1 minute, then remove from the pan and crush them. Mix them with 225ml (8fl.oz) water then strain and set aside.

Boil the 475ml (16fl.oz) water with the salt and monosodium glutamate. Add the squid and cook for 2 minutes. Remove the squid and set aside. Add the prawns (with the shell on) and cook for 2 minutes. Take out the prawns, then remove the shell from the prawns, leaving the tails on. Set aside. Add the cubed pork to the liquid and cook for 15 minutes. Remove and set aside to cool. When cooled, slice into thin strips.

Pour the prawn liquid from the initial stage into the stock, then boil until the stock has reduced to 475ml (16fl.oz). Strain and set the mixture aside.

Frying the noodles: Fry the noodles in 2 halves. Heat the lard in a large wok. When very hot, add 2 eggs to scramble, then add half the bean sprouts and half the noodles. Add 1 tablespoon reserved stock to the noodles, stir-fry and cover. Cook for 1 minute. Remove the lid, add half the prawns, half the pork and half the squid. Cover and cook for a further 2 minutes. Remove the lid and stir-fry the noodle mixture for 1 minute.

Push aside the noodle mixture. Add 2 tablespoons vegetable oil and fry 3 teaspoons garlic until light brown. Add 1 tablespoon soy sauce and 2 tablespoons stock. Stir in the noodle mixture and mix well. Add half the chives and stir to mix. Remove the pan from the heat and keep warm.

Repeat with the second half of the mixture, then mix together and garnish with the chillies and limes. Serve hot.

The Imperial City Chinese Restaurant

Royal Exchange, Cornhill, London EC3V 3LL. Tel: 0171 626 3437

THE IMPERIAL CITY CHINESE RESTAURANT has been very successful, probably due to its guidance by Ken Horn in the kitchen. Ken approves all the chefs and therefore his style of food is very much in evidence, as he devises the menu himself too. Here he shares with us two recipes which he finds are very popular with customers in this City restaurant.

Chiu Chow Style Sweet and Sour Pork

Serves 4

450g (1lb) fatty minced pork
1 egg white
4 tablespoons cold water
175g (6oz) peeled fresh or canned water chestnuts, coarsely chopped
2 tablespoons light soy sauce
1 tablespoon dark soy sauce
2 tablespoons Shaoxing rice wine or dry sherry
1½ tablespoons sugar
2 teaspoons salt
½ teaspoon freshly ground black pepper
225g (8oz) caul fat for wrapping
115g (4oz) green pepper
115g (4oz) red pepper
50g (2oz) spring onions
cornflour for dusting
450ml (¾ pint) groundnut oil

For the sauce:
150ml (¼ pint) chicken stock
1 tablespoon light soy sauce
2 teaspoons dark soy sauce
2 teaspoons sesame oil
1½ teaspoons salt
1 teaspoon freshly ground white pepper
1 tablespoon sugar
75g (3oz) canned or fresh lychees
orange segments, to garnish

Mix the pork with the egg white and mix by hand – the mixture should be light. Do not use a blender as this would make the texture too heavy. Add the water, water chestnuts, soy sauces, rice wine or sherry, sugar, salt and pepper and mix for a few seconds. Divide the pork into small balls, the size of golf balls. Wrap the caul fat around each ball.

Cut the green and red peppers into squares. Peel and thinly slice the carrots on the diagonal. Cut the spring onions into thin pieces. Bring a pan of water to the boil and blanch the peppers for about 4 minutes or until tender. Drain and set aside.

Dust the pork balls with cornflour, shaking off any excess. Heat the oil in a deep, large wok until it is slightly smoking. Deep-fry the pork balls in batches ffor 5-7 minutes until they are crisp. Drain well on kitchen paper.

Combine the sauce ingredients in a pan. Bring to the boil. Add the carrot and spring onions and stir well. Boil for a few minutes, stirring. Turn the heat down so the mixture is simmering. Add the lychees and pork balls. Mix well. Turn the mixture onto a platter and serve at once with plain rice and a stir-fried vegetable dish. Garnish with orange segments.

Steamed Salmon with Black Beans

Serves 6

450g (1lb) boneless salmon fillet,
skinned and divided into
4 equal pieces
1 teaspoon salt
¼ teaspoon freshly ground
white pepper
2 tablespoons black beans,
rinsed and chopped
1½ tablespoons finely
chopped garlic
1 tablespoons finely chopped
fresh ginger
1½ tablespoons Shaoxing rice wine
or dry sherry
1 tablespoons light soy sauce

For the garnish:
3 tablespoons finely chopped
spring onions
small handful of fresh coriander,
chopped
1½ tablespoons groundnut oil

Sprinkle the salmon pieces evenly with salt and pepper. Combine the black beans, garlic and ginger in a small bowl. Put the fish fillets on a deep heatproof plate and evenly scatter the black bean mixture over the top. Pour the rice wine or dry sherry and soy sauce over the fish.

Set up a steamer or put a rack into a wok or deep pan and fill it with 5cm (2 inch) of water. Bring the water to the boil over a high heat. Carefully lower the fish and plate into the steamer or on to the rack. Reduce the heat to low and cover the wok or pan tightly. Steam gently for 8-10 minutes, depending on the thickness of the fish fillets. Top up with boiling water from time to time.

When the fish is cooked, remove the plate from the steamer or wok and scatter the spring onions and coriander on top of the fish to garnish.

Heat a wok or large frying pan until it is very hot. Add the oil and when it is very hot and slightly smoking pour this over the fish fillets. Serve at once.

Jin

16 Bateman Street, London W1. Tel: 0171 734 0908

JIN IS ONE OF THE FEW KOREAN RESTAURANTS in London. Although the waiters don't always speak great English, the food has exciting tastes, often with a simple cooking technique. Here Tony Li gives an unusual recipe from his restaurant.

Barbecued Chicken

For the marinade:
½ fresh peeled pear
150ml (¼ pint) orange juice
1 clove garlic
2.5cm (1 inch) piece of fresh root ginger
1½ tablespoons soy sauce
1 tablespoon caster sugar
1 teaspoon sesame oil

1 chicken breast weighing about 175g (6oz), cut into bite-sized pieces
½ lemon

Whizz all the marinade ingredients together in a blender or food proceessor and pour over the chicken. Cover and leave to marinade for at least 3 hours.

Cook on a preheated barbecue or griddle pan, squeezing the lemon juice or a little rice wine (sake) over the chicken, for about 15 minutes turning regularly.

Serve with boiled rice or a salad.

The Lebanese Restaurant

60 Edgeware Road, London W2 2EH. Tel: 0171 262 9585

Mr Diab, the manager of The Lebanese Restaurant on the Edgware Road, gives us his recipes for two classic dishes he serves in the restaurant. An Arabic cook is often measured by his or her Kibbeh and the second classic dish is Tabbouleh, both of which are very popular in the restaurant. These recipes come from the Syrian and Lebanese kitchen.

Tabbouleh

Serves 6-8

115g (4oz) flat-leaf parsley
50g (2oz) fresh mint
300g (10oz) bulgur (cracked wheat)
salt and freshly ground black pepper
juice of 2 lemons
125ml (4fl.oz) virgin olive oil
5 spring onions, finely chopped
2 large tomatoes

Finely chop the parsley and mint together. Place the bulgur in a bowl and cover with cold water. Leave for 30 minutes. Drain well through a sieve, pressing with the back of a spoon to squeeze out the excess moisture. Spread over a clean dry tea towel to absorb any more excess water.

Mix the bulgur, parsley and mint mixture, seasoning, lemon juice, olive oil and spring onions together. Chill for 30 minutes. Peel and de-seed the tomatoes, then dice them. Stir the tomatoes into the bulgur mixture just before serving as a starter or an accompaniment.

Kibbeh

Serves 6

2 onions, finely chopped
50g (2oz) clarified butter
50g (2oz) pine nuts
225g (8oz) coarsley ground lamb
freshly ground black pepper and salt
¼ teaspoon ground cinnamon
½ teaspoon ground allspice
115g (4oz) bulgur (cracked wheat)
1 teaspoon cumin seeds
1 teaspoon coriander seeds
1 small onion, chopped into quarters
50g (2oz) butter, melted
25g (1oz) pine nuts, to garnish

Preheat the oven to 180°C/350°F/gas mark 4.
Traditionally the meat for Kibbehwas pounded with a pestle and mortar: this was a ritual associated with preparing the dish.

Gently fry the onion in the clarified butter until softened but not coloured. Add the pine nuts and gently fry until golden brown. Turn up the heat and add the lamb. Brown well, remove from heat and add the seasoning, cinnamon and allspice, then set aside.

Soak the bulgur for 15 minutes in cold water. Drain well and place in a blender or food processor with the cumin seeds, coriander seeds and onion. Season well and process until smooth.

Layer the bulgur and meat mixture in a greased 28 x 33cm (11 x 13in) baking/roasting dis, making two layers of each. Drizzle over the melted butter and scatter over the pine nuts. Slash into diamond shapes. Sprinkle over 2 tablespoons water. Bake in the preheated oven for 45 minutes–1 hour, sprinkling lightly with water 3 or 4 times during cooking. Serve hot or cold with yogurt and salads.

Ken Lo's Memories of China

Chelsea Harbour Yard, Chelsea Harbour, London SW10 0QD. Tel: 0171 352 4953

KEN LO'S NAME IS SYNONYMOUS with Chinese cooking in London. His recent death was a sad loss to the cooking world. His gentle nature and huge knowledge will be sorely missed.

He was educated at Cambridge and played tennis at Wimbledon in the 1940s. But his main career was Chinese food, writing numerous books on the subject and teaching through cookery lessons first at his Ebury Street School, then continuing at Chelsea Harbour. I remember the visually spectacular lessons at Ebury Street where industrial ovens used in authentic Chinese kitchens, housed the wok beautifully, heating the pan evenly and quickly for great demonstrations. Now lessons are continued at Chelsea Harbour

by a group of teachers, notably his great friend Deh-Ta Hsiung who worked with Ken for many years. Deh-Ta is a very good cook and cookery author in his own right and is carrying on the tradition of teaching from a huge knowledge and experience of Chinese food.

Ken said of his lessons 'I believe that to fully appreciate Chinese cuisine you have to understand how to eat it as well as how to cook it.' Therefore all teaching sessions finish with a feast of different dishes to tempt your palette. Ann Lo, Ken's widow, is still very much at the helm of the cooking legend of restaurants and cookery classes and she shares here with us three of Ken's favourite recipes.

Aromatic Crispy Duck

Serves 4-6

For the cooking sauce:
1.2 litre (2 pints) good stock
6 tablespoons sugar
6 slivers fresh root ginger
10 tablespoons soy sauce
4 tablespoons yellow bean paste
6 tablespoons dry sherry
6 star anise
1½ teaspoons five spice powder
salt and pepper

1.8–2.25kg (4-5lb) duck
vegetable oil for deep frying

Mix all the ingredients for the cooking sauce together in a large saucepan. Clean the duck thoroughly and cut in half down the backbone. Place into the liquid and submerge.

Simmer the duck gently for about 40 minutes, then remove the duck from the cooking liquid and set aside to cool. When required, heat the oil in a wok or a deep fat fryer. Lower the duck gently into the oil and fry for 10-15 minutes. Drain well and then place the duck onto a large serving platter. Serve by taking the meat off the carcass and serve it with pancakes, spring onions, cucumber and plum sauce.

Shredded Beef with Ginger and Onions

Serves 4-6

450g (1lb) beef steak, e.g. rump,
fillet or sirloin
seasoning
1½ tablespoons cornflour
1 egg white
3 medium onions
3 slices fresh root ginger
4 tablespoons vegetable oil
25g (1oz) lard
2 tablespoons soy sauce
1 tablespoon sugar
3 tablespoons good stock
1½ tablespoons dry sherry
2 tablespoons cornflour, blended
with 2 tablespoons water

Using a very sharp knife, cut the beef into thin slices, then cut again into matchstick-size shreds. Season with salt and pepper. Toss in the 1½ tablespoons cornflour and coat in the egg white.

Peel and thinly slice the onions and shred the ginger. Heat the oil in a wok or frying pan. When hot, stir-fry the beef over a high heat for 1½ minutes. Remove and set aside. Add the lard to the pan. When hot, stir-fry the ginger and onions over high heat for 1½ minutes. Add the soy sauce, sugar and stock and stir together for 30 seconds. Return the beef to the pan, add the sherry and blended cornflour and continue to stir-fry for 30 seconds. Serve immediately.

Sliced Beef in Black Bean and Chilli Sauce

Serves 4-6

450g (1lb) beef steak
seasoning
2 tablespoons cornflour
1 egg white
1 medium onion
2 dried chillies
1 small red pepper
1 small green pepper
1½ tablespoons salted black beans
4 tablespoons vegetable oil
15g (½oz) lard
3 tablespoons good stock
2 tablespoons sherry
1 tablespoon soy sauce
½ teaspoon cornflour blended with
1 tablespoon water

Cut the beef into thin slices and rub evenly with salt and pepper. Toss in the cornflour and coat in the egg white. Peel and thinly slice the onion. Finely chop the chillies. Cut the red and green peppers into 2.5cm (1 inch) pieces. Soak the black beans in 4 tablespoons cold water for 3 minutes, then drain.

Heat the oil in a wok or frying pan. When hot, stir-fry the beef over a high heat for 1 minute. Remove and set aside. Add the lard to the pan. When hot, stir-fry the onion, black beans, chillies and peppers. Squash the softened black beans with a metal spoon against the edge of the wok or pan. Stir in the stock, sherry and soy sauce over a high heat. Return the beef to the pan and add the blended cornflour. Heat through and simmer for 3 minutes, then serve.

Ma Goa Restaurant

244 Upper Richmond Road, Putney, London SW15 6TG. Tel: 0181 780 1767

SUE KAPOOR OF Ma Goa Restaurant in Putney cooks many Goan delicacies, along with her husband, but she feels that this dish reflects Goan cooking at its best. Xachutti is a traditional Goan dish made with roasted spices to impart a unique and delicious flavour. This uses coconut milk and palm vinegar, both of which are dominant ingredients in Goan cookery.

Goan Xachutti

Serves 4-6

6 whole cloves
1 teaspoon black peppercorns
5cm (2 inch) stick of cinnamon,
broken up
1 teaspoon skinned sesame seeds
1 teaspoon poppy seeds
¼ teaspoon red 'Ghatti' chillies
(dried red chillies)
10cm (4 inch) piece fresh root
ginger, peeled
6 cloves garlic, peeled
1 medium onion
6 tablespoon oil
1 medium chicken weighing 0.9-
1.4kg (2-3lb), cut into 8 pieces
salt to taste
125ml (4fl.oz) palm vinegar or
cider vinegar
225ml (8fl.oz) fresh or tinnned
coconut milk
225ml (8fl.oz) water
fresh coconut and fresh coriander,
to garnish

Roast the cloves, peppercorns, cinnamon, sesame seeds, poppy seeds and chillies in a frying pan or 'tara' with no oil until the aromas of the spices are released. Grind the roasted spices in a coffee grinder until fine.

Make a paste with the ginger and garlic in a food processor (blend with a little water). Chop the onion finely and fry in the oil until golden brown. Add the chicken pieces and cook for about 10 minutes, before adding the ground spices and salt to taste. Cook for a further 5 minutes, stirring continuously. Add the palm or cider vinegar and coconut milk and simmer for about 5 minutes. Add the water and leave to simmer over a medium heat for about 15 minutes or until the chicken is tender.

Garnish with wafers of fresh coconut and fresh coriander leaves. Serve with plain boiled rice.

Matsuri

15 Bury Street, London SW1 6AI. Tel: 0171 839 1101

MR KANETURO TAKASE IS the head chef at the Matsuri, St James's. He was born into a family of restaurateurs in Tokyo and his job at the Matsuri is his first outside his native Japan. He's worked in restaurants as a chef for over 30 years, with experience in a well-known French restaurant in Tokyo, his own restaurant and the famous Tsunahachi restaurant, again in Tokyo. Masashi Yamashita, the manager, comes from the capital city of northern Japan, Sendon.

The Matsuri restaurant is a joint ownership between the Central Japan Railway Company and Kikkoman Corporation, the giant soy sauce company. The foods served in the restaurant are both traditional and modern tastes of Japan through its Sushi and Teppan-Yaki cuisine.

Teppan-Yaki is a form of post-war Japanese cuisine which in the 1960s and 70s became extremely popular abroad, particular in the USA. It has now become the most popular form of Japanese restaurant dining throughout the world, including Japan. It is a very visual form of dining as personal chefs on each table cook food on Teppans (hot plates) at 180°C/350°F while guests watch. Extremely fresh ingredients include seafood, duck, chicken and vegetables.

Sushi is rice flavoured with vinegar mixed with thinly sliced raw fish, shellfish, vegetables and eggs with seaweed added to it. Its origins are over 200 years old, having been developed as a way of preserving fish, it graduallybecame a dish in its own right and is now a fashionable and healthy form of cuisine known throughout the world. Matsuri serves about 20 different types of fresh seafood in its sushi bar, from salmon and tuna to the more unusual but delicious sea urchin. Tasty pickled ginger is served to cleanse the palette between different types of fish. A green horseradish paste of Wasabi adds spice to the Sushi. Mr Takase shares one of his recipes with us below.

Chawan Mushi

Serves 6

6 eggs, beaten
750ml (1¼ pints) consommé
50g (2oz) cooked chicken
5 prawns
25g (1oz) bamboo shoots
15g (½oz) kinko nuts
1 teaspoon coriander
25g (1oz) oyster mushrooms

Heat the eggs for a few minutes, then strain and pour into the heated consommé. Place the chicken, prawns, bamboo shoots, nuts, coriander and oyster mushrooms into a small earthenware bowl and pour the soup mixture over this. Cover the bowl and place in a steamer. Steam for 15 minutes, then serve immediately.

New Soraya Restaurant

36 Gloucester Road, London SW7 4QT. Tel: 0171 589 0271

IN THIS WELL-ESTABLISHED Persian restaurant the menu and the dishes are regularly updated. Authentic ingredients, classic recipes and well-trained chefs continue to create great Persian dishes. Below they give one of their traditional recipes.

Mirza Ghasi

Serves 4

450g (1lb) aubergine
115g (4oz) butter
¼ teaspoon turmeric
4 cloves garlic, crushed
115g (4oz) peeled tomato, diced
2 eggs, beaten
salt and pepper

Place the whole aubergine in a pan and dry fry until the skin is burnt. Allow to cool and then peel off the burnt skin. Pound the flesh to a very fine and creamy paste. Fry the aubergine paste in the butter until brown. Add the haldi, the garlic and the diced tomato. Cook for 10 minutes, then add the eggs, salt and pepper. Mix well and serve hot with pitta bread.

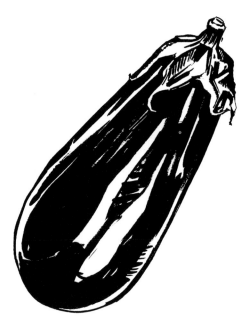

Rasa South Indian Vegetarian Restaurant

55 Stoke Newington Church Street, London N16 0AR. Tel: 0171 249 0344

DAS PADMANABHAN gave us this recipe from the Rasa restaurant in north London, which is one of the best vegetarian Indian restaurants in or around London. The dish, Avial, is a famous Keralan feast dish and is the ultimate recipe for coconut masala with green chilli and cumin seeds. Fresh green vegetables are steamed in turmeric-scented water then mixed with fresh coconut and thick yogurt. It is best served with lemon or plain rice.

Avial

Serves 6

2 carrots, peeled
2 potatoes, peeled
2 plantains, peeled
50 g (2oz) green beans, tailed
1 fresh coconut, peeled and grated
4 green chillies, de-seeded and
finely chopped
1 teaspoon cumin seeds
¼ teaspoon black peppercorns
½ teaspoon turmeric powder
salt to taste
150ml (¼ pint) thick yogurt
a few curry leaves

Chop all the vegetables into 3cm (1¼ in) pieces. Grind together the coconut, chillies, cumin seeds and peppercorns in a coffee grinder with a little water to form a paste.

Cook the vegetables with the turmeric powder and enough water to cover. Add salt. Mix the coconut paste with the vegetables and add the yogurt. Add the curry leaves and simmer for 10 minutes. Remove from the heat and serve immediately.

Shree Krishna South Indian Restaurant

192-194 Tooting High Street, London SW17 0SF. Tel: 0171 672 6903

T. HARIDAS HAS GIVEN US this recipe from the Sri Krishna restaurant which is well-known in South London. It is the only South Indian restaurant specialising in Keralan cuisine, promoting rarely available authentic South Indian dishes from the region of Kerala on the Malabar Coast. South Indian food is distinctive because of the unique combination of freshly ground spices and herbs in its preparation, with the use of a minimal quantity of oil or fat.

Chicken Malabar

Serves 4

½ coconut (fresh)
1 teaspoon cumin seeds
1 teaspoon turmeric powder
2 garlic cloves
1cm (½in) fresh root ginger
15 curry leaves
450g (1lb) spinach leaves
1 teaspoon mustard seeds
2 tablespoons oil
2 onions, sliced
5 green chillies
1 tablespoon chilli powder
2 tablespoons ground coriander
2 tomatoes, chopped
900g (2lb) roasting chicken, cut into pieces
salt and freshly ground pepper

Blend together the coconut flesh, whole cumin seeds, turmeric powder, garlic, ginger, 10 curry leaves and spinach with 3 tablespoons water. Mix well.

In a pan, fry the mustard seeds in the oil until they pop. Add the onion and chillies and fry until golden brown. Add the remaining curry leaves, chilli powder and ground coriander and fry until the mixture becomes dry. Add the tomato and chicken and simmer gently until the chicken is cooked.

Season and serve hot with rice.

Stir Crazy

120 Marylebone Lane, London W1. Tel: 0171 486 7070

THIS MONGOLIAN RESTAURANT is very much based on the do-it-yourself theory and the whole experience is enjoyable, taking part in cooking your own food. The choices of ingredients in the dish are entirely up to you. You select your own vegetables, meat, fish, spices, oils and sauces. All you have to do is create a stir-fry.

Rashim Danchan gave us this typical recipe from the restaurant, entitled Balti Bomber. It has a lot of Indian influences and you will really have fun creating it for yourself, especially if you serve it for a crowd of friends.

Balti Bomber

Serves 8

2 tablespoons oil
225g (8oz) onion, chopped
1 teaspoon ground cumin
pinch of rye seeds
1 large tin tomatoes
1 teaspoon mint sauce
1 garlic bulb, finely chopped
2 tablespoons root ginger, finely chopped
5 fresh ground chillies
pinch of black pepper
1 tablespoon sesame seeds
1 teaspoon tumeric
1 teaspoon chilli powder
1 teaspoon ground cumin
½ teaspoon garam masala
1 teaspoon salt
450g (1lb) boneless chicken or lamb, cut into small pieces
115g (4oz) fresh seasonal vegetables per person
finely chopped fresh coriander leaves

Pour the oil into a pan. Add the onions, cumin and rye seeds and fry until golden brown. Add the tinned tomato, mint sauce, garlic, ginger, chillies, pepper, sesame seeds, spices and seasoning. Add the meat and vegetables. Cover and simmer for 30 minutes. Garnish with fresh coriander and serve with basmati rice or naan bread.

The Tibetan Restaurant

17 Irving Street, London WC2. Tel: 0171 839 2090

LLAMO DOLMA IS THE CHEF at the only Tibetan restaurant in London, serving authentic dishes which are all well worth trying out. He has given us here the recipe for the most popular dish in Tibet, Momo. It resembles a mini cornish pasty, as the meat is wrapped in pastry.

Momo

Serves 6

For the filling:
2 onions (medium size), finely chopped
450g (1lb) lean minced beef
½ teaspoon ground ginger
½ teaspoon ground coriander
½ teaspoon ground cumin
½ teaspoon soy sauce
½ teaspoon salt
1 clove garlic, finely chopped
a drop of oil
3 tablespoons of water

350g (12oz) plain flour
350g (12oz) self-raising flour
approximately 350ml (½ pint) water

Mix together the onion, meat, spices, soy sauce, salt, garlic, oil and 3 tablespoons water; set aside. In a separate bowl, mix the flours together. Add the water slowly, making a dough that has elasticity and is neither too wet or dry. Take a small amount of dough, approximately the size of a ping pong ball, and roll it out into a neat round approximately 8cm (3in) in diameter, leaving the centre slightly thicker than the edges (to avoid splitting.)

Place a teaspoon of the meat mixture into the centre of the flattened dough and fold and crimp the edges.

Prepare a steamer by coating the inside base with a thin coat of oil to prevent the momo sticking. Place the momos on the base of the steamer and cook over a pan of boiling water for 20 minutes.

Serve with hot chilli sauce and a green salad.

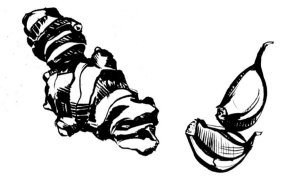

Veeraswamy

99-101 Regent Street, London W1R 8RS. Tel: 0171 734 1401

THIS INDIAN RESTAURANT HAS a long history. It was one of the first Indian restaurants to open in London (founded in 1927) and started with authentically dressed waiters and waitresses in Indian costumes. The menu has developed over the years, as has the palates of the British Indian tastes – customers can now eat their curries much hotter. Here they share one of their favourite recipes with us.

Lobster Peri Peri

Serves 6

4 lobsters

For the peri peri paste:
15 whole red chillies
15g (½oz) cumin seeds
1 teaspoon turmeric
12 cloves
2 cinnamon sticks
15g (½oz) ginger paste
15g (½oz) garlic paste
4 tablespoons malt vinegar
6 tablespoons water
salt and pepper, to taste

2 tablespoons groundnut oil
115g (4oz) chopped onions
2 teaspoons tomato paste
2 tablespoons chopped fresh coriander
lime twists, to serve

Boil the lobster, allow it to cool down and then cut it in half lengthwise. Remove all the meat and dice roughly. Wash out the shell and keep for later.

Place the ingredients for the peri peri paste in a blender and blend together to make a smooth paste.

Heat the oil in a Kadai or wok, add the chopped onions and cook until brown. Add the tomato paste and sauté for 30 seconds. Add the blended paste and sauté until all the fats are burned off. Then add the diced lobster and cook for 2-3 minutes, stirring continuously. Finally add the chopped coriander, check for seasoning and then remove from the heat.

Return the lobster meat to their shells, cover with sauce and serve with lime twists.

The Yohan Plaza

399 Edgware Road, Colindale, London NW9. Tel: 0181 200 0009

THE YOHAN PLAZA is a large Japanese shopping centre in Colindale which opened in 1993. The only place of its kind in Europe, it caters primarily for the Japanese expatriate community, of which there are about 30,000 in London. It is highly regarded by the Japanese; regular shopping trips by coach are even made by Japanese residents in Brussels.

On the upstairs section of the Plaza there are three restaurants. Within the supermarket itself is, without doubt, the best selection of Japanese ingredients in London. For me, the most interesting part of the supermarket is the array of fish on display, prepared in such a precise and attractive package. The meats available are also prepared in this way, invaluable for immediate use in Japanese cooking. It would be very difficult to prepare the wafer-thin meat to this standard at home, and there must be a team of very skilled Japanese chefs behind the scenes. The fresh vegetable produce too, such as the green, pointed *ohba* leaves, is specifically Japanese. A food counter with several stalls also sells several unusual snacks and street food from Japan.

Tempura (Deep Fried Seafood and Vegetables)

Serves 4

150g (5oz) dashi (see opposite)
4 spring onions. peeled
1 aubergine, salted
1 small sweet potato
1 carrot
4 shiitake mushrooms
8 king prawns
1 squid body
225g (8oz) white fish fillet
4 tablespoons soy sauce
3 tablespoons mirin (see opposite)
6 tablespoons finely grated dalkon
(see opposite)
2 teaspoons finely grated root ginger
1.7 litres (3 pints) vegetable oil,
for frying
2 egg yolks
475ml (16fl.oz) iced water
300g (10oz) tempura flour
(or other plain flour)
65–150g (2½-5oz)
flour, for coating
1 lemon, cut into segments
salt, to taste

Prepare the dashi with 'dashi no motto', following the instructions on the packet just like an ordinary stock cube. Cut the spring onions in half. Cut the aubergine into quarters lengthwise, leaving 1cm (½in) of flesh on the skin. Slice into fan shapes. Cut the sweet potato crosswise into 5mm (¼in) slices. Place in a bowl or on a plate and add the diced carrot and the mushrooms.

Remove the shell but leave the tail on the king prawns. Make 2-3 short, deep cuts on the inner curve to prevent curling during cooking. Press slightly to straighten. Clean and skin the squid, cutting through both layers crosswise to form rings. Cut the white fish fillets into 5 x 2.5cm (1 inch) pieces. Pat all the fish dry.

To make the dipping sauce, bring the dashi, soy sauce and mirin to the boil, reduce the heat and keep warm. Place 1½ small rounded tablespoons of dalkon in each of 4 serving bowls, top each round with ½ teaspoon ginger.

Heat the oil in a deep fat frier to 170°C/ 325°F and maintain the temperature. Prepare the batter, beating egg yolks in a bowl, then adding the iced water. Beat lightly, add the flour and stir well.

Coat the ingredients individually in flour. Shake off any excess and dip into the batter. Cook in the hot oil for 2-3minutes, drain and place on a plate. Pour a little dipping sauce into each bowl with the dalkon and ginger. Each person then dips the hot food into their sauce. Add lemon juice and salt to season, as desired.

Mirin: a rice cooking wine, similar to sherry.
Soba noodles: the basis of many Japanese dishes, often used in salads
Wasabi paste: often mixed with soy sauce, this paste is made from green horseradish root.
Dalkon: white radish.
Nori (roasted seaweed sheets): a light dry seaweed used in *sushi*, it can be chopped and sprinkled over soups or other Japanese dishes.
Dashi: a stock base made from dried *bonito* (tuna) flakes and kelp (a seaweed used as flavouring in *sushi* rice).
Dashi no motto: a stock cube.
Konbu: a form of dried kelp.

Sushi

Serves 6

For the sushi rice:
450g (1lb) short-grain rice
plenty of cold water
1 piece dried kelp, 8cm (3 inch) square (see above)
1.4 litres (2½ pints) water
2 tablespoons sake
5 tablespoons rice vinegar
2 tablespoons sugar
2 teaspoons salt

For the nigiri sushi:
125ml (4fl.oz) water
1 tablespoon vinegar
wasabi paste (see above)
smoked salmon or raw fish fillet of your choice (e.g. tuna, salmon, turbot, shrimps)
soy sauce

Wash the rice in cold water 4 or 5 times until the water is almost clear. Leave to drain for 1 hour. Wipe the kelp gently with a damp cloth to remove any sand (not the white powder). Cut the kelp into 4 equal strips. Place the rice in a saucepan (with a close-fitting lid) and add the water and sake. Place the kelp on top of the rice, then replace the lid and bring to the boil. Remove the kelp just before the water boils, then reduce the heat, cover and simmer for another 15 minutes until the liquid is absorbed.

Remove from the heat and leave to stand for 15 minutes. Gently fluff the rice using a wooden spoon. Place a clean kitchen towel over the pan, replace the lid and leave for 10 minutes. Mix the vinegar, sugar and salt in a pan over the heat until the sugar dissolves. Cool, then place the rice in a large, shallow, plastic bowl. Sprinkle the vinegar mixture over the rice and mix in gently, fanning the rice for 5-10 minutes. Cover with a damp cloth.

To make *nigiri sushi* (hand-formed sushi): First moisten your hands with 'lezu' (125ml/8 fl.oz water mixed with 1 tablespoon of vinegar). Place 1 tablespoon of the sushi rice across the cupped fingers of one hand. Gently close the fingers about the rice and mould into an oval or finger shape. Place a small dab of *wasabi* on the top centre of the rice. With the other hand, place slices of fish lengthwise along the rice. Using two fingers, press gently but firmly on the rice. Roll the sushi over so that the fish is on the top and press. Turn the sushi to the reverse ends, press and place on a plate. Dip the sushi, fish side down, in the soy sauce and enjoy!

African Cooking

The large continent of Africa has many diverse culinary traditions, some of which are relatively well known in Europe and others which are only recently establishing themselves outside their native areas. The cultural differences in the dishes and recipes are well illustrated. In north Africa, particularly Tunisia, Egypt and Morocco, the ingredients, spices and cooking techniques are closely linked with those of other countries surrounding the Mediterranean; the African influence of cooking in Sicily, for example, is marked. However, the cooking of sub-Saharan Africa is much less familiar to London audiences; it is an area of cuisine still largely unexplored by the capital's restaurants, although this is now starting to change.

There are a few good authentic restaurants developing which feature food predominantly from Guyana and Ethiopia. However, the strongest evidence of African food in London is still to be found in the markets, where an abundance of West African produce is available, from yams, breadfruit, limes, coconuts, bonnet chillies and plantains to the salt cod and other exotic fish used in traditional recipes.

Plantains and bananas in Brixton's street market.

Ali Baba Restaurant

32 Ivor Place (off Gloucester Place), London NW1. Tel: 0171 723 7474/723 5805

THIS EYGPTIAN RESTAURANT serves dishes from Eygpt as well as dishes with other African origins. Dishes such as falafel are often served in a mezze-style with the Arabic flat bread, Khoubiz.

Khoubiz has a conveneint pocket for the same kind of fillings as go into pitta breads. Other typical North African dishes include Tabouleh and Fried Kibbi Balls.

Molikhia (Lamb in Spinach Sauce)

Serves 6

1.6kg (3½lb) leg of lamb or whole chicken
1 onion, peeled and chopped
1 tablespoon ground coriander
salt and freshly ground pepper
3 kg (7lb) spinach, washed and chopped
2 cloves garlic, crushed, to garnish

Put the lamb or chicken in a saucepan of water, together with the onion, coriander and salt and pepper and bring to the boil. Simmer for about 1 hour, then take the meat out of the liquid and cut up into bite-size pieces.

Add the chopped spinach to the meat and mix well. Garnish the Molikhia with crushed garlic, fried in a little oil until golden.

Serve hot, with rice.

Felafel

Serves 4

1kg (2.2lb) skinless brown beans (to be soaked in water for 20 minutes)
1 onion, chopped
1 bunch spring onions, chopped
1 bunch fresh coriander, chopped
1 bunch parsley, chopped
2 cloves garlic, peeled
1 chilli pepper, chopped
salt and pepper
2 teaspoons ground cumin
1 teaspoon bicarbonate of soda
oil, for frying

Drain the soaked beans and place them in a food processor. Blend all the ingredients together to form a paste. Roll into walnut-sized balls and flatten slightly. Fry in oil in batches.

Eutens Restaurant and Bar

4-5 Neal's Yard, Covent Garden, London WC2H 9DP. Tel: 0171 379 6877

Eutens is a new African restaurant set up in Covent Garden serving a selection of dishes originating from all across the African continent. Members of the alliance of black chefs, the restaurant is always very keen to employ authentic chefs from the regions whose food they are cooking. If goat (mutton) is unavailable, the following recipe works well with chicken breast.

Eutens Curried Goat

Serves 6

1.4kg (3lb) mutton, diced
1½ teaspoons cumin seeds
1½ teaspoons coriander seeds
1 teaspoon ground turmeric
2 tablespoons lime juice
2 bunches spring onions, finely sliced
3 cloves garlic, crushed
1 chilli, finely chopped
1 tablespoon salt
1 teaspoon pepper
50g (2oz) butter or oil, for frying
900ml (1½ pints) chicken stock

Wipe the mutton and place it in a stainless steel container.

Using a pestle and mortar, crush the cumin and coriander seeds and add them to the goat meat. Add the turmeric, lime juice, spring onions, garlic, chilli, salt and pepper. Mix well, cover and leave to marinate in the refrigerator for at least 24 hours – this tenderises the meat.

Place the meat and marinade in a heavy-based saucepan with some butter or oil and sauté for about 5 minutes. Add the stock, bring the mixture to the boil, then reduce the heat and simmer until the meat is tender (about 1½ hours). Skim off and discard any impurities which will rise to the top.

Remove the meat and keep hot. Boil the sauce to reduce and thicken it. Return the meat to the pan and reheat. Serve with boiled long grain rice.

Eco Pizzeria

162 Clapham High Street, London SW4 7UG. Tel: 0171 978 1108

SAMI WASY IS A STRONG CHARACTER who has very definite ideas about food and restaurants. This introduction to his recipe ideas represents the driving force behind Eco, one of my favourite local restaurants.

Sami was born and grew up in Egypt and from the age of 10 was involved in the family business, a shoe factory. Used to being with skilled craftsmen, he learned by watching some of their techniques, such as sharpening knives to cut leather – he can still produce a sharper knife than most chefs.

For business reasons his father entertained two or three times a week. Sami's mother, with a couple of helpers, used the family's wood-burning oven to produce delicious food for 20-25 people. Fresh breads, fish, produce from the family farm, and game caught locally were the foundation of Sami's love of food and hospitality.

Sami's academic skills were sharpened by a degree in commerce. He first went to Italy but decided to settle in England, where, despite being appalled by what was known here as pizza, he instantly liked the simplicity and quality of traditional English food. Running restaurants, mainly in hotels, he spent time watching the chefs. Uniquely for a restaurant manager, he would call the hotel manager when a sudden rush threatened to overwhelm the operation, hand over control of the seating, and go behind the scenes to assist the chef. No one ever realised he had no formal training in the kitchen.

He believes in doing rather than reading (there is, he says, still no adequate book on making a pizza), he has studied and experimented extensively with flours and doughs. Unlike formally- trained chefs, he has no fear of introducing new ideas into traditional concepts – he is extraordinarily painstaking to ensure that the flavour combinations are exactly right, by adding something to the original cuisine, not merely setting a trend or being fashionable. He strives obsessively for balance, finding ingredients that work together harmoniously and contribute to the whole. He will try absolutely any new ingredient, but only the outstanding flavour combinations get past the daily experimentation sessions and onto the menu.

This approach extends to the whole restaurant environment; his operation must have an edge, must provide new experiences and incorporate the most modern thinking – but at the same time must always give traditional standards of comfort, food and service. Customers should go home excited by the decor and delighted by the food. He fervently believes that a restaurateur has a duty to educate the public, to present novel surroundings and truly tasty food that challenges preconceptions and raises expectations – and encourages people to understand what makes some meals so good.

Sami also runs a fantastic pizzeria in Brixton Market on Electric Avenue. You can sit inside or out, and the pizzas really melt in your mouth.

Sun-Dried Tomato and Aubergine Pizza

Serves 2

3 tablespoons olive oil
1 aubergine, cut into slices
5mm (¼ inch) thick

For the tomato sauce:
900g (2lb) plum tomatoes, chopped
salt and freshly ground pepper
1 tablespoon sugar

3-4 sun-dried tomatoes, in oil
250g (8oz) Mozzarella, grated
pinch dried oregano

Preheat the oven to 220°C/425°F/gas mark 7.

Grease the pizza pan and put it in the oven to heat up before plac-ing the dough in. Heat the olive oil in a frying pan and dip the aubergine slices in; fry them until golden and crispy. Leave the slices to cool.

To make the tomato sauce: Simmer together the tomatoes, salt, pepper and sugar until reduced to a thick, pulpy sauce. Spread the sauce on the pizza, leaving at least 1cm (½ in) all round the edge; don't use too much tomato sauce. Sprinkle over the grated Mozzarella. Place 4 or 5 slices of aubergine on top, then 3-4 pieces of oil-soaked sun-dried tomato.

Bake for about 20 minutes in the preheated oven. Sprinkle over the dried oregano before serving.

Mandola Café Restaurant

139 Westbourne Grove, London W11 2RS. Tel: 0171 229 4734

GHEE IS AN INGREDIENT much used in African cooking. Ghee is simply butter that has been so clarified that you can deep-fry in it, without it burning. It has a very special, nutty taste and it is now widely available in supermarkets, African and Indian shops. If you cannot buy ready-made ghee, you can make your own.

Using 450g (1lb) of best-quality unsalted butter, put it in a small pan and let it melt over a low flame. Simmer on a low heat for 45 minutes or until the milky solids turn brownish or cling to the sides of the pan. Strain the ghee through layers of cheesecloth. Home-made ghee should always be stored in the refrigerator.

Adas (Lentil Stew)

Serves 6

4 onions, chopped
6 cloves garlic
vegetable oil
2 x 375g (14oz) cans chopped tomatoes
1 small can tomato purée
1 teaspoon salt
1 teaspoon ground cumin
1 teaspoon ground coriander
1 teaspoon black pepper
1 teaspoon powdered garlic
450g (1lb) split lentils
1 tablespoon bicarbonate of soda
3 glasses water
2 tablespoons ghee (clarified butter) or vegetable oil

Fry the chopped onions and 2 cloves of chopped garlic in the oil until softened. Add the tomatoes and tomato purée and cook over a medium heat for 5 minutes. Add the salt and all the spices and mix well.

Place the split lentils in a bowl and wash and drain them several times to remove the starch. Add the bicarbonate of soda and soak for 5 minutes, then drain.

Place the lentils in the pot with the onions, tomatoes and water, mix well and cook until the lentils are beginning to break, which means they are cooked. Allow to cool slightly. Place the lentil mixture in a blender or food processor and blend until smooth. Set aside.

Crush the remaining 4 cloves of garlic and place them in a frying pan with the ghee or vegetable oil and fry until caramelized. Pour in the lentil sauce and mix well. This is now ready to serve.

Calabash

The Africa Centre, Covent Garden, London WC2E 8JS. Tel: 0171 836 1976

WITHIN THE AFRICAN CONTINENT there are a huge number of different influences. This dish comes from Morocco, where coucous is as much a staple of the cuisine as potatoes are in this country. The mixture of spices in the recipe below is typical of Moroccan cuisine and the dish is often served in the base of a traditional-shaped 'tagine'. This cooking pot has a shallow base, with a high domed lid which peaks at the top, a bit like a teepee. This allows the special dish called a Tagine (often made from lamb) to cook with the steam gathering in the peak of the pot, keeping the meat tender and not allowing it to overcook.

Moroccan Rabbit

Serves 6

900g (2lb) rabbit pieces
salt and freshly ground pepper

For the stock:
400g (14 oz) tinned chick peas
4 tablespoons olive oil
2 large onions, chopped
2 sprigs of fresh thyme
3 large cloves garlic, peeled
4 small turnips, cut in half
2 teaspoons paprika
¼ teaspoon cayenne pepper
1 teaspoon ground cinnamon
pinch powdered saffron
2 tablespoons tomato purée, mixed
with a little hot water
1 green pepper
6 tablespoons chopped fresh
coriander

450g (1lb) couscous

For the garnish:
½ teaspoon paprika
½ teaspoon cayenne pepper

Season the rabbit pieces with salt and pepper. Drain the chick peas, rinse them and remove the skins.

Place the rabbit, chick peas and all the stock ingredients except the green pepper and coriander into the base of a steamer. Add about 2 pints of water and mix well. Bring to the boil, then reduce the heat, cover and simmer for 20 minutes. Add the chopped and deseeded green pepper and coriander to the rabbit and cook for a further 25 minutes. Steam the couscous over the rabbit for the last 20 minutes.

Arrange the rabbit in the middle of the couscous and sprinkle over a little extra paprika and cayenne pepper to serve.

Central and South American Cooking

This large area covers a wide range of exciting cuisines poised to become a major food trend in London. The cooking traditions of Chile, Columbia and Peru, together with Mexico and the islands off the coast of central America, are varied and reflect the different colonial or other influences that have shaped their respective pasts. These cuisines are dominated by spices and the often unusual combinations of ingredients, both native and those imported from foreign parts. Corn, capsicum peppers, many kinds of beans, pumpkin and all kinds of squashes, turkey, pineapples, chocolate, vanilla and peanuts are among the most frequently used.

In London, the number of restaurants serving this type of cuisine is increasing. Specialist food shops provide specific ingredients for home cooking, also offering valuable supplies for the chefs in the many Embassy kitchens. The popularity of certain Latin American-style restaurants, has grown offering good authentic dishes at reasonable prices.

Tex-Mex cooking as served here in TGI Fridays, is heavily influenced by Central American cooking.

Chilean Embassy

12 Devonshire Street, London W1N 2DS. Tel: 0171 580 6392

CHILEAN GASTRONOMY is the result of two culinary traditions, founding and giving life to the so called 'Creole cuisine'. Major contributors were the Indian traditions and their products, such as potatoes, corn and beans, along with Spanish habits and usages brought by the conquerors, and foreign culinary influences such as French, German, Italian and British. The combination of the Spanish conquerors' wives' knowledge and that of their employed Indian cooks produced copies of Spanish dishes which contained less meat but which were enriched with such ingredients as corn in Humitas, cornmeal and potato in dishes such as Lacro, Charquican and Valdiviano, which is pumpkin seasoned with chilli and cooked with lard.

The most representative of this mixed cuisine is, however, its sweet dishes which have a definite Hispanic-Moorish-Jewish influence. Typical Chilean dishes include rolled meats, tumoras, spicy pork ribs and beef with cranberry beans.

Fresh fruit played a large part in the Chilean cuisine and during the time of the Spanish conquerors, cherimoyas (custard apple), egg fruit and strawberries were very much in evidence. Cherimoyas and egg fruit were sent to Peru in exchange for sugar and strawberries were Chile's greatest contribution to Europe. A French engineer, Arnédée Frézier took them to France at the beginning of the 18th Century and had them planted in the gardens of Versailles. Cherimoyas, or custard apples, have the most delicious creamy coloured flesh but contain very large, shiny stones. To prepare them, cut in half, scoop out the flesh and stones and rub through a sieve, removing the stones, then use the fruit pulp for the recipe. The fruit should be soft to the touch (like a ripe peach) when it is ripe enough to eat.

The following recipes recommended by Jacqueline Tichauer of the Chilean Embassy, where she's the Cultural and Press Attaché, are great and typical Chilean dishes.

Tomatican

Serves 6

1 tablespoon oil
250g (9oz) beef sirloin, diced
3 onions, finely sliced
2 garlic cloves, crushed
2 tablespoons paprika
6 large ripe tomatoes, peeled and
chopped, with their juice
3 fresh corn on the cob,
kernels only
salt and freshly ground pepper
dried oregano

Heat the oil in a frying pan and sauté the beef, onions, garlic and paprika until the meat is browned and the onions are tender. Add the tomatoes and corn kernels, then season with salt, pepper and oregano to taste.

Cover and cook over a low heat for 2 hours, adding more tomato juice if necessary. The stew should be quite thick.

Serve with cooked potatoes.

Corn and Meat Casserole

Serves 12

6 fresh corn on the cob
8 leaves fresh basil, chopped
salt and freshly ground pepper
3 tablespoons butter
750ml (1¼ pints) milk
3 tablespoons oil
4 onions, finely minced
450g (1lb) ground beef
1 teaspoon ground cumin
4 hard-boiled eggs, sliced
200g (7oz) black olives
200g (7oz) raisins
12 cooked pieces or joints of
chicken, e.g. leg, wing, breast
2 tablespoons sugar

Preheat the oven to 200°C/400°F/gas mark 6.

In a large saucepan heat the corn (grated kernels), basil, salt, pepper and butter. Slowly add the milk, stirring constantly until the mixture thickens. Cook over a low heat for 5 minutes, then set aside.

In a frying pan, heat the oil, add the onions and sauté until the onions are transparent. Add the ground beef and cook until lightly browned. Season with salt, pepper and cumin and cook for a few more minutes. Spoon the meat mixture into a baking dish, then arrange the egg slices, olives and raisins in layers over the meat. Place the chicken pieces on top and cover with the reserved corn mixture.

Sprinkle with sugar and bake in the preheated oven for 30-35 minutes or until golden brown.

Empanadas (Baked Meat Turnovers)

makes 20 empanadas

575g (1¼lb) plain flour
1 tablespoon baking powder
salt
1 egg yolk
1 whole egg, beaten
350ml (12fl.oz) warm milk
225g (8oz) melted shortening
2 tablespoons oil
1 teaspoon paprika
4 onions, finely chopped
½ teaspoon each of chilli powder,
cumin and oregano
450g (1lb) ground beef
3 hard-boiled eggs, sliced
20 black olives
40 large raisins

Preheat the oven to 200°C/400°F/gas mark 6.

To prepare the dough: Sift the flour with the baking powder and salt. Add egg yolk, egg, milk and shortening. Mix to make a stiff dough, then divide the mixture into 20 pieces and roll each thinly into a circle.

For the stuffing or pino: Heat the oil in a frying pan with the paprika and sauté the onions until soft. Add the chilli powder, cumin, oregano and salt. Add the beef and mix with the onions. Cook until the meat is no longer pink.

Prepare the empanadas by placing a spoonful of stuffing on one half of each dough circle, then top with slices of egg, olives and raisins. Fold the dough over the filling, wet the edge with milk, fold over again and seal.

Bake in the preheated oven for 25 minutes until cooked and lightly browned. Serve hot.

Chilean Embassy

12 Devonshire Street, London W1N 2DS. Tel: 0171 580 6392

Sopaipillas

Makes 20 sopaipillas

450g (1lb) cooked pumpkin or butternut squash, puréed
150g (5oz) plain flour
1 tablespoon baking powder
2 tablespoons margarine
¼ teaspoon salt
oil for frying

In bowl mix together the pumpkin or squash, flour, baking powder, margarine and salt until the mixture forms into a ball, without kneading. Roll out the dough to 1cm (½ inch) thick and cut out round sopaipillas, each approximately 8cm (3in) in diameter. Prick with a fork.

Fry in hot oil until golden brown, then drain onkitchen paper. Serve hot with pebre sauce or sweet syrup. Makes 20 pieces.

Mote with Dried Peaches

Serves 4

12 whole dried peaches
sugar
cinnamon stick
250g (9oz) wheat

In a bowl, soak the peaches in cold water overnight.

The next day place them in saucepan with the soaking water, add sugar to taste and the cinnamon. Cook until tender, then allow to cool in the cooking liquid.

To prepare the mote: In a saucepan, put the wheat in water with the ashes from a eucalyptus or cypress tree and boil to loosen the skin. Drain and rub the wheat with your hands to remove the skin; wash in cold water and boil again. Drain and cool.

In a serving dish, place the peaches with the juice and sprinkle with cooked mote.

Happy Cherimoya Juice

Makes 2 cups

1 small cherimoya, peeled and seeded
225ml (8fl.oz) orange juice
125ml (4fl.oz) water
sugar to taste

In a blender or food processor blend all the ingredients together until smooth.

Refrigerate until very cold, then serve with ice.

Cherimoya Meringue

Serves 4

350ml (12fl.oz) orange juice
1 tablespoon sugar
1 cherimoya (1kg/2lb 2oz in weight),
peeled, seeded and chopped
115g (4oz) caster sugar
2 egg whites

In a deep serving bowl, mix together the orange juice and 1 tablespoon sugar, add the cherimoya and stir to mix. Set aside.

In a saucepan prepare the syrup with 115g (4oz) sugar. Heat it gently on its own until it reaches the fine-thread stage (about 120°C).

In a bowl, whisk the egg whites until stiff, then slowly add the syrup, beating until cool. Cover the cherimoya and orange juice mixture completely with the meringue. Refrigerate before serving.

Salmon and Vegetable Ceviche

Serves 6

750g (1½ lb) salmon, skinned and
cut into small cubes
450g (1lb) scallops, cubed
450ml (16fl.oz) lemon juice
400g (14oz) peeled tomatoes, diced
200g (7oz) spring onions, chopped
50g (2oz) finely chopped green chillis
16 green olives, sliced
115ml (4fl.oz) olive oil
50ml (2fl.oz) dry white wine
2 tablespoons white wine vinegar
a few drops of Tabasco, to taste
1 teaspoon dried oregano
3 tablespoons chopped parsley

In a large, non-metallic bowl, place the salmon and scallops. Add the lemon juice and marinate for at least 6 hours. In another bowl mix the rest of the ingredients for the dressing

Drain the salmon and scallops and mix with the prepared dressing. Cover and refrigerate for 2-4 hours. Serve on a bed of lettuce leaves and garnish with sliced avocados.

Chilean Embassy

12 Devonshire Street, London W1N 2DS. Tel: 0171 580 6392

Chilean Salad

Serves 6-8

750g (1½lb) onions, finely sliced
750g (1½lb) tomatoes, peeled and
finely sliced
salt and freshly ground pepper
3 tablespoons olive oil
12g (½oz) fresh coriander, chopped

Rinse the onions in thoroughly in cold water and drain. into a bowl. Mix the tomatoes with the onions and season to taste with salt and pepper. Add the olive oil and mix well. Sprinkle with chopped coriander and serve.

Prebre Sauce

Makes 1 cup

2 hot red chillies
2 garlic cloves, peeled
115g (4oz) fresh coriander,
finely chopped
4 spring onions, finely chopped
1 teaspoon dry oregano
2 tablespoons olive oil
2 tablespoons red wine vinegar
salt and freshly ground pepper

In a blender purée together the chillies and garlic cloves. Then add the coriander, spring onions, oil , oregano and vinegar, salt and pepper to taste. Blend well and add 50-100ml (2-4fl.oz) of water if the sauce is too thick.

Porotos Grandados

Serves 8

2kg (4½lb) fresh cranberry beans
50ml (2fl.oz) oil
½ teaspoon paprika
450g (1lb) butternut squash, peeled
and cut into small cubes
375g (12oz) chopped onions
2 garlic cloves, crushed
2 fresh corn on the cob, kernels only
5 leaves fresh basil
salt

In a large saucepan cook the beans in plenty of salted water for 1 hour. Drain and reserve 1 cup cooking liquid.

In a frying pan heat the oil and paprika; add the squash, onion and garlic and sauté until tender. Add this mixture and the rest of the ingredients, including the reserved cooking liquid, to the beans. Cook them over a low heat for 1 hour, or until the beans are tender and soft. Add some chicken broth if necessary. Add the corn kernels 5 minutes before serving and continue cooking.

Serve hot, garnished with basil leaves, with a tomato salad if desired.

Consulate of Columbia

Flat 3a, 3 Hans Crescent, London SW1X 0LR. Tel: 0171 589 9177

GENOVERA VILLANDA from the Consulate of Columbia shares these Columbian recipes. Columbia has a cuisine that is a product of Spanish and African influences, so that a typical Columbian dish does not really exist. Each region has developed its own gastronomic delicacies, according to what is grown locally, and incorporating ancestral traditions and customs. Many of the dishes are based on fish, shellfish and coconut. Sancocho de Sabalo is prepared in coconut milk with strips of fish, potato, plantain and yam, served with coconut rice.

Sancocho de Sabalo (Fish Stew)

Serves 6-8

900g (2lb) onions, peeled and
roughly chopped
1 green pepper, deseeded and
roughly chopped
seasoning
½ teaspoon ground cumin
1.3kg (3lb) fresh white fish fillets,
roughly chopped
900g (2lb) yam, peeled and
roughly chopped
900g (2lb) potatoes, peeled and
roughly chopped
3 large plantain, peeled and
roughly chopped
2 x 400g cans coconut milk

Place the onions, green pepper, salt, pepper and cumin into a large pan with 300ml (½ pint) boiling water and simmer for about 10 minutes. Add the fish, yam, potatoes and plantain; cover and cook gently for 30 minutes.

Stir in the coconut milk and simmer for a further 5 minutes, then serve with coconut rice.

Arroz Con Conco (Coconut Rice)

Serves 6

3 tablespoons vegetable oil
2 coconuts, broken open, milk
reserved, flesh cut finely
1 teaspoon caster sugar
450g (1lb) long grain rice
½ teaspoon salt
350g (12oz) small black grapes

Heat the oil in a pan, add the coconut flesh to the oil and sauté until lightly golden. Stir in the sugar and rice, then sauté for 2 minutes.

Add 1.2 litres (2 pints) water and salt. Bring to the boil, cover and simmer for about 10 minutes, until the rice is tender. Stir in the grapes and serve.

Dominican High Commission

1 Collingham Gardens, London SW5 0HN. Tel: 0171 370 5194

PAULA GINAND from the Office of the High Commissioner for the Commonwealth of Dominica shares two favourite Dominican recipes she cooks. Christophines are hard, green pear-shaped vegetables with a very shiny skin and pale cream flesh. To prepare, remove the skin and stone. Plantains look like green bananas but have quite hard flesh.

Christophine Pie

Serves 6-8

4-5 christophines
¼ teaspoon salt
1 green pepper
2 tablespoons chopped chives
115g (4oz) cheese, grated
fresh parsley, chopped

For the cheese sauce:
50g (2oz) butter
75g (3oz) plain flour
300ml (½ pint) evaporated milk
%0g (2oz) Cheddar cheese, grated
1 teaspoon onion, finely grated

Preheat the oven to 180°C/350°F/gas mark 4.
Wash and peel the christophines. Slice lengthwise and core, then cut into strips and steam with salt for 20 minutes or until tender.

Arrange the christophine slices in a buttered dish, layering it with some strips of green pepper, chopped chives, grated cheese and parsley. Place all the cheese sauce ingredients in a saucepan. Heat gently, whisking continuously, until the sauce comes to the boil and thickens. Simmer for 5 minutes, whisking. Pour the sauce over the christophine mixture.

Garnish the edge, corners and/or centre of the dish with some more chives, green pepper and parsley.

Bake in the preheated oven for 35 minutes or until the cheese sauce is set and firm to the touch. Serve hot.

Stuffed Plantain Rings

Serves 6

5 ripe plantains
oil, for frying
Philadelphia cream cheese
fresh parsley sprigs
cherry slices

Slice the ripe plaintains lengthwise in thin, even slices (approximately 4-5 slices for 1 ripe plaintain. Fry in the oil until golden brown but not dry. Place in full length on absorbent paper. Roll immediately into a tight ring (even while still hot) and arrange on a platter.

Pipe rosettes of cream cheese or another filling on to the ring. Garnish the cream filling with a sprig of parsley and/or a slice of cherry to make an attractive decoration. Serve.

Estilo Kitchen

37 High Street, Wimbledon Village, London SW19 5BY. Tel: 0181 314 6868

WIMBLEDON'S ESTILO KITCHEN SHOP is a very stylish kitchenware and cookshop, which sells good specialist foodstuffs from all over the world. Their expert knowledge of the US gourmet market is reflected in their stock.

The principal buyer and owner is Marion Araji. She treats her customers to regular 'tasters' in the shop to encourage an interest in new tastes and flavours. She has given us her special tips for quick snack ideas.

Coriander Dip

1 teaspoon minced coriander, fresh or from a jar
juice of ½ lemon
black pepper

Mix the minced coriander, the lemon juice and a generous grinding of black pepper for a delicious dip to serve with crudités.

Baked Nachos

1 jar ready-made salsa sauce
1 packet tortilla chips
75g (3oz) Cheddar cheese, grated
preserved chillies (optional)

Preheat the oven 180°C/350°F/gas mark 4.
Scatter tortilla chips over the base of a shallow ovenproof dish, spoon over ready-made salsa sauce and a handful of grated cheese. Repeat the layers twice, finishing with a layer of cheese. Bake in the preheated oven for 15 minutes. For those who enjoy a hotter flavour, add a few preserved chillies from a jar in between the layers.

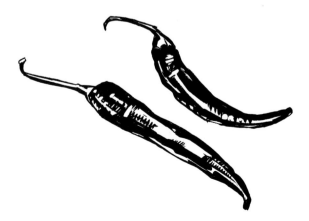

Fate

12 Maida Vale Avenue, London NW6. Tel: 0171 706 2620

ATOIME AT THIS NEW AFRO-CARIBBEAN restaurant in Maida Vale has shared with me his recipe for Chicken St. Lucia. One of the typical ingredients in Caribbean cooking and in particular in his restaurant, is cinnamon.

The sticks and the ground form of this highly aromatic spice is derived from the bark of the *Cinnamomum* tree. Ground cinnamon adds a distinctive sweet, spicy flavour to the dishes in which it is used.

Chicken St Lucia

Serves 8

For the marinade:
6cm (2½ inch) piece of fresh
ginger, peeled and grated
1 clove garlic, crushed
1 teaspoon chopped fresh thyme
1 teaspoon ground cinnamon
1 tablespoon chopped fresh coriander
400g (14oz) can of coconut milk
1 tablespoon rum
6 chicken breasts, sliced into pieces

To make the marinade: Place all the marinade ingredients in a bowl and mix together thoroughly. Add the chicken pieces, mix well, cover and leave to marinate in the refrigerator overnight.

Remove the chicken pieces from the marinade and pan fry for 5 minutes. Serve with boiled rice and sprinkle over some flaked or desiccated coconut and chopped parsley before serving.

Suggestion: Sieve the used marinade, bring to the boil and reduce for a sauce accompaniment to serve hot with the chicken.

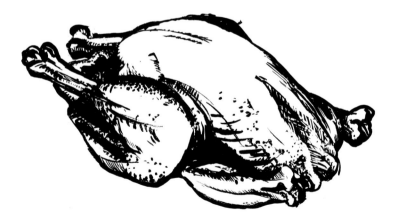

High Commission of the Bahamas

Bahamas House, 10 Chesterfield Street, London SW1X 8AH. Tel: 0171 408 4488

THE HIGH COMMISSION OF THE BAHAMAS in London have shared with us some of their favourite dishes from their native land.

Peas 'n' Rice, in one form or another, is a very traditional dish which can be found throughout the Caribbean. Howeve, in the Bahamas it is usually made with pigeon peas and is served alongside most entrées. If necessary, black-eye beans or even kidney beans can be used as a substitute for pigeon peas.

Peas 'n' Rice

Serves 6-8

50g (2oz) salt pork or bacon, diced
1 small onion, minced
1 green pepper, diced
1 stick celery, diced
4 tablespoons tomato paste
1 x 250g (8oz) can pigeon peas
thyme
salt and pepper
200g (7oz) rice
475ml (16fl.oz) water

Fry the salt pork or bacon in a saucepan until it is crisp. Add the onion, green pepper and celery and cook until the mixture is pulpy.

Add the tomato paste and cook until most of the liquid in the pan has evaporated. Add the drained pigeon peas, thyme, salt and pepper and cook for a further 2 minutes. Add the rice and pour in enough water to cover. Cover the pan tightly and allow the mixture to simmer for 20 minutes until all the liquid has been absorbed. Serve hot.

Curried Goat

Serves 6

900g (2lb) mutton
1 teaspoon salt
1 tablespoon ground black pepper
1 large onion
2 teaspoons curry powder
2 tablespoons cooking oil
475ml (16fl.oz) water
2 diced green peppers
450g (1lb) diced potato

Clean the mutton and cut it into 2.5cm (1in) cubes. Season well with salt and pepper, then add the onions. Add the curry powder and allow to stand for approximately 30 minutes.

Remove the meat cubes and fry briskly in heated oil until slightly browned. Add water, cover tightly and allow to cook for 1½ hours, until the meat is tender. Add the peppers and potatoes, then the seasonings in which the meat was marinated and cook over a low heat for 30 minutes.

Serve with steamed white rice or boiled green bananas.

High Commission of the Bahamas

Bahamas House, 10 Chesterfield Street, London SW1X 8AH. Tel: 0171 408 4488

John Cake

Serves 6-8

115g (4oz) lard or other shortening
700g (1½lb) plain flour
2 tablespoons sugar
1 teaspoon salt
water

The origins of this simple, sweet bread are hazy; some say that the name derives from 'Journey Cake', the term used by spongers (the crew of ships employed in collecting sponges) who prepared it over a small burner during long sea voyages. Traditionally served with Boiled Fish, John Cake is delicious warm and lightly buttered.

Preheat the oven to 180°C/350°F/gas mark 4.

Rub the shortening into the flour, then stir in the sugar and salt. Add enough water to make a soft but firm dough and knead for about 2 minutes, or until the dough is smooth and cohesive.

Shape the dough into a round and place on a greased baking sheet. Bake in the preheated oven for 45 minutes, until golden brown.

Boiled Fish

Serves 6

900g (2lb) grouper (or firm-fleshed white fish e.g. monkfish or cod)
salt and pepper
2 medium onions, sliced
115g (4oz) salt pork, diced
6 potatoes, quartered
2 limes
50g (2oz) butter
300ml (½ pint) water

This delicious fish soup is a traditional breakfast dish and is reputed to be particularly efficacious after a late night! Serve with fresh John Cake and grits for full effect.

Cut the grouper into serving pieces and season with salt and pepper (and hot pepper, if desired). Place all the ingredients in a deep saucepan and simmer for 15-20 minutes. Add more water and adjust the seasoning, if required, then continue to cook over a medium heat for a further 15 minutes, or until the potatoes are cooked through. The fish should still be firm. Serve hot.

Grits

Serves 6

175g (6oz) grits
¼ teaspoon salt
900ml (1½ pints) water
knob of butter

Also served with Boiled Fish, Grits are bleached cornmeal and when cooked are similar to semolina or porridge. This dish is thought to have originated in the southern states of America.

Stir the grits into boiling salted water, reduce the heat and cook for 3-5 minutes.

Remove from the heat, cover and let the mixture stand to thicken. Serve topped with a knob of butter.

Chicken Souse

Serves 8

1 medium-sized chicken, jointed
2 medium onions, sliced
2 cloves garlic, crushed
5 potatoes, peeled and quartered
7 carrots, scraped and thickly sliced
4 tablespoons lime juice
25g (1oz) butter
water
1 bird pepper or 2 tablespoons
hot pepper sauce
about 6 allspice berries

You will often find pig's feet or sheep's tongue instead of chicken in a souse! Serve with grits and John Cake (see previous recipes).

Skin the chicken portions, if desired, and place them with the onions, garlic, potatoes, carrots, lime juice and butter in a large saucepan, adding sufficient water to cover. Break up the bird pepper and add it to the pan together with allspice to taste.

Bring to the boil and simmer for about 1 hour or until the chicken falls off the bone and the potatoes are cooked through. Serve while hot.

Jamaican Information Service

Jamaican High Commission, 1/2 Prince Consort Road, London SW4 2BZ. Tel: 0171 823 9911

LOWERN REID, the Information Officer at the Jamaican Information Service in London, cooks these recipes at home. She's based them on recipes from Norma Benghients' *Traditional Jamaican Cookery*. One of the ingredients used in the recipe is the sweet potato. This very versatile vegetable came originally from tropical South America, and is often mistaken for yam.

Jamaican Rum Punch

Serves 6-8

1 part sour (lime juice)
2 parts sweet (sugar, syrup)
3 parts strong (rum)
4 parts weak (water or any fruit juice)

Mix all the ingredients together well and serve on crushed ice, decorated with slices of pineapple, lime or lemon.

Sweet Potato Pudding

Serves 8

900g (2lb) sweet potatoes
250g (8oz) brown sugar
750ml (1¼ pints) coconut milk
2 teaspoons vanilla essence
1 teaspoon grated nutmeg
1 teaspoon ground cinnamon
1 tablespoon butter
1 medium coconut, grated flesh only
225g (8oz) raisins
1 teaspoon butter, for greasing

Preheat the oven to 180°C/350°F/gas mark 4.
Grate the sweet potatoes. Add the sugar and coconut milk a little at a time, to the potatoes. Stir in the vanilla, nutmeg, cinnamon, butter and coconut. Add the raisins. The mixture should be runny rather than thick, so make sure you add enough coconut milk.

Place in a greased baking tin and bake in the preheated oven for approximately 1 hour or until a skewer run through the middle comes out clean. Delicious served warm or cold.

Mexican Embassy

42 Hertford Street, London W1Y 7TF. Tel: 0171 499 8586

Alejandra de la Paz is the Minister for Cultural Affairs at the Embassy of Mexico in Mayfair. He shares one of his country's most popular dishes.

Tortillas can now be bought ready-made and kept in the freezer for up to a month. Allow to thaw before using. Any type of hard cheese can be used for the topping, but try to use Cheshire cheese as it has a distinctive tang.

Tortillas Stuffed with Cheese

Serves 4

For the chilli sauce:
750ml (1¼ pints) tomato purée (not concentrated)
1 small onion, finely chopped
1 clove garlic, chopped
2 fresh hot green chillies, or more, to taste, seeded and chopped
salt
pinch sugar
2 tablespoons vegetable oil
225ml (8fl.oz) soured or double cream

To assemble:
oil for frying
12 corn tortillas
350g (12oz) grated Cheshire cheese
1 onion, finely chopped
fresh coriander, finely chopped

Preheat the oven to 180°C/350°F/gas mark 4.

Making the chilli sauce: In a blender, combine the onion, garlic, chillies, tomato purée, salt and sugar and reduce to a purée. In a large frying pan heat the oil and pour in the purée. Cook, stirring, over a moderate heat for about 10 minutes until the sauce is thick and well blended. Cool the sauce slightly, then stir in the cream. Set the sauce aside.

Assembling the dish: In a large frying pan, heat the oil and fry the tortillas, one by one, for about 30 seconds on each side. Drain on kitchen paper.

Warm the chilli sauce but do not let it boil as it will curdle. Dip the tortillas one by one in the sauce, then fill with some cheese and top with some onion. Leave enough cheese and onion for the garnish.

Fold the tortillas and put them into an ovenproof dish. Pour the remaining sauce over the tortillas, sprinkle with the rest of the cheese and onion and put the dish into the preheated oven for about 10 minutes to heat through. Garnish with chopped coriander and serve as soon as possible as enchiladas go soggy if left to stand. These enchiladas can also be stuffed with shredded cooked chicken.

Paulo's

30 Greyhound Road, London W6 8NX. Tel: 0171 387 9264

PAULO OWNS THIS BRAZILIAN RESTAURANT near Hammersmith, to which he has given his name. He gives us the recipe for one of the most popular desserts served in the restaurant.

If you can't buy sponge fingers, use Rich Tea biscuits instead. As a variation, try using pineapple chunks and brandy instead of the chocolate sauce.

Pavé

Serves 10

397g (14oz) can condensed milk
900ml (1½ pints) milk
5 eggs, separated
5 dessertspoons milk chocolate powder (Cadbury's drinking chocolate powder)
5 dessertspoons caster sugar
450g (1lb) can Nestlé cream
1 packet of 12 sponge finger biscuits

In a saucepan mix together the condensed milk, 600ml (1 pint) milk and the egg yolks. Stir and bring to the boil. Set aside to cool. In a separate saucepan, place the chocolate powder and 300ml (½ pint) milk. Stir and bring to the boil. Set aside to cool. In a mixing bowl whisk the egg whites until stiff. Gradually whisk in the sugar, then fold in the Nestlé cream.

Pour the condensed milk mixture into individual trifle glasses or one large one. Place sponge fingers over the top. Pour the chocolate sauce over the sponge fingers, then top with the whisked egg white and cream mixture.

Place in the refrigerator, then slice and serve when cold.

Salsa

96 Charing Cross Road, London WC2. Tel: 0171 379 3277

GAVIN HEALY FROM SALSA, a Mexican Restaurant in central London gives us two of their most popular recipes. Chillies are a frequent ingredient at Salsa and there are now many varieties available in London.The snub chilli used in this recipe has a medium hotness of flavour. Vary the chilli content to the heat you want, adding the seeds too if you prefer a really hot flavour.

Peanut Chicken

Serves 6

400ml (14fl.oz) vegetable oil
50ml (2fl.oz) sesame seed oil
12 small snub chillies
1 tablespoon lemon grass
1 tablespoon grated root ginger
50ml (2fl.oz) soy sauce
1 clove garlic, crushed
6 chicken breasts

Combine all the ingredients except the chicken and leave to stand for at least 2 hours.

Slice each chicken breast into 5 long strips and place in the marinade in the refrigerator for 8 hours, or overnight if possible. Skewer each of the strips onto a separate skewer and grill for 5-7 minutes until cooked. Serve hot with the peanut dip (see below).

Peanut Dip

Serves 6

400ml (14fl.oz) milk
25ml (1fl.oz) coconut milk
150g (5oz) peanut butter
½ red snub chilli, finely chopped
37ml (1½fl.oz) soy sauce
25ml (1fl.oz) sesame oil
¼ teaspoon crushed chillies
salt and freshly ground
black pepper

Combine the milk and coconut milk together and warm through gently in a saucepan. Add all the remaining ingredients and whisk together over a gentle heat. Bring to the boil, remove from the heat and leave to cool before serving with the chicken.

New World Cooking

The Pacific Rim and Australasia combine a whole mixture of cuisines which mould the New World food influence in London. There are a lot of Antipodean chefs working in the capital, who bring a host of fresh ingredients and new cooking styles to London restaurants and cafés. The Far East is a key source of inspiration for many of these chefs, and it is reflected in their selection of ingredients: lemon grass, chillies and coriander. Unusual native ingredients, such as kangaroo and emu, not to mention the celebrated smoked crocodile, have also found their way on to London menus in recent years. However, it is still difficult for many people to obtain indigenous products from Australia and New Zealand on a regular basis as supplies tend to be erratic.

The United States was, of course, regarded historically as the New World, and recipes from it are included here as part of this young and developing food scene. American restaurants, as well as the long-standing burger bars, are increasing in number in London and continue to be popular. Many shops also cater for the needs of homesick American expatriates.

Delicious Blue – Australian owned and run, with innovative menus.

Christopher's

18 Wellington Street, London WC2E 7DD. Tel: 0171 240 4222

CHRISTOPHER'S PRODUCES AN EXCELLENT all-American brunch and continues with the US flavour running throughout the menu. And the portions for the starters are large, so just beware. The sweet delicacies include pancakes with maple syrup and bacon, which are delicious. For extra sweet-toothed diners, the slab of New York Cheesecake is essential. Everything is served by American waiters and waitresses. Here, Christopher Gilmour shares a favourite dish.

Christopher's Lobster Coleslaw

Serves 6

1 tablespoon good mayonnaise
pinch of sugar
pinch of celery salt
115g (4oz) cooked lobster meat
1 small Chinese lettuce, stalks
removed and cut crossways
as finely as possible
2 large carrots, peeled and
finely grated
8-10 large spinach leaves, blanched

To make the coleslaw, place all the ingredients except the spinach leaves in a bowl and mix together. Lay some clingfilm on a sushi mat and cover with blanched spinach leaves. Lay some lobster coleslaw along the middle to create a roll approx. 2.5cm (1 inch) thick. Roll up as for Japanese teriyaki, remove clingfilm and cut into three at a slight angle.

Arrange on a plate with a little green salad garnish and serve immediately.

Terry Farris

Tel: 0181 744 9260.

TERRY FARRIS HAS LIVED IN LONDON for 5 years, after following a career as a newspaper photographer in the States. Trained at Leith's School of Food and Wine, Terry now enjoys freelance cooking projects including assisting TV cook Glynn Christian in producing a series on microwave cookery for the BBC, acting as relief cook to ex-King Constantine and HM Queen Anne Marie of Greece, as well as cooking for plenty of private dinner parties. Terry has given me her favourite recipe, one that reminds her of her United States home.

Breakfast Burritos

Serves 2

1 tablespoon light oil
2 medium potatoes, peeled and cut into 1cm (½ inch) cubes
1 onion, finely chopped
1 chilli, deseeded and finely chopped
salt and pepper
2 tomatoes, deseeded and chopped
small handful of fresh coriander, roughly chopped (optional)
25g (1oz) butter
4 wheat tortillas
knob of butter (for scrambling eggs)
4 eggs

Heat a little oil in a frying pan (cast iron is best) over a medium to high heat. Add the potatoes and cook – they may stick to the bottom but don't worry, just scrape and stir to cook evenly. Reduce the heat to medium.

After 8-10 minutes, add the onion, chilli, salt and pepper. You can cover the pan now if you like – this cooks it faster and makes it moist and slightly mushy. Lower the heat even more so that the mixture doesn't catch on the bottom. Stir occasionally.

When the mixture is cooked (probably about 15-20 minutes), remove from the heat and stir in the chopped tomatoes and coriander. Transfer to a bowl and keep warm. Wash the pan.

Melt a quarter of the butter in the pan. When sizzling, fry both sides of a tortilla just long enough to soften and give a little colour. Repeat with the rest of the butter and tortillas. Keep warm under tin foil to prevent them from drying out.

Wipe out the pan, add a small amount of butter and scramble the eggs. Season with salt and pepper.

To assemble, divide the egg and potato mixtures evenly between the warm tortillas. They can be rolled (like a fat cigar) or simply folded over in half. Serve warm.

Variations: Sprinkle a little cheese over the filling before folding or rolling. Use a Mexican salsa (Pace Picante Sauce is best or make you own) and pour it over the fillings. In this case, omit the tomatoes. Or add chopped, fried bacon bits to the scrambled eggs.

Delicious Blue

75 Beak Street, Soho, London W1R 3LF. Tel: 0171 287 1840

MARK O'HARA IS THE AUSTRALIAN chef at this intimate restaurant on Beak Street in London's Soho. His Australian roots are reflected in his choice of ingredients in these two recipes. Mark does, however, cook with foods and ingredients from his experiences of the cuisines of different countries, which he learnt during his extensive travels before settling in London to cook.

Seared Emu and Candied Sweet Potatoes and Pan-Fried Spiced Figs

Serves 4

For the candied sweet potatoes:
6 sweet potatoes
225g (8oz) unsalted butter
2 tablespoons caster sugar
salt and pepper
2 tablespoons demerara sugar
225g (8oz) pecan nuts, chopped

For the spiced figs:
115g (4oz) unsalted butter
2 tablespoons olive oil
10 fresh figs
2 tablespoons ground cumin
2 tablespoons ground coriander

For the rosemary and Madeira sauce:
150ml (¼ pint) Madeira
600ml (1 pint) beef stock
2 tablespoons chopped fresh rosemary

450g (1lb) emu

Preheat the oven to 180°C/350°F/gas mark 4.

Place the sweet potatoes in a pan and cover with water. Bring to the boil for about 10 minutes, until tender. Drain and mash with two-thirds of the butter and caster sugar. Season to taste. Place the mixture in a baking tray. Scatter over the demerara sugar, pecan nuts and remaining butter and bake in the oven for 20 minutes, until the potatoes are golden.

Meanwhile make the spiced figs. Heat the butter and oil in a frying pan, slice the figs in half and place them in the pan, flesh side down. Add the spices and fry for 2 minutes. Turn over, place in a baking tray and bake in the oven for about 15 minutes.

Place the Madeira in a pan and reduce by half. Add the stock and reduce for 15 minutes until the sauce is a thick consistency. Add the rosemary and simmer for 5 minutes.

To cook the emu, sear each side in a hot frying pan for 2 minutes. Remove from the pan and allow to rest for 2-3 minutes.

Slice the emu and serve with the spiced figs and candied sweet potatoes alongside.

Kangaroo Rump with Tomato and Olive Sauce

Serves 4

olive oil
450g (1lb) kangaroo rump

For the sauce:
2 tablespoons extra virgin olive oil
2 shallots, finely chopped
1 tablespoon chopped garlic
115ml (4 fl.oz) red wine
4 ripe plum tomatoes, chopped
175ml (6 fl.oz) tomato juice
salt and pepper to taste
6 fresh basil leaves, chopped
75g (3oz) sliced black olives

To cook the kangaroo, heat some oil in a frying pan. Add the kangaroo and fry it until it is cooked to your liking.

Meanwhile, make the sauce. Place the oil, shallots and garlic in a pan and simmer for 10 minutes. Add the red wine and reduce by two-thirds. Add the chopped tomatoes and juice. Simmer for 10-15 minutes. Season to taste, add the basil and olives and stir well.

Serve the cooked kangaroo with the warm sauce.

The Maple Leaf

41 Maiden Lane, Covent Garden, London WC2. Tel: 0171 240 2843

MARC CHARUTT, HEAD CHEF at The Maple Leaf restaurant in Covent Garden, finds that native Canadians enjoy eating something familiar when travelling abroad. The Canadian flavour in this busy pub includes a classic Canadian brunch dish of pancakes, good classic maple syrup, ham and eggs, which are by tradition fried sunny side up. The following three recipes are cooked at the restaurant. Marc feels that they reflect their most popular and typically Canandian dishes.

Corn Chowder Bisque

Serves 6

4 bacon slices
1 medium onion, chopped
2 tablespoons flour
300g (10oz) diced potato
2 x 398ml (14oz) cans creamed corn
or tomatoes
a 284ml (10oz) can tomato soup
500ml (17fl.oz) chicken stock
salt and pepper
fresh parsley, chopped

Fry the bacon until crispy. Remove and set aside. Sauté the onion in the remaining bacon fat until soft, then. stir in the flour. Add the potato, corn or tomatoes, tomato soup, chicken stock and reserved bacon. Mix well and simmer for 15 minutes or until the potato is tender. Add salt and pepper to taste.

Serve immediately, sprinkled with chopped parsley.

Maple Syrup Dumplings

Serves 6

For the dumplings:
300g (10oz) self-raising flour
2 dessertspoons butter, softened
3 tablespoons milk

For the syrup:
450ml (¾ pint) water
115g (4oz) sugar
1 tablespoon golden syrup
3 tablespoons maple syrup
1 dessertspoon lemon juice

Knead together the flour, butter and milk until the mixture is well-combined.

Bring a large saucepan of water to the boil. Spoon in the dumplings using 2 spoons, then reduce the heat. Cover with a lid and simmer for 10 minutes.

Meanwhile, make the syrup. Place the water and sugar in a saucepan and heat gently until the sugar has dissolved. Add the syrups and lemon juice and heat the mixture through.

Drain the dumplings and serve immediately with the warm syrup.

Meatloaf with BBQ Sauce

Serves 6

450g (1lb) sausagemeat
700g (1½lb) minced steak
115g (4oz) breadcrumbs
2 onions, finely chopped
2 teaspoons curry powder
1 tablespoon tomato purée
salt and pepper
1 tablespoon chopped parsley
1 egg
175ml (6fl.oz) milk
125ml (4fl.oz) water

For the BBQ sauce:
225ml (8fl.oz) water
175ml (6fl.oz) tomato ketchup
75ml (3fl.oz) Worcestershire sauce
2 tablespoons vinegar
50g (2oz) brown sugar
1 teaspoon instant coffee powder
25g (1oz) butter
2 tablespoons lemon juice

Preheat the oven to 180°C/350°F/gas mark 4.

Combine the sausagemeat, minced steak, breadcrumbs, chopped onion, curry powder, tomato purée, salt, pepper, parsley and lightly beaten egg in a bowl. Beat until the mixture is well combined. Gradually add the milk and water and continue beating until the mixture is very smooth.

Shape the meat mixture into a loaf, place in a greased baking dish and bake in the oven for 30 minutes. Remove from the oven and carefully pour off any surplus fat.

Combine all the sauce ingredients in a saucepan, bring slowly to the boil, then reduce the heat and simmer for 10 minutes. Pour the BBQ sauce over the meatloaf, return to the oven and bake for a further 45 minutes, basting frequently with the sauce. Serve hot with vegetables or cold with salad.

Montana

125 Dawes Road, Fulham, London SW6. Tel: 0171 385 9500

KEN FINCH IS THE PROPRIETOR of Montana, in Fulham, which offers contemporary and innovative American cooking and Southern Western food, which takes its influences from Native American, Hispanic, Cajun and Creole cuisines.

Montana is well regarded for its drinks as well as its food. Try the Pisco Sour, their best-selling cocktail.

Blackened Salmon on Watercress Salad with Tomato, Lime and Jalapeno Salsa

Serves 4

4 salmon fillets (weighing approx 150g/5oz each)
3 tablespoons Cajun Blackening Spice (available from good supermarkets)
4 plum tomatoes
2 limes, skinned and segmented
1 red onion
25g (1oz) chopped fresh coriander
125ml (4fl.oz) extra virgin olive oil
salt and pepper
50g (2oz) sliced jalapenos (from good supermarkets)
1 bunch watercress

For the vinaigrette:
115ml (4fl.oz) extra virgin olive oil
50ml (2fl.oz) balsamic vinegar

lime segments and fresh coriander leaves, to garnish

Coat the salmon fillets with blackening spice, cover with clingfilm and refrigerate for 30 minutes. Meanwhile, make the salsa. Chop the tomatoes into 1cm (½ inch) dice and put in a mixing bowl, Add the chopped red onion, olive oil, finely chopped coriander and salt and pepper. Segment the limes and add to the mix with the roughly chopped jalapenos. Mix all the ingredients, cover with clingfilm and set aside.

Watercress salad: Toss the watercress in vinaigrette and divide between 4 plates.

Blackened salmon: Heat a frying pan until almost smoking hot and then add 2 tablespoons of olive oil and the salmon fillets. Wait until they start to smoke, then turn and continue cooking for about 4-5 minutes or until the fish feels firm. Place the salmon on the watercress and spoon some salsa over the top. Garnish with the lime and the coriander leaves.

Pisco Sour

2 shots Pisco
1 egg white
1 fresh lime

Place the pisco in a shaker and then add ice nearly to the top.
Add the egg white and the juice of 1 lime plus the skin. Shake
well and strain into an old fashioned cocktail glass, to serve.

Peach Julep

1½ measures peach pulp
½ shot peach liqueur
1 dash peach bitters
crushed ice
2 shots Makers Mark
peach slice and a sprig of mint,
to garnish

Pour the peach pulp, liqueur and bitters over crushed ice into a
tall glass. Stir vigorously and top with Makers Mark. Decorate
with a peach slice and a sprig of mint.

Parsons Restaurant

311 Fulham Road, London SW10. Tel: 0171 352 0651

PARSONS IS A LIGHT AND AIRY American-style restaurant dotted with lots of mirrors, palms and bentwood chairs. Burgers feature heavily on the menu, with ten different varieties available. They also concoct some great milkshakes – the pistachio one is particularly delicious. Here, Patrick Horsley of Parsons Restaurant shares a popular recipe, great for feeding a crowd.

Tuna Fish Pie

Serves 30

3kg (7lb) large Spanish onions, chopped in rings
6 cloves garlic, finely chopped
1 teaspoon ground chilli
300g (10oz) butter
1.7 litres (3 pints) béchamel sauce
2 bunches spring onions, chopped
900g (2lb) red peppers, sliced in rings
900g (2lb) button mushrooms, halved
1.4kg (3lb) good quality tinned tuna in oil (not brine)
900g (2lb) puff pastry, rolled out to fit the baking tin

Preheat the oven to 190°C/375°F/gas mark5.
Fry the onions, garlic and chilli in butter till the onion is soft. Add the spring onions, peppers, and mushrooms and fry for a further 5 minutes.

Heat the béchamel sauce and season. Add the chopped vegetables, cook for a further 5 minutes, then stir in the flaked tuna. Pour into a large baking tin, add the puff pastry top and bake in the preheated oven for 45-60 minutes, until cooked. Serve immediately, cut into slices.

PJ's Bar and Grill

52 Fulham Road, London SW3. Tel: 0171 581 0025

PJ's BAR AND GRILLE HAS A typical New York mix of Mediterranean and Californian appeal with soft-shell crabs and excellent Caesar salad. Their head chef, Richard, has introduced great brunch dishes too, including Eggs Benedict Royale. This is my favourite brunch restaurant on a Sunday. The best place to sit is downstairs so that you can watch the world go by through the window as well as see all the drinks being mixed at the bar.

With a huge airplane propeller and engine hanging over the centre of the downstairs bar, this place has an airy, relaxed atmosphere – I highly recommend it.

Eggs Benedict Royale

Serves 4

5 egg yolks
2 x 225g (8oz) packets butter, melted
115ml (4fl.oz) orange juice
12 small eggs
225g (8oz) smoked salmon
12 small pieces of toast
butter, for toast

First make the hollandaise sauce: Over a bain-marie, whisk the egg yolks until they are very pale and frothy and form a ribbon. They will be hot, but still cool enough to touch.

Gradually add the melted butter, whisking all the time, until all the oil is amalgamated. (Use about half the milk residue from the butter as well). Set the sauce aside in a warm place so that it does not separate. Meanwhile, soft-boil the eggs. Drain well.

Butter the toast, and cover with smoked salmon. Carefully place the soft-boiled egg on top of each toast and put 3 pieces of toast on each plate. Spoon over the hollandaise sauce so that all the eggs and most of the toast and smoked salmon is covered. Put under a preheated hot grill until the hollandaise just begins to brown. Serve immediately.

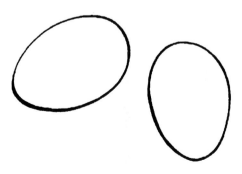

Seattle Coffee Company

12a Weargate Terrace, London W10 2BJ. Tel: 0171 370 7713

THE SEATTLE COFFEE COMPANY is a UK-based company, operating from London, which brings the gourmet coffee 'craze' to the British public. The company was formed by a consortium of UK and US partners, led by Ally Svenson from Seattle who came to the UK five years ago and, finally tired of waiting for a good cup of coffee to arrive in London, decided to set up her own coffee bar. Ally thought it best to include the recipe for one of their cold coffee drinks so that readers could make the drink at home without sophisticated espresso equipment.

Iced Vanilla Latté

50g (2oz) freshly extracted espresso
25g (1oz) vanilla syrup
ice
milk

Fill a 350g (12oz) cup with crushed or cubed ice. Layer the bottom of the cup with vanilla syrup, followed by the darkly roasted espresso. Fill the remainder of the glass with well chilled milk. Mix well and serve immediately.

This refreshing drink can also be made with strong, dark-roast (Italian or French) coffee as a substitute for the espresso – not everyone has the luxury of their own machine.

Shoeless Joe's Sports Bar & Grill

555 King's Road, London SW6 2EB. Tel: 0171 384 7222

THIS IS A NEW SPORTS BAR and grill in the King's Road Sports bars were first conceived in the United States in the 1920s, when sporting stars such as Jack Dempsey and the late Mickey Mantle started their own bars. Since then they have been through many permutations, but to this day the most famous are still linked with sporting celebrities.

Victor Ubogo, prop forward for Bath and England, and Christopher Gilmour of the eponymous Christopher's (see page 184) have joined together to create the bar and grill.

One of the main features in the bar is a 17ft x 6ft (33.5 x 29m) video wall made up of 17 digital rear projection cubes. There are six smaller monitors at various points around the bar, together with an extensive range of sporting memorabilia, photographs and artwork. There are also a number of television monitors in the restaurant. These monitors will be silent except when showing major sporting events.

The menu, which is served in the bar and also in the private members' club room, has been created by pulling together the very best of American East and West cuisine. This recipe which appears below for delicious Seared Tuna with Red Pepper Salsa has been given to us by Shoeless Joe's chef.

Seared Tuna with Red Pepper Salsa, Apple Endive Salad and Soy Dressing

Serves 4

4 red peppers
½ small cucumber, peeled and finely diced
2 small chillies, very finely chopped
½ Spanish onion, finely chopped
4 tablespoons roughly chopped coriander leaves
juice of 4 limes
salt and freshly ground pepper
4 thick steaks of tuna, approx 200g (7oz) each
75ml (3fl.oz) medium sherry, mixed with 75ml (3fl.oz) soy sauce for the dressing
olive oil to taste
1 head of curly endive, washed (yellow part only)
1 Granny Smith apple, halved, cored and very thinly sliced

Grill the peppers until they are black, then put them in a bowl and cover with clingfilm until cool. Peel off the black skin, remove the core and pips, then finely dice the peppers. Add the remaining salsa ingredients (cucumber, chillies, onion, coriander, lime juice) and mix well. Cover and set aside for 2 hours, then adjust the seasoning to taste.

Season the tuna. Grill the steaks until they are seared on the outside and raw in the middle. (The tuna can be cooked through if you prefer.)

Meanwhile, place some salsa around 4 plates, leaving the middle clear. Drizzle some soy dressing and extra virgin olive oil over the salsa. Mix the curly endive and sliced apple together and dress with a little soy dressing.

Cut the tuna steaks in half, place one half on top of the other, then put these into the centre of the plates. Place a little endive salad on top of the steaks. Top the salad with a few coriander leaves for garnish. Season with ground black pepper and serve.

Café Suze

1 Greenwich Street, London NW1 5PG. Tel: 0171 935 3827

SUE GLYNN HAS LIVED AND COOKED in London for about 20 years. Her extensive travelling, practical experience in the kitchen and flair with food resulted in a great desire to practise these skills in her own establishment. Café Suze was opened by Sue and her husband Tom in 1989.

A New Zealander by birth, Sue enjoys trying to use and promote their products. The main problem in London is with the erratic supply. She believes that the New Zealand suppliers don't fully understand the importance of consistency and reliability of supply. She raves about the seafood, especially the green mussels and orange ruffe which are sporadically available through her brother Mark's butcher's shop in Kensington. She also buys New Zealand lamb and New Zealand venison from him. The venison comes over chilled, and she uses it in this recipe.

Sue and her brother Mark often share staff members: a sausage-maker at Mark's butcher's shop often doubles up as a chef at Café Suze! New Zealand honeys and jams are now available in this country and, after being in New Zealand myself, I can assure you their fresh produce is top-notch stuff.

Barbecued New Zealand Venison Kebabs with a Spiced Mango Salsa

Serves 4

For the marinade:
225ml (8fl.oz) teriyaki marinade
150ml (¼ pint) sherry or juice from tinned mangoes
2 teaspoons clear honey
50g (2oz) finely grated root ginger
salt and pepper
4 New Zealand venison steaks
2 red peppers, deseeded and cut into 2.5cm (1 inch) pieces
16 shallots, peeled

For the spiced mango salsa
425g (15oz) tin mango slices, drained, *or* 2 large mangoes, peeled
2 teaspoons tandoori spice
rind and juice of 1 lemon
1 tablespoon chopped fresh coriander
1 teaspoon finely grated root ginger
salt and black pepper

Whisk the marinade ingredients together until thoroughly mixed. Cut the venison steaks into 2.5cm (1 inch) cubes. Pour the marinade over, cover and leave to marinade for 1 hour.

Drain the marinade from the venison and thread the venison cubes onto skewers (if wooden, soak first), alternating them with the pieces of pepper and the shallots.

Cook on a preheated barbecue for 5-8 minutes, turning and basting with the marinade mixture.

Meanwhile, make the salsa. Place all the salsa ingredients in a blender or food processor and blend together. Transfer to a serving dish, cover and chill.

Serve the venison kebabs on savoury rice with the mango salsa drizzled over them.

The Outback Inn

11 Henrietta Street, Covent Garden, London WC2E 8PS. Tel: 0171 379 5555

AS ITS NAME SUGGESTS, The Outback Inn is a pub run by Australians. It bases its menu on dishes that Australians eat back at home. Damien Jackson, the head chef, has been creating a great selection of home-made hamburgers based on a recipe containing lots of garlic and herbs.

The entrées in the pub include king prawns and New Zealand green-lipped mussels, as well as mushrooms and onion rings. Here, Damien shares one of his favourite recipes, with influences from the Pacific Rim as well as from Australia.

Paradise Chicken Fillet

Serves 4

50g (2oz) butter
1 onion, finely chopped
1 teaspoon crushed garlic
1 bunch fresh basil leaves, chopped
1 bunch fresh coriander, chopped
3 fresh red chillies, deseeded and chopped
250ml (9fl.oz) sweet white wine
150ml (¼ pint) lemon juice
375ml (13fl.oz) coconut milk
250ml (9fl.oz) chicken stock
salt and freshly ground black pepper
4 boneless chicken breasts
1 red pepper, deseeded and cut into matchsticks
1 green pepper, deseeded and cut into matchsticks
1 yellow pepper, deseeded and cut into matchsticks
sprigs of coriander, to garnish

Preheat the oven to 220°C/400°F/gas mark 6.
In a medium saucepan melt the butter and sweat the onion, garlic, herbs and chillies. Add the wine and lemon juice. Bring up to the boil and simmer for 10 minutes until the sauce has reduced by half. Add the coconut milk and chicken stock, bring to the boil, then reduce to a simmer. Season well and simmer for 10 minutes.

In a frying pan, pan-fry the chicken breasts for 20 minutes until golden brown. Remove the chicken breasts to a roasting tin and place in the oven for 8-10 minutes.

Serve with the sauce, boiled wild rice and freshly steamed vegetables of your choice. Garnish with finely sliced peppers and a sprig of coriander.

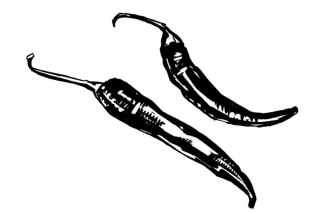

Sheila's Bar-Barbie

41 King Street, Covent Garden, London WC2E 8JS. Tel: 0171 240 8282

THIS IS THE PLACE FOR AUSTRALIANS and other Antipodeans to meet up in central London. With the Australian decoration inside the restaurant, you could imagine you are in a bar in the outback. With classic dishes such as Pavlova to enjoy with an Australian beer – soak up the atmosphere.

Chook Wings

Serves 4-6

12 small chicken joints, e.g. wings, thighs or drumsticks

For the marinade:
1 clove garlic, finely chopped
2.5cm (1 inch) piece root ginger, peeled and finely chopped or grated ½ teaspoon chilli sauce
4 tablespoons bottled barbecue sauce
salt and black pepper

Preheat the oven to 180°C/450°F/gas mark 4. Arrange the chicken joints in a shallow dish in a single layer. Mix together the garlic, ginger, chilli sauce, barbecue sauce and seasoning. Spoon over the chicken joints. Cover the dish with clingfilm and leave to marinate for several hours in the refrigerator.

Lift the joints from the marinade and place in a roasting tin. Cook in the oven for 30-45 minutes until cooked through. Serve hot with the following dressing.

Soured Cream and Chive Dressing: Mix together 150ml (¼ pint) fresh soured cream and 2 tablespoons fresh chives, snipped into small pieces with scissors. Season to taste and serve, sprinkled with a little paprika pepper.

Grilled Tuna Steak with Mango and Peach Salsa

Serves 4

4 x 225g (8oz) fresh tuna steaks

For the marinade:
2 cloves garlic, crushed
1 tablespoon chopped fresh herbs: thyme, rosemary, chervil or parsley
a small glass white wine
2 tablespoons olive oil
salt and black pepper

For the mango and peach salsa:
1 mango
4 peach halves, fresh or canned
1 small red-skinned onion, chopped
1 tablespoon chopped coriander

Wipe the tuna steaks with damp absorbent paper. Place side by side in a shallow dish. Mix together the garlic, herbs, wine, olive oil and seasoning. Spoon over the fish. Cover loosely with clingfilm and leave to marinate for several hours in the refrigerator.

Preheat the grill. Lift tuna steaks from marinade and place on a grill rack. Grill for 10-15 minutes until the fish is just cooked through, turning once.

Serve hot with the following salsa.

To make the salsa: Peel the mango and cut the flesh away from the centre stone. Chop the mango flesh and peach halves into tiny cubes. Mix with the onion and spoon into a small bowl. Sprinkle with chopped fresh coriander and serve.

Boomerang Baked Chocolate Bread Pudding

Serves 4

75g (3oz) butter, softened
75g (3oz) light, soft brown sugar
1 egg, beaten
50g (2oz) dark chocolate, finely chopped or grated
75g (3oz) fresh breadcrumbs (brown or white)
25g (1oz) ground almonds
50g (2oz) self-raising flour
50g (2oz) sultanas

For the chocolate sauce:
175g (6oz) dark chocolate, broken into small pieces
25g (1oz) butter
2 tablespoons orange juice or brandy
2 tablespoons water
1 teaspoon instant coffee granules

A dreamy chocolate steamed sponge pudding!

Lightly grease 4 individual pudding basins or old cups and line the base of each with a disc of greaseproof paper.

In a mixing bowl, cream the butter and sugar together until light and fluffy. Beat in the egg, then stir in the chocolate, breadcrumbs, ground almonds, flour and sultanas until evenly mixed. Divide the mixture between the basins or cups.

Cover tightly with greaseproof paper and foil and secure with string. Steam over a pan of simmering water for 1 hour, keeping the steamer topped up with hot water, as necessary.

Uncover puddings and turn out onto serving plates. Serve hot with the chocolate sauce.

To make the chocolate sauce: Place the chocolate in a heatproof bowl and melt over a pan of hot (not boiling) water. When melted, stir until smooth. Add the butter, cut into small pieces and stir in with the orange juice or brandy, water and instant coffee. Spoon over the puddings and serve immediately.

Pavlova

Serves 8

4 egg whites
225g (8oz) caster sugar
½ teaspoon vanilla essence
½ teaspoon vinegar
1 teaspoon cornflour
300ml (½ pint) double cream
fresh or canned fruit, to decorate

Preheat the oven to 140°C/275°F/gas mark 1.

Draw a 23cm (9 inch) circle on a sheet of baking parchment and place on a baking sheet.

Whisk the egg whites until standing in stiff peaks. Gradually whisk in the sugar until the mixture is very stiff and shiny. Finally whisk in the vanilla essence, vinegar and cornflour.

Spread the meringue over the marked circle on the baking parchment and bake in the oven for about 1 hour or until it is crisp and dry. Cool in the turned off oven. Whip the cream until it holds its shape. Place the cooked meringue on a serving dish and spread with cream. Top with a selection of fresh or canned fruits.

Londoners at Home

Hidden in the privacy of their own homes, there are many passionate, practical and talented cooks. They are often people cooking for family or friends, who may never have had any practical training, and who certainly are not professional cooks. Yet they are inspired by a love of good food and the scope afforded by a kitchen well stocked with fresh and dry ingredients from all over the world. The recipes in this chapter come from home cooks who are making full use of the abundance of ingredients now readily available at a reasonable price. Happily without the constraints of customer requirements or restaurant style, home cooks are uniquely able to cook purely for pleasure, to create their own delightful combinations and to develop their own enthusiasms and ideas.

Cooking at home for friends and family.

Mary Flowers

MARY FLOWERS, A KEEN COOK, links music and food and here she shares two inspirational ideas. 'Among the fondest memories of my youth, are the concerts I attended in London, and the late supper after we got home. It seems but yesterday that I drank a cup of steaming consommé with the slow movement of Brahm's Violin Concerto singing in my ears or bit into a tangy Welsh Rarebit after hearing a piece by Ralph Vaughan Williams. I also remember losing my appetite completely after the last movement of Tchaikovsky's Pathétique.

'The memory of one concert is stamped indelibly on my mind. We heard Rachmaninov playing his own great Third Piano Concerto. There was a reception for him afterwards and I retain a clear image of this impressive yet modest and intensely courteous musician. It was far too late for any

Rachmaninov Rolls

Serves 4

12 thin rindless rashers of smoked bacon
2 firm parsnips
1 medium-sized cooking apple
1 teaspoon Dijon mustard
fresh black pepper
300ml (½ pint) red wine
1 tablespoon redcurrant jelly
salt, if needed

Separate the rashers and stretch them with the flat of a knife. Peel the parsnips and cut them into little sticks 1cm (½ inch) thick and 4cm (2inch) long. Peel the apple and cut into sticks to match. Spread them all with the mustard and sprinkle with black pepper. Take a stick of parsnip and one of apple and roll together very carefully in the bacon. Secure each one with a solid cocktail stick (don't be tempted to use toothpicks – they break).

Put a large, preferably non-stick, frying pan or one that is very lightly oiled on a gentle heat and cook the bacon rolls very slowly, turning them constantly and watching them so they don't burn. When they are crisp on the outside and tender in the middle when pierced with a skewer, turn them on to a dish and keep warm.

Deglaze the pan with wine and redcurrant jelly; add a pinch of salt only if needed. Reduce a little and serve the resulting sauce separately.

supper when we returned and I have often wondered what would have been appropriate to serve on that occasion.

'This snack seems to suggest itself as rich, spicy, yet fruity and romantic. It is substantial and strong on flavour. All the main ingredients could be found in the composer's native land.'

For the sweet course Mary continues her musical connections. Here is a dish that is light and sweet, one that imparts the serenity of Arcadian delights. It has an unusual yet markedly pure and pastoral flavour. Like the music, it implies effortless grace rather than scintillatng technique. Listen, while preparing it, to one dance from Christopher Gluck's opera 'Orpheus and Eurydice'. The Blessed Spirits calm and please the soul in a way that I hope this simple recipe will calm and please the palate!

Gluck's Lemon Meringues

Serves 4-6

3 large eggs, separated
120g (5oz) caster sugar
rind of one large lemon
5 tablespoons lemon juice
2 tablespoons fresh garden mint,
very finely chopped
1 teaspoon Cointeau (optional)
1 packet powdered gelatine
(dissolved in hot water)
165g (6oz) raspberries or
blueberries

Beat the egg whites until they stand in peaks. Beat the yolks and sugar until pale and fluffy. Add the lemon rind, juice, mint, Cointreau and gelatine to the yolk mixture quickly, then gently fold in the egg whites. Pour into a glass bowl and refrigerate until set. Finallly spread the berries on top and serve with a selection of crisp, sweet biscuits.

Be sure to use fresh, free-range eggs and start with everything at room temperature.

Food File

Channel 4 TV, 124 Horseferry Road, London SW1P 2GX. Tel: 0171 396 4444

AMANDA URSELL, A STATE REGISTERED DIETICIAN, nutritionist and presenter of Channel 4 TV's 'Food File' programme, has strong views on healthy eating. She emphasises that healthy eating need not compromise on taste, colour and texture: 'it does not have to be rabbit food'. Amanda's motto is 'It's not hell to be healthy,' and she illustrates this well in sharing with us her favourite of all the different recipes that she cooks at home.

Garlic and Herb Pasta

Serves 4

1 tablespoon olive oil
3 leeks, washed and sliced
1 onion, sliced
2 cloves garlic, crushed
300g (10oz) dried green tagliatelle
50g (2oz) reduced-fat garlic-and-herb cream cheese
3 tablespoons chopped fresh coriander
freshly ground black pepper
2 tablespoons low fat natural yogurt

Heat the olive oil in a frying pan, stir in the leeks, onion and garlic and cook until softened and golden (this takes about 5 minutes).

Meanwhile cook the pasta in boiling water for 10-12 minutes or until tender. Drain well. Stir the cheese into the onion mixture and gently heat for 2 minutes to melt. Mix in the coriander, black pepper and yogurt. Toss the pasta well in the sauce.

Serve with a mixed tomato salad, made with a mixture of halved ripe cherry tomatoes, sliced ripe salad tomatoes and quartered ripe plum tomatoes, seasoned well with salt and freshly ground black pepper. Stand at room temperature for 15 minutes before serving.

Looking at the meal from her healthy perspective, Amanda shares her thoughts on why she chose the ingredients for this dish.

The garlic aids efficient circulation of blood around the body and by using low-fat garlic-and-herb cheese the fat content of the dish is cut down without compromising the taste.

There is a good source of calcium in the yogurt and she emphasises how important the ratio of pasta to sauce is in the dish. More carbohydrate from the pasta is good health sense. Serving with the tomato salad provides a good source of vitamin C and balances this meal nutritionally. Her advice: 'Cook quick, simple dishes with fresh ingredients'.

Amanda Grant

Flat 6, Kings Court Mansions, 713 Fulham Road, London SW6 5PB. Tel: 0171 731 6478

AMANDA GRANT, as well as being a competent assistant to me on food photography shoots, works in the development kitchens of Loseley real dairy ice-creams. Although her culinary skills as a trained home economist envelop all types of cooking, she has a definite affinity with desserts so gave me this delicious recipe which she often cooks at home for dinner parties.

This dessert is a sumptuous combination of crisp coconut, tangy lime and sweet, crunchy meringue. The flavours and textures complement one another perfectly!

Crunchy Coconut Cream with Swirls of Tangy Lime

Serves 4

For the coconut ice cream:
300ml (½ pint) milk
300ml (10fl.oz) double cream
4 eggs, separated (reserve 2 egg whites for the meringue)
115g (4oz) caster sugar
300ml (½ pint) coconut milk (or reconstituted creamed coconut)
115g (4oz) desiccated coconut, toasted

For the lime cord ripple:
grated rind and juice of 1 lime
1 egg
25g (1oz) butter
75g (3oz) caster sugar

For the meringues:
2 egg whites (reserved from the coconut ice cream)
115g (4oz) icing sugar

To make the coconut ice cream: Bring the milk and cream to the boil. Remove from the heat. Whisk the egg yolks and sugar together until pale and thick. Stir in the milk mixture and return to the pan. Cook the custard over a gentle heat, stirring all the time, until it thickens very slightly (it should coat the back of a wooden spoon). It is important not to let the custard boil or it will curdle. Leave the mixture to cool.

Stir in the coconut milk and desiccated coconut and freeze the ice cream mixture in an ice cream machine. Alternatively, pour the mixture into a shallow freezer container, cover and freeze for about 2 hours or until just frozen all over. Spoon into a bowl and quickly mash with a fork to break down the ice crystals. Return the mixture to the freezer and freeze for a further 2 hours.

To make the lime cord ripple:. Place all the ingredients in a bowl and place over a pan of simmering water. Stir until the sugar has dissolved and continue heating gently for about 20 minutes, until the cord thickens. Do not boil or it will curdle. Strain into a bowl and leave to cool.

To make the meringues: Preheat an oven to 110°C/225°F/gas mark ¼. Whisk the egg whites until stiff in a grease-free bowl. Whisk in the icing sugar, a tablespoon at a time. Once all the sugar is added, the meringue should be thick and glossy. Spoon, in dessertspoons, onto a baking sheet lined with non-stick baking parchment. Cook for 2 hours or until dry. Leave to cool.

Soften the ice cream slightly, add lime cord and the crushed meringues. Freeze for about 2 hours before serving. Remove from the freezer 20 minutes before scooping out to serve.

Felicity Harrison

Private Address

FELICITY HARRISON (RAINES) IS AN ACTRESS who has always filled out-of-work stints with other things, mostly to do with food! Even when appearing in the West End in 'Godspell' and as Frenchy in the original production of 'Grease', she was cooking lunches for 80 engineers!

'I cook dishes from all over the world, perhaps mostly Italian and French, and love all the new influences from California and the East.'

This recipe is simple and flavourful and easy to assemble when friends are round, with some preparation beforehand. I chop and change the ingredients, sometimes I use Parma ham, Parmesan cheese and double peeled broad beans with lots of basil, and sometimes a completely vegetarian version with more roasted vegetables.

Quantities are difficult to gauge, it depends on the size of the tartlets, your own taste and vegetables can always be eaten another time.

The tartlets can be served either as a first course before a light main dish or as a lunch dish with salad.'

Mediterranean Tartlets

Serves 6-8

For the pastry shells:
225g (8oz) plain flour
pinch of salt
150g (5oz) butter, very cold and cut into bits
1 egg yolk
3 tablespoons cold water

For the filling:
(for 4 large shells)

2 aubergines
salt
olive oil
2 red or yellow peppers
115g (4oz) good salami, in one piece
115g (4oz) mozzarella
about 12 sun-dried tomatoes
garlic
a handful of rocket
about 10 olives

Preheat the oven to 180°C/350°F/gas mark 4.

In a food processor, mix the flour, salt and butter briefly until you get a texture of breadcrumbs. Add the egg yolk and water and process again until the dough forms a ball, but do not overmix. Chill for at least 1 hour, roll out and line 6-8 large individual tartlet tins.

Chill again for 30 minutes, fill with foil and beans and bake blind in the preheated oven for about 10 minutes. Remove the foil and cook again until light brown. Cool for 5 minutes, then gently remove from the tins and set the pastry cases aside on a baking tray.

Slice the aubergines thickly, about 4 slices to each, sprinkle with salt and leave to drain for 30 minutes. Wash thoroughly, dry with a tea towel and brush with olive oil. Grill on both sides on a ridged grill to get a good char-grilled effect. When cool cut into largish dice.

Quarter and deseed the peppers and grill with the skin side down, until black. Put in a plastic bag until cool, then skin and slice.

Dice the salami and mozzarella, chop some sun-dried tomatoes and garlic, tear the rocket into large pieces and halve the olives.

Fill the pastry cases with the aubergine, peppers, mozzarella and salami, then sprinkle generously with the tomatoes, garlic, rocket and olives. Finally dribble over some olive oil. Heat shells in a hot oven until the mozzarella melts. Sprinkle with basil or chives before serving if you like.

Simon Ibbitson

Private Address

SIMON IBBITSON, NOW AN INVESTMENT BANKER, was a pork butcher in the north-east of England. He shares with us a recipe he often cooks at home for himself and friends in London.

With a comprehensive training in butchery at Smithfield, he knows his meat and would recommend sourcing a good butcher, getting to know him and learning where he gets his meat from.

Bacon Spare Ribs with Cabbage

Serves 4

1.4kg (3lb) bacon spare ribs (ask the butcher for chops cut into15cm/6in squares)
1 white hard cabbage, cut into quarters
1.4kg (3lb) new potatoes, peeled and halved

Place the spare ribs into a large pan and cover with cold water. Bring to the boil. Throw the water away then cover the ribs with fresh boiling water and simmer for 30 minutes or so until the meat is nearly tender.

Add the white cabbage and potatoes and cook for 20 minutes – the meat should be soft and can easily be taken from the bone. Serve immediately.

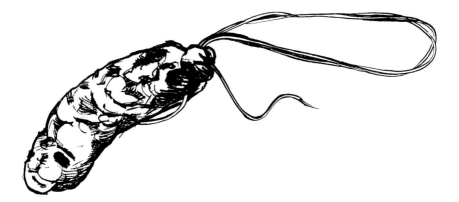

Pip Landers

Private Address

PIP LANDERS is product development manager for Pizza Hut UK, where she utilises her training as a home economist and in food marketing to their full potential. Her creative culinary talents are also practised on her friends at home in Clapham, where I have enjoyed this salad on more than one occasion. It is accompanied by copious glasses of wine.

Goat's Cheese with Tomato and Basil

Serves 2-3 as a starter

2 beefsteak tomatoes, sliced
125ml (¼ pint) olive oil
1 tablespoon capers
4 spring onions, chopped
1 tin anchovies, chopped
fresh basil (the amount depends on taste but at least 1 tablespoon)
125g (4-5oz) goat's cheese, cut into 4 or 5 slices

Preheat the oven to 200°C/400°F/gas mark 6.

Cover the bottom of an ovenproof dish with a layer of sliced tomatoes (one third of the total quantity). Sprinkle with half the olive oil, capers, spring onions, anchovies, basil and salt and pepper. Repeat for the second layer, and finish with the remaining tomatoes on top. Place slices of goat's cheese on the top and place in the pre-heated oven on the top shelf, for 20-25 minutes until the cheese is golden brown.

Serve with warm ciabatta bread.

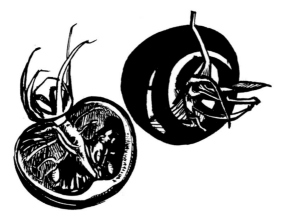

Michelle's

Information on Special Diets, 5 Lawn Road, London NW3 2XS. Tel: 0171 722 3136

MICHELLE BERRYDALE JOHNSON started life as a food historian (she has five historical cookery books to her credit) and a caterer. (Dinner for 180 with period table settings at Osterley House madam? Or would you prefer a medieval banquet complete with jousting at Penshurst Place?) But six years ago her career took an entirely different turn when her family developed dairy product allergies.

What many would have seen as a disaster Michelle took as an interesting challenge: how do you make tasty and exciting foods without some of the staple items of our diet – milk, butter, cheese, cream, yogurt? Her researches led her to realise that there were a substantial number of people with food allergies far worse than those of her family who were struggling to find anything worthwhile to eat. She therefore decided to go commercial!

A totally dairy-free ice cream, made from organic tofu (soya bean curd) and honey was launched and although it did not in the long term prove commercially viable, it did grace the freezer cabinets of a number of our larger super-markets for several years. She then experimented with dairy, gluten and egg-free vegetarian ready meals (her meals, under Berrydales brand, are to be found in health food stores), followed by dairy-free chocolate – important because it is almost impossible to get genuinely dairy-free chocolate in the UK. The dairy-free chocolates have now been joined by diabetic and carob chocolates in a flourishing mail order business.

Meanwhile, Michelle received so many enquiries about her dairy-free foods, that in 1991 she started a magazine/newsheet about dietary problems and ways to help them and, a year later, published a small special diet cookbook. This has recently been expanded into a book for Sainsbury's.

The following cake recipe makes an excellent wholesome and very tasty chocolate cake. (If you are neither gluten nor dairy allergic, the cake is still delicious, but in that case, substitute butter for the dairy-free margarine and use ordinary cocoa powder and baking powder. You could also, if you are not allergic, substitute 75g (3oz) semolina for the ground almonds).

Rice Flour Chocolate Cake

Serves 6-8

75g (3oz) dairy-free margarine
250g (9oz) dark muscovado sugar
4 tablespoons gluten-free
cocoa powder
3 eggs
115g (4oz) ground rice or rice flour
1 teaspoon gluten-free
baking powder
75g (3oz) ground almonds

Preheat the oven to 180°C/350°F/gas mark 4.
Line a 20cm (8in) cake tin with greaseproof paper.
Beat together the fat and the sugar until light and fluffy. Bring 75ml (3fl.oz) water to the boil, pour onto the cocoa, mix well, then beat into the creamed mixture. Beat in the eggs, adding a spoonful of rice flour with each. Mix the baking powder into the remaining rice flour and ground almonds and fold into the mixture.
Spoon the mixture into the tin and bake in the preheated oven for approximately 35 minutes or until the cake is firm to the touch. Cool on a wire rack before cutting.

Wild Food

by Roger Philips

ROGER PHILLIPS' *WILD FOOD*, published in 1985, is a book I have been inspired by, both in the natural photography style and as a reference book for wild food in the U.K. He wrote *Wild Food* as a basic reference for all the well-known recipes traditionally associated with wild food, but also he explored and developed some of the other fascinating sources of wild food, such as seaweeds and mushrooms. He wanted to show how several areas had been left largely unexploited, yet provide some of the most delicious nutritious recipes.

He places great importance of selecting a definitive recipe for each plant. With mushrooms he devised recipes which he thinks best suits the flavour and texture of that particular mushroom. Here he shares some interesting facts about chanterelles, and gives a simple recipe for chanterelle omelette.

The chanterelle – *Cantriarellus cibarius* – is an egg-yellow to orange, funnel-shaped fungus sometimes smelling mildly of fresh apricots. It grows in all kinds of woodland, particularly under oaks and conifers.

Chanterelles, or *girolles* as the French call them, are one of the most popular and best-known fungi on the continent and throughout Scandinavia, where they are served in restaurants and sold in shops and markets. The name is derived from the French dimunitive of the Greek *Kantharos* (cup).

They keep well for a few days and can also be successfully dried. Clean with a damp cloth, trim away dirty stems, cut in half and dry in the sun or in a food dryer. Chanterelles are superb when cooked with eggs or potatoes. When cooked they tend to give off rather a lot of liquid, especially if picked in wet weather.

CAUTION: Never eat any mushroom until you have positively identified it as edible.

Chanterelle Omelette

Serves 2

3 spring onions
450g (1lb) chanterelles
1 tablespoon butter
salt and freshly ground black
pepper to taste
4 eggs

Skin the spring onions and chop them very finely. Wash the chanterelles and dry them with kitchen paper. After cutting off the stem bases, chop the chanterelles into smallish pieces. Melt the butter in a frying pan, add the spring onions and mushrooms and sauté over medium heat for about 5 minutes, then pour off excess liquid. Flavour the mixture until salt and pepper to taste, cover to keep hot, and put to one side. Now prepare a large omelette with the 4 eggs, well beaten.

When the outside is cooked but the inside is still a bit runny, pour the chanterelles onto one half and flop the other half over the top. Serve piping hot.

Pete Smith

PETE SMITH GAVE ME THIS RECIPE which is very much his style – quick and easy. Pete comes from Australia, but has been in Europe for the past 15 years. For the last 12 years, he has been preparing food for TV. As a food stylist he has been preparing food for many companies, from fast-food restaurants to Birds Eye products and supermarket food packaging. Working in photography studios is Peter's life and he has pre-pared the food for many photographic cook books. Always accompanied by his dog on shoots, Pete has a reputation for being fun to work with.

One of the most famous pictures Pete worked on was presenting Albert Roux's head on a plat-ter for an American Express advertment. His experience has also developed into writing recipes for *New Woman* magazine for 2½ years.

Onion Tart with Apples and Calvados

Serves 4 as a main course
or 6 as a starter

115g (4oz) frozen puff pastry, thawed
115g (4oz) butter
225g (8oz) red onions, very
thinly sliced
grated black pepper
2-3 pinches freshly grated nutmeg
450g (1lb) cooking apples, peeled,
cored and chopped into cubes
50g (2oz) brown sugar
150ml (¼ pint) Calvados

Preheat the oven to 200°C/400°F/gas mark 6.
Roll the pastry out on a lightly floured board into a large rectangle, approximately 30 x 15cm (12 x 6 inches). Place the pastry on a baking sheet and place into the fridge to relax. Melt 50g (2oz) butter in a frying pan, add the onions and cook gently until the onions are soft and creamy in texture but not brown; add the pepper and nutmeg and stir for 1 minute. Remove the onions from the pan and set aside.

Melt the remaining butter in the pan and add the apples and brown sugar. Cook for 2 minutes and then pour in the Calvados and cook for a minute or so longer. Remove the apples with a slotted spoon and set aside. Boil the Calvados and butter for a minute or two more, or until the mixture has reduced and started to become sticky.

Remove the pastry from the fridge, spread the onions over it, leaving 1cm (½ inch) gap around the edges. Pile the apples over the onions and pour or brush over the Calvados glaze. Bake in the preheated oven for 20-25 minutes or until the tart is crispy and brown.

The tart can be eaten hot, warm or cold; try shaving Parmesan cheese over the top with some chopped fresh herbs. Serve the tart with a mixed salad.

'London's Finest'

Expertise of all kinds abounds in the capital and the food world is no exception. Drawing both upon well established traditions, yet also flexible and accommodating to new ideas, styles and ingredients, expertise is one of the most dynamic areas of London life. Within the cafés, restaurants, shops and food suppliers are a lot of people with unrivalled knowledge in their specialist areas. Fruit and vegetable sellers know from years of experience exactly what produce is in season or available from the markets at any particular time. Butchers and fishmongers are highly skilled in selecting their merchandise and are happy to pass on invaluable tips to their customers. London's thousands of restaurants are adept at recognising current trends in eating and adapting their menus – and even their interiors – to reflect them. London also has some of the world's finest food shops, often at the forefront of culinary innovation, and with the flair to create new customer demand with imaginative new products. This chapter introduces many of these experts and enables us to share and benefit from their knowledge and experience.

Harrods a London mecca for food lovers.

Food in London Life

FOOD – AND DRINK – have played an important role in London's economic development. The capital's famous food markets – Billingsgate for fish, Smithfield for meat, Spitalfields and Covent Garden for fruit and vegetable produce – have been in existence for centuries and continue to thrive today, although Covent Garden Market has been re-located to Nine Elms, south of the Thames (between Battersea and Vauxhall). The markets are essential for London's contemporary catering trade, offering good quality fresh produce at resonable prices. Menus at some of the most successful restaurants in London are determined by what is available in the markets on a particular day, ensuring that their core ingredients are as fresh as possible.

Traditionally London's markets provided an important trading centre for those outside the city as well as its inhabitants. From Medieval times cattle, sheep, poultry and pigs, for example, were herded into London in huge 'droves' which often lasted for months as the animals made their way over considerable distances on foot. Smithfield Market (the name deriving from the descriptive 'smooth field') was the usual destination of these animals, who were sold on, directly or indirectly, into London slaughterhouses. These, rather unpleasantly, were located in the heart of the city itself; the celebrated 'Pudding Lane', for example, where the Great Fire of 1666 broke out, has nothing to with desserts. It was named for the black and white pig's puddings created by the many slaughterhouses in that street.

The institutions of the City of London often have traditional connections with the capital's food scene. With the arrival of coffee as a beverage in the eighteenth century, coffeee houses became popular places in which to conduct business. One of the City's most enduring institutions, Lloyds of London, began life as a coffee house in which a range of negotiations and transactions were undertaken. Another great London name, Twinings, ironically started out as a coffee house itself, before diversifying into the tea blending and trading for which it was to become famous.

As overseas trade developed in the eighteenth and nineteenth centuries, London's importance as a port meant that a wide range of imported and exported foodstuffs passed through its docks. Tea clippers, such as the famous *Cutty Sark*, now restored in dry dock at Greenwich, raced one another to be the first to arrive in Britain with the new season's crop of tea from India and Sri Lanka. Foods were also imported from the countries of the rapidly-expanding British Empire. Tropical fruits and vegetables, spices, meats, and indeed whole concepts of cooking were introduced into London through colonial commerce and influences from the eighteenth century onwards.

Perhaps the one consistent element in London's rapidly changing cuisine has been its eagerness to absorb new flavours, dishes and traditions, and to adapt its eating habits to accommodate the fashions of the day. Nowadays, from its exotic food halls to its lively markets, from formal afternoon tea to a multitude of late-night eateries, London's food reflects with enthusiasm and ingenuity the demanding and often wide-ranging tastes of its hungry (or thirsty) inhabitants.

Buchans

62-64 Battersea Bridge Road, London SW11 3AG. Tel: 0171 228 0888

A SMALL RESTAURANT BASED ON THE SCOTTISH ancestral-home cook, Buchans does a roaring trade in these potent and spicy bloody Marys, especially at the weekends. Here are their recipe tips for making a bloody good bloody Mary!

Their only real competition for the best bloody Mary in London is at The Grenadier pub (18, Wilton Street, London SW1). However, this secret recipe is passed down from licensee to licensee, so you must go there yourself to taste one.

Buchans's Bloody Mary

vodka
creamed horseradish
lemon juice
salt
Worcestershire sauce
tomato juice

First you need plenty of ice. Fill a third of a long glass tumbler with ice, then cover the ice with a good splash of vodka. Stir in a teaspoon of creamed horseradish, a good splash of lemon juice, a pinch of salt and several shakes of Worcestershire sauce (Lea and Perrin's is recommended). Top up with tomato juice and stir well to serve.

Cuan Oysters

0171 978 2151

OYSTERS HAVE BECOME A LUXURY FOOD, but, along with jellied eels and other seafood, they were traditionally cheap and eaten by the London poor. Nowadays many oysters are imported to the capital; those from Ireland are considered to be particularly fine.

Jonathan Dunhill, is the marketing force behind Cuan Oysters, the leading wholesaler of Irish oysters in London. Here are his guidelines on buying, handling and storing oysters, along with some of his favourite recipes.

Buying Oysters

Oysters can be bought fresh from your local fishmonger or supermarket fish counter. They are also increasingly available chilled in the half-shell, or as oysters that are gaping and do not close when tapped.

Handling and Storing Oysters

Store oysters in a fridge or cool place, cup shell down and covered with a damp cloth. Fresh oysters will keep for one to two weeks if stored correctly. Topless oysters and oyster meats will keep in a fridge for a maximum of six days after shucking (opening).

Freezing Oysters

Oysters can be kept frozen in their shells for up to three months. What's more, the shells open automatically on thawing! Ready frozen oyster meats are also available. It is also a good idea to keep an eye open for frozen oyster recipe dishes in your local supermarket.

Opening Oysters

Oysters may be opened at the side and at the hinge, the aim being to cut the muscle attaching the meat to the top flat shell. Most good fish recipe books include diagrams – but the easiest method is simply to freeze the oysters overnight and then let them open by themselves on defrosting. Microwaving the oysters for 30 seconds on high heat or 4 minutes on warm makes it easier to insert the knife.

Oysters for Health

Oysters are an excellent source of vitamins and minerals, especially zinc (essential for an active sex life!) They also contain Omega 3, a special type of polyunsaturated fatty acid. This is medically proved to reduce the risks of heart disease and strokes. Oysters also contain Taurine, an amino acid good for lowering blood pressure and relieving arthritis.

Oysters Mornay

Serves 12

24 oysters
mornay sauce
cheddar cheese, grated
parsley, chopped
cayenne pepper

Spoon a little Mornay sauce over half-shell oysters and place under a medium grill for 2–3 minutes. Remove from the heat and sprinkle some grated cheese over the top of each oyster. Turn the grill up to high and heat the oysters for a further 2-3 minutes until golden brown. Garnish with a little chopped parsley or cayenne pepper and serve piping hot.

Angels on Horseback

Serves 12

1 lemon
12 oyster meats
12 pieces bacon
cayenne pepper
black pepper

Squeeze some lemon juice on to oyster meats. Wrap each meat in a thin rasher of bacon (lightly smoked streaky is best). Skewer the meat and bacon parcels with a cocktail stick, and then grill the parcels under a medium heat until the bacon is cooked.
Serve hot on a cocktail stick, or arrange on toast and sprinkle with cayenne or black pepper.

Carpetbag Steak

Serves 4

4 rump or fillet steaks
12 oyster meats
25g (1oz) butter
clove of garlic, crushed
black pepper
sprig of parsley, chopped

Slit the steaks lengthways with a sharp knife, forming a pocket in the steaks. Mix together oyster meats, butter, garlic, freshly ground black pepper and parsley. Fill each pocket with the mixture, using three oyster meats per steak.

Seal the opening with a cocktail stick and grill or barbecue as for an ordinary steak.

House of Commons

Westminster, SW1

MANY OF LONDON'S MAJOR INSTITUTIONS have excellent dining facilities attached. David Dorriot cooks at the House of Commons, where M.P.s of all parties rely on his delicious and very sustaining recipes to keep them going through all-night parliamentary sittings.

Salad of Steamed Natural Smoked Haddock with young Spinach Leaves and Coriander

Serves 4

1 teaspoon coriander, chopped
3 tablespoons Greek yogurt
salt and pepper
575g (1¼ lb) skinless natural
smoked haddock
1 teaspoon parsley, chopped
4 brioche, sliced
2 plum tomatoes, peeled and
deseeded cut into small neat dice
115g (4oz) young spinach leaves,
washed
50ml (¼ pint) champagne
vinaigrette
150ml (¼ pint) fish cream sauce

Champagne vinaigrette
2 teaspoons champagne vinegar
2 tablespoons olive oil
salt and pepper

Fish Cream Sauce
150ml (¼ pint) fish stock
75ml (3fl.oz) white wine
1 bay leaf
15g (½oz) shallots, peeled and
sliced thinly
a few parsley stalks, washed
200ml (7fl.oz) double cream
salt and pepper

Mix the chopped coriander with the Greek yogurt. Season with salt and pepper and leave to infuse for 30 minutes. Meanwhile, place the haddock on a plate. Set it in a steamer to cook for approximately 8 minutes.

Take the concasse, mix with a little of the champagne vinaigrette (see below) and season with salt and pepper. Remove the haddock from the steamer, retaining the cooking liquid. Flake one-quarter of the haddock into small pieces and place in a bowl on one side. The remaining prtion of haddock is then flaked into large pieces. Take the fish cream sauce (see below) and add the chopped parsley, the cooking liquid and a little vinaigrette.

Mix the small flakes of haddock from the bowl with the yogurt/coriander mixture from the bowl. This mixture (known as a rillette) should be still quite firm. Toast the brioche.

To serve, imagine your plate as a clock face with 12 at the top. Dress the young spinach leaves in the champagne vinaigrette and arrange around the centre of the plate leaving a hole 7cm (coin) in diameter. In the centre, place the large flaked smoked haddock. Assemble the rillette and toasted brioche. Pour the fish cream sauce over the flaked haddock. Place a neat pile of concasse on the centre of the smoked haddock and serve.

Champagne vinaigrette: Combine the champagne vinegar and olive oil. Whisk gently until all is thoroughly combined and season with salt and pepper to taste

Fish Cream Sauce: Cook the fish stock, white wine with bay leaf, shallots and parsley stalks in a thick bottomed saucepan until the mixture has reduced by two-thirds. Add the double cream and reduce again to one-half of this volume. You should have about 150ml of sauce. Season to taste. Pass the sauce through a fine strainer and allow to cool.

Pret à Manger

Over 30 in London, the largest in Covent Garden, 77-78 St Martins Lane, WC2N. Tel: 0171 379 5335

JULIAN METCALFE IS THE FOUNDER of the successful *Pret à Manger* group of high-quality sandwich shops which have sprung up all over the capital in recent years. Here he gives some personal tips on successful sandwich making.

'At *Pret à Manger* the emphasis is on quality. You can certainly buy many of the ingredients we put into our sandwiches much more cheaply – but you cannot buy the same quality cheaper. A key turning point for *Pret à Manger* was the day we discovered a farm able to supply us with ham that was neither shiny nor wet. That allowed us to get away from the traditional British sandwich. We take care always to choose suppliers who won't compromise on quality.'

Tips

For a perfect sandwich

Always make the sandwich as freshly as possible prior to eating.

Always use the best quality ingredients possible.

Always ensure that all the ingredients are as fresh as possible.

Try to make the sandwich interesting and colourful. Always try to includean ingredient which will be crunchy. Texture is essential to a good sandwich.

Randalls Butchers

118, Wandsworth Bridge Road, Fulham, London SW6 2TE. Tel: 0171 736 3426

BRIAN RANDALL NOW PRESIDES over this independent butcher's shop in Fulham. A long established butcher, he is a member of the prestigious 'Q' Guild (see page 000). Membership of the Guild is subject to so many conditions it cannot but inspire confidence in their members' skills.

The 'Q' Guild is recognised as the association of progressive, independent meat retailers in Great Britain who offer top-quality meat, customer service, hygiene and innovation. In order to qualify for the Guild award premises and staff have to pass an exacting independent inspection conducted by the Meat and Livestock Commission.

The quality of the produce in this small butcher's reflects their commitment to providing meat of the highest standard. All 'Q' Guild butchers know where the animals come from and control the maturing of the meat very carefully. A lot of Randalls meat is free-range, additive-free and organic. Delicious Scotch, grass-fed beef is one of their range and here Brian gives his hot tips to roast a joint of beef perfectly.

Tip

For a perfect Sunday Roast

Buy a piece of beef from the fore rib, with the exposed bone trimmed off to give a manageable joint to carve. It will still have the base of the bones attached. This is important as it achieves the added flavour bonus of the meat being cooked on the bone.

Heat the oven up well before starting to cook. Follow the 'Delia Smith' way of smothering the fat with good English mustard – for great flavour.

Roast the beef for 15 minutes to the 450g (1 lb), basting well throughout the cooking process. (Note that this timing will give a pink rare beef. If you like it well done, continue roasting until the juices run clear when the meat is pierced with a fork).

When cooked, wrap the beef in foil and leave to stand for 15 minutes. This enables the meat to tenderise a little before serving.

Meat Matters

2 Blandy's Farm Cottages, Letcombe Regis, Wantage, Oxon OX12 9LJ. Tel:

LONDON HAS HAD A LONG AND PROUD MEAT tradition which is reflected in the importance of Smithfield Market (see page 214). The capital's cooks, butchers and producers have proved skilful in adapting to prevailing trends and health concerns. Demand for organic meat continues to grow, and this company from just outside London will deliver their produce direct to your door. To tempt you, here is the perfect warming recipe for a winter day.

Venison on Orange and Brandy Sauce

6 tablespoons cooking oil
1.4kg (3lb) diced venison
450g (1lb) peeled button onions
2 cloves garlic
4 tablespoons plain flour
600 ml (1pint) venison or beef stock
3 oranges
6 tablespoons brandy
2 tablespoons tomato purée
2 tablespoons black treacle
good pinch coriander
salt and pepper
50g (2oz) butter
225g (8oz) button mushrooms

Preheat the oven to 170°C/325°F/gas mark 3.
Heat the oil in the pan and seal the venison. Transfer the meat to a casserole dish. Fry the onions and garlic in the same fat until lightly browned. Transfer the mixture to the casserole dish.

Add the flour to the fat in the pan and cook for 1 minute. Then stir in the stock and bring to the boil. Pare the rind from three oranges and cut into thin matchstick strips. Add the rind to the sauce with the juice of the oranges. Add the brandy, tomato purée, treacle, coriander and seasoning. Stir and then pour the mixture into the casserole dish.

Cover the casserole tightly and cook for 2½ hours. Fry the mushrooms in the butter for a few minutes, then add to the casserole. Taste, adjust the seasoning and cook for a further half hour or until the meat is tender.

Serve with potatoes and green vegetables.

Breakfast Time

LONDON IS A 24-HOUR CITY, and the need for a good breakfast is acute in those who have worked a very early start to the day. Many places continue to serve the traditional full English breakfast: bacon, eggs, sausage and tomatoes, washed down by strong, hot tea. Once maligned as unhealthy and unimaginative, modern lighter ingredients can render the English breakfast a real feast – and arguably more appealing to the seriously hungry than the Continental version!

Futures (0171 638 634) is a vegetarian take-away outlet and delivery service in the heart of the City, with one branch in the Broadgate development and another near Monument (see page 21). Their porridge is a renowned breakfast dish amongst those working nearby – including, one suspects, dealers in the financial markets who begin work very early in the day.

Futures Porridge

Serves 4

300ml (½ pint) of milk
75g (3oz) regular small oats
2 dessertspoons clear honey

Heat the milk in a saucepan to boiling point. Then add in the oats and continue to cook on a high heat. Stir the mixture vigorously for 3 minutes, then turn the heat down and cook for a further 2 minutes. Stir in the clear honey to sweeten, and serve piping hot.

Tip Good breakfast spots

For a summer breakfast, or for those who prefer some-thing lighter in the morning, good coffee and croissants or bagels are hard to beat. Some of my favourite places are included here, guaranteed to shave off hunger pangs wherever you may find yourself!

Bagel King
280 Walworth Road, London SE17.
Tel: 0171 252 5057.

Ridley Bagel Bakery
13-15 Ridley Road, London E8.
Tel: 0171 923 0666.
The bagels served in these two outlets are quite delicious and available with a wide range of fillings.

Bar Italia
22 Frith Street, London W1.
Tel: 0171 437 4520.
A great variety of coffees to choose from for your first caffeine fix of the day.

Cullens Patisserie
108 Holland Park Avenue, London W11.
Tel: 0171-221-3598.
Now under the guidance and advice of the Roux Brothers, this patisserie serves a memorable great almond croissant for a delious breakfast snack.

L'Express at Joseph
16 Sloane Street, SW1
Tel: 0171 235 1991
L'Express café downstairs from the Joseph store in Sloane Street was started up over a decade ago, and I think after a croisant, orange juice and good coffee I feel ready to tackle a good mornings shopping in the heart of Knightsbridge.

Informal Afternoon Tea

SOME WONDERFUL AFTERNOON TEASHOPS and cafés have sprung up in London in recent years, providing a welcome addition to the capital's food life. They generally feature coffees and fruit juices. Eatables include the traditional scones and fruit breads, cakes of varying degrees of sweetness (and consequent calories!), cookies and biscuits, and often delicate fruit tarts. Some also feature more savoury dishes, although not generally the full high tea. They are very relaxed places to sit in and chat, and are particularly attractive to families.

The Tea House
College Farm, 45 Fitzalan Road,
London N3 3PG.
Tel: 0171 240 9577.
This charming haunt is defined in the Tea Council's *Guide to British Tea Shops*. It is a very prestigious entry, as there are only 67 listed tea shops (located in England, Scotland and Wales) in the Tea Council's guide.

Teatime
21 The Pavement, Clapham Common,
London SW4.
Tel: 0171 622 4944.
A cosy tea-time café, which also does good brunches. A relaxed atmosphere and good tasty food, totally unpretentious and a great place to spend time on a Sunday with the newspapers.

Annabel's
33 High Street, London SW19.
Tel: 0181 947 4326.
This is a formal salon de thé with good high quality patisserie and savouries. It is also a great place to relax and watch the world go by.

Patisserie Valerie
There are now three branches of this famous patisserie (see page 110) which provide the perfect accompaniment to afternoon tea. The café at Old Compton Street in Soho, where it has been located since the early 1950s, has retained the original décor of the period and contains Toulouse-Lautrec cartoons and paintings to gaze at while you indulge. The other locations are in Knightsbridge, at 215 Brompton Road, and in central London, at 105 Marylebone High Street. A visit to sample the delicious pastries, coffee and teas is a memorable experience.

Patisserie Valerie makes a wide range of cakes and gâteaux of French, Italian and Austrian origin, as well as traditional fruit wedding cakes. All are given an inspirational touch by the influence of the Sicilian chef. Exclusive cakes sold include the Cortina cake, an adapted and simplified recipe for which is given on page 110. (The full professional version is a work of art, and the patisserie reserves the secret of its creation!)

Formal Afternoon Tea

ONE OF LONDON'S FINEST TRADITIONS is formal
afternoon tea, which is served in most of its
large hotels. You don't have to stay there to go
and enjoy the restful atmosphere and discreet
service, as well as delicious food, that
characterise the best of them. Clothes may be
fairly casual, but should not be scruffy or untidy
– leave your jeans or shorts at home, and at least
bring a tie. The food is usually a meal in itself,
including assorted sandwiches and savouries,
scones with cream and jam, cakes and other
sweetmeats. (A high tea is a larger proposition,
and will involve at least one cooked savoury
course). Most of these hotels offer a set price
menu for their afternoon teas, so you can
indulge to your heart's – or stomach's – content!

Brown's Hotel
33-34 Albermarle Street, London W1.
Tel: 0171 493 6020
Served in the Lounge 3.00 – 6.00 p.m. daily.
Brown's is a discreetly renowned place to take
tea. Service is excellent and the food plentiful
and good; Brown's Hotel is also known to be a
wonderfully atmospheric place to watch dusk
falling on the elegant street outside in the
autumn and winter months.

The Capital
22 Basil Street, London SW3.
Tel: 0171 589 5171.
Served in the sitting Room 3.30 – 5.30 p.m.
daily. This wonderfully discreet but central
hotel is a great place for tea with tasty
sandwiches, delicious cakes and scones. The
food is made under the command of the Chef
Philip Britten, whose food in the newly
nlarged restaurant and Metro downstairs
is excellent.

The Hyde Park Hotel
Knightsbridge, London SW1.
Tel: 0171 235 2000
A delightful room overlooking Hyde Park which
has a piano playing through your tea-time. The
hotel provides a quite delicious tea which is
served impeccably.

The Landmark
222 Marylebone Road, London NW1.
Tel: 0171 631 8000.
Served in the Winter Garden, 3.00 – 6.00 p.m.
daily. With three varieties of teas available,
his attractive menu is served in the very
airy atrium.

The Ritz

Piccadilly, London, W1.
Tel: 0171 493 8181.
The famous afternoon tea at
the Ritz is served in the Palm
Court 2.00 – 6.00 p.m. daily.
Note that you do usually have
to book. Tea at the Ritz is an
experience which lives up to
expectations, but need not
break the bank – it offers
unlimited sandwiches and
cakes for a set price.

Tea-Time at Twinings

216 Strand, WC2. Tel: 0171 353 3511

TEA, ENJOYED THROUGH-OUT THE WORLD and known particularly as the traditional British brew, has had a long and che-quered history in the capital. In 1684 a man called Thomas Twining left his West Country home to seek his fortune in London. He complet-ed an apprenticeship as a weaver – a trade was essential in order to become a freeman of the City of London – and in 1706 he opened Master Tom's Coffee House at the sign of the Golden Lion in the Strand. His 'gimmick' was that he served tea as a sideline ,and his business soon flourished as his reputa-tion as a tea blender and merchant spread.

He was followed into the tea business by his son Daniel. Today Sam Twining OBE presides over this very famous tea company. Its tea shop in the Strand still marks the importance of Twinings' presence in London, with a well-stocked shop and a small museum at the rear.

Tea was at first a luxury in Britian. Twinings sales ledgers of the period which have been pre-served through the years show that prices ranged from six shillings to thirty six shillings a pound (30p – £1.80). This was an extortionate price by our standards, when you consider that £1 in the late 18th century would be worth about £20 today! Nonetheless, demand increased.

The popularity of tea continued to spread, but it was not until 1839 that the first shipment of Assam Indian tea was landed by the tea clip-per *Calcutta*. Previ-ously only China tea was available, and the Chinese had not permit-ted the seeds or seed-ling of the plant to be exported. However, it had now been discov-ered growing wild in India. A healthy trade with India was soon established, and 'tea clippers', such as the *Cutty Sark*, were reach-ing the peak of their sailing days. In 1879 the first shipments of tea from Ceylon began to arive. By 1880 this had been firmly established alongside Indian and China teas, giving us the same broad range of teas that we know today.

London is still the centre of the trade, and indeed Twinings still have a shop on the site of the original Tom's Coffee House at 216 The Strand. However, the company has expanded considerably. With the benefit of two and a half centuries of experience, they still blend and market a wide range of teas – Earl Grey, Lapsang Souchong, Ceylon, Darjeeling, Assam and many others are exported to tea lovers in over ninety countries. The name of Twining remains synonymous with quality and tradition across the world.

Tea-Time Secrets

THE TRADITIONAL BRITISH RATIO for making tea is one spoonful of leaves per cup of water plus a spoonful for the pot. But how large is the spoonful? Should it be level or heaped? Do you take your tea with milk or lemon?

There are no precise answers to these questions. It is best to experiment and arrive at your own conclusions – which will probably vary with each different tea blend. The only rule is to make the tea strong enough. Strong tea can be diluted with hot water. Tea that is made too weak is beyond repair.

Generally speaking, small-leaf teas, such as Assam and Irish Breakfast, need about 3 minutes brewing time. Medium-leaf teas (for example, Darjeeling and Orange Pekoe) brew in 4 to 5 minutes. And large-leaf teas, such as Green Gunpowder and Prince of Wales, require 5 to 7 minutes to bring out their full flavour.

The better quality the tea, the more cups it will produce. A pound of quality loose tea will produce 240 cups, compared to the 200 cup average for ordinary tea. By the same token, a fine tea bag has enough character and enough tea in the bag for most tastes to yield two full-flavoured cups.

Tips

Steps to a Perfect Cup

Bring a kettle of freshly drawn cold water just to the boil.

As the water approaches the boil, pour a little into the teapot to warm it well.

Empty the teapot. Add the tea: one teaspoon for each cup, plus 'one for the pot'. If using tea bags, two bags will usually serve three cups.

Bring the teapot up to the kettle. As soon as the water begins to boil, pour it over the tea leaves in the teapot. Stir, cover and leave to brew. Allow a minute or two for tea bags, three to seven minutes for loose tea.

If you prefer lighter tea, add some more hot water to weaken the brew.

To produce perfect tea, freshness is as important as quality. A sealed tin has a minimum shelf life of at least two years. After initial opening, the tin should be firmly closed each time that it is used. Scented teas, such as Earl Grey and Blackcurrant, should never be left uncovered, or their delicate bouquet will dissipate. Tea bags should be transferred to an airtight container to ensure freshness.

Food Halls

THE FOOD HALLS OF LONDON'S MOST FAMOUS department stores – Fortnum and Mason, Harrods, Harvey Nichols and Selfridges – are justly celebrated in their own right. Stocked with produce from all over the world, they offer a bewildering array of delicious ingredients and a fascinating visual experience. Each has its own atmosphere and flavour to reflect that of the wider store, from the traditional to the very modern and glamorous. They are not the cheapest places to buy food by any means, but they are an invaluable source of exotic, luxury or just good quality foodstuffs all the year round.

Harvey Nichols is the jewel in the crown of new food shopping in central London. Highly design-led, this food floor at the top of the Knightsbridge store has a great selection of fresh and store cupboard foods. Its airy layout, with specialist fish, cheese, meat and bakery departments along with the central grocery store, allows interesting shopping. A coffee bar, café, chocolate section, and separate, well-stocked wine shop, not to forget the stylish bar and trendy but solid cooking in the restaurant, complete this high tec modern food emporium.

Selfridges on Oxford Street also needs to be considered, as it has a unique layout and accessibilty about it which makes it one of the easiest food halls to use in central London. With specialist counters designated to ready-made Jewish, Chinese and Indian foods, there is also the traditional fruit and vegetable section, grocery, frozen foods, butchery and fishmongers. An impressive bakery and quick-flowing checkouts make it easy to shop here. With a Pret à Manger (see entry on page 219) sandwich bar

and an oyster bar – the food section at Selfridges has recently been completed with a restaurant ('Premier') on the second floor.

Fortnum and Mason and, of course, Harrods form the old established food stores in the capital, and each of their individual styles is internationally well known.

Fortnum and Mason specialise in high-quality foods, tending very much towards the traditional. The Food Hall itself is dark wood, with classic shelving for dry goods, and you are attended by formally dressed men and women in long black aprons. The fruit and vegetable section can only be described as exotic. It contains a wealth of jars, tins and bottled foods as well as the fresh fruit, and is a great place to hunt out 'foodie' presents for tourists to take home. One particular favourite of mine is Patum Pepanum (also known as Gentleman's Relish). Teas and coffees still remain one of the favourite gift purchases.

The **Harrods** food halls have been renowned the world over for decades, and they are still very impressive. The meat and fish hall is surrounded by models of hanging meat, with a superb fish display by the working fountain in one corner. The bakery department has recently moved to house a pizza restaurant. A juice bar, oyster bar and sushi bar now are intermingled with the food for sale on the shelves and in the fridges. The prepared delicatessen foods, charcuterie, cheeses and specially prepared ready-made foods create a startling display. Now the confectionery, chocolates, patisserie, cakes and other Harrods delicacies mean that you simply cannot visit London and not take a walk around!

Harvey Nichols food Hall

Fashion and Food

THE IMPORTANCE OF STYLE AND ENVIRONMENT is regularly pointed out as the link between restaurants and fashion. People who like stylish clothes generally care for an equally fashionable eating environment.

The idea of a café within a clothes shop is a relatively recent phenomenom in London, and to have proved a great success. Nicole Farhi recently opened a café in her shop in Bond Street, now the enormously popular Nicole's (see below). A juice bar in the same street at DKNY is also successful.

On a much larger scale Harvey Nichols introduced a whole floor in the top of their fashion store, (see page 228) .A restaurant bar and food store – linking the whole ethos of the store's fashion-led success, where previously only a small Joseph café existed in the basement. Selfridges are the latest store to catch on to the trend; they are due to open their restaurant as we go to press.

However, the first fashion house to develop the idea of a café within a clothes shop, and to invest in a full blown stand – alone restaurant is Jones. Jones restaurant in Covent Garden opened this year and has achieved considerable success. The restaurant has a similar interior design to the Jones mensware shop, and it seats about one hundred people.

Wagamama, the enormously successful Japanese noodle bar in Bloomsbury is working the opposite way around. It has become the first restaurant to develop a clothing label gaining a foothold in the fashion industry with the instantly recognisable T-shirts worn by the staff.The T-shirt designers of past years, Paul Smith and John Richmond, regularly eat there.

Wagamama's new 20-piece clothing range will adopt a workwear style typical of the utilitarian style of the restaurant. The simple Wagamama philosophy of eat well, live well, will be reflected in the clothes when they hit the streets in 1996.

Other designers and restaurants have linked together in subtle ways. The waiters in Emporio Armani Express wear a version of the Italian bell-boy suit designed, of course, by Giorgio Armani. This adds a degree of glamour and prestige to the restaurant.

Independent restaurants have also enlisted the help of the fashion world. In 1992 Bella Freud designed uniforms for the trendy Chinese restaurant Zen, whilst Jasper Conran designed the uniforms for the staff of Bibendum, Quaglinos and Mezzo.

From a completely different angle, themed restaurants, such as The Hard Rock Café and Planet Hollywood, make more money from their clothing ranges, than they do from their burgers. The clothing falls into T-shirt, key-ring and baseball cap category – all complete with the essential ingredient, the logo, on the front.

How the link between fashion and food will develop in the London of the 21st century remains to be seen, but it will undoubtedly continue in some form.

Nicole's at Nicole Farhi
158 New Bond Street, London W1.
Tel: 0171 499 8408.

DKNY
27 Old Bond Street, W1.
Tel: 0171 499 8080.

Harvey Nichols
Knightsbridge, London SW1.
Tel: 0171 235 5000.
Selfridges
400 Oxford Street, W1.
Tel: 0171 629 1234.

Wagamama
4 Streatham Street, WC1.
Tel: 0171 323 9223.

Emporio Armani Express
191 Brompton Road, SW3.
Tel: 0171 823 8818.

Zen
85 Sloane Avenue, SW3.
Tel: 0171 584 9219.

Bibendum
81 Fulham Road, SW3.
Tel: 0171 581 5817.

Quaglinos
16 Bury Street, SW1.
Tel: 0171 930 6767.

Hard Rock Café
150 Old Park Lane, W1.
Tel: 0171 629 0382.

Planet Hollywood
13 Coventry Street, W1.
Tel: 0171 287 1000.

Nicole's at Nicole Fahri

Markets

MARKETS ARE AN ESSENTIAL FEATURE of London's food life. In all areas of the city, from Brick Lane in the East End to Berwick Street in Soho to the North End Road Market in Fulham, West London, they offer a fascinating array of produce from all over the world. Each has its own character and specialities, which make them wonderful places to wander through and browse. The market traders themselves are well informed on current food trends in London, and – if not too busy – are happy to discuss them with interested customers.

Brick LaneMarket
E1 and E2.
Open Sundays 6am – 1pm.

There are several good fruit and vegetable stalls on the junction of Brick Lane, Sclater and Cheshire Street, where bargains of large quantities of good-quality fruit and vegetables are always up for grabs.

Brick Lane Bagel Bakery, at the top of the market near Bethnal Green Lane, is famous. Open 24 hours, it is a reliable haunt of all-night party revellers. It's an experience going into this shop, as at the back you can see all the bagels being made – a process which continues non-stop throughout the day and night.

Brixton Market
Electric Avenue, Brixton Station Road, SW9.
Open 8.30am – 5.30pm Mon, Tue, Thurs, Sat.
Open 8.30am – 1pm Wed.

Electric Avenue was one of the first streets to get electricity in the 1880s. It is now full of fruit and vegetable shops and stalls, as well as lots of fascinating butchers and grocery shops which complement the market.

On Pope's Road is a fantastic array of fruit and vegetables form all over the world – the friendly stall holders and Afro-Caribbean music pulsating from the back of the stalls reminds you of the huge West Indian population and culture based in Brixton. Obviously the different varieties of yams, chillies and unusual looking fruit, such as christophenes and breadfruit, are present in abundance.

Granville Arcade is the largest arcade in Brixton. It is very light and bright, with more interesting grocery shops as well as fantastic fish displays. There is a lot of preserved salt cod for sale, but also the fresh fish stalls selling unusual varieties, such as St. Peter's fish and smoked angera. There is also a great variety of frozen fish for sale too.

Arcade bakeries sells the best sweetbreads and the more adventurous of you can search for delicacies like goat's meat, cow's foot and tripe up the Electric Avenue.

Cafés are popular in Brixton market, my favourite being The Pizzeria and Coffee Bar on Electric Avenue, where they serve the best Calzone on Saturday brunch time – my favourite time. Watch out though, as there are a lot of regulars and a queue can form quite quickly!

Berwick Street Market
Berwick Street and Rupert St, W1
Open 9am – 6pm Mon – Sat.

As I became a regular visitor to this market when I worked around the corner in Broadwick

Street, I know the market traders well. The price and quality varies enormously with several stalls just selling one type of fruit or vegetables – pile them high and sell them cheap being the motto. Real market traders can be seen here shouting slogans to sell their produce; I've often seen them wheeling their barrows out of the lock-ups to set up their wares in the morning. Dennis has to have the best presentation on his stall; he takes great pride in setting up every morning, wrapping his goods in coloured tissues all up the front side of his barrow. He supplies many of the local Soho restaurants and it's not unusual to bump into a chef clad in his whites buying the herbs he needs for the lunchtime service or the shiitlake or oyster mushrooms proudly displayed up front. Dennis's strategic position, just in front of Fratelli Carmisa, provides a good corner – I used to pop in for a piece of home-made foccacia (bought by the weight) to nibble on as I went around the stalls and shops in the area collecting my ingredients for the recipes I was going back to the kitchen to create.

Further along, over Brewer Street and into Rupert Street, there are two more excellent fruit and vegetable stalls. This area surrounding Berwick Street is a great 'foodie' area, In Old Compton Street, look up Carmisa and the Patisserie Valerie (see pages 110 and 223); in Brewer Street seek out Lina Stores (see page 76) and Slater, Cooke and Bisney at no.68. These are truly professional butchers, in their clean stainless steel and functional shop with the unique, old-fashioned method of paying the cashier on the way out once you've chosen and collected your meat. Watch out, as it though closes early on Saturdays at 1pm.

Greenwich Market

SE10
Open: Saturday and Sunday 9 – 5pm.

In the undercover Bosun's Yard, Greenwich Church Street, there is a very good food stall selling all sorts of pickles, mustards and flavoured cooking oils.

Portabello Road

W11
Open 8.30am – 5.30pm Mon-Sat

During the week this is a favourite foodie area of mine, not least because of its close proximity to 'Books for Cooks' on Blenheim Crescent (see page 12). Here I can be found browsing for about 2-3 hours at a time and, can never make it out of the door without at least one or two books under my arm!

The fruit, vegetable, fish and eggs stalls are open during the week, with the more famous bric-à-brac part of the market opening up at weekends.It has great cafés, delis such as Mr Christians on Elgin Crescent (see page 17), the Lisboa patisserie and delicatessen further down Portabello (see page 100) and Garcia's the Spanish delicatessen at the bottom end of the road going towards Golborne Road. Just opposite Elgin Crescent there's a good selection of food stalls which are great for finger food.

Chapel Market

N1
Open: Tuesday, Wednesday, Friday and Saturday 9 – 5pm, Thursday and Sunday 9 – 12.30pm.

A busy market in the heart of Islington, close to

Markets

Marks and Spencers, Sainsburys and Woolworths, it's a well-stocked shopping corner. The fish stall is very good, selling good basic fish varieties at reasonable prices. The fruit and vegetables are of good quality, but just a good basic variety (with no exotic or unusual ingredients from abroad), at the Liverpool Road end.

Alpino's at No. 97 Chapel Street, is known for its cheap pasta dishes. The Bhel Poon House has good value Indian vegetarian dishes. Manze's pie and mash shop at No. 74 is an institution, and allows you to experience the local flavour.

Spitalfields Market

E.1.
Organic market 11 – 3p.m. Fridays,
9 – 3p.m. Sundays,
General market 11 – 3p.m. Monday to Friday,
Sunday 9 – 3p.m.

This was the original site for London's largest wholesale fruit, vegetable and flower markets, now based at Temple Mills. The original site covers five acres, and the warehouse is now used as an entertainment and shopping centre. Only a small part of the warehouse is used. Crafts and antique stalls are set up during the week, but on Fridays and Sundays the market becomes busy. This organic food market really sells fruit and vegetables as well as free-range farm eggs, bread, pastries and home-made jams and chutneys.

Ridley Road Market

Ridley Road, London E.8.
Open: 9 – 3 pm Monday to Wednesday, 9 am – 12.00 Thursday 9 – 5pm. Friday and Saturday

Ridley Road is a fun, multi-cultural market with a great mix of stalls. It's been a market since the 1880s, with Afro-Caribbeans, Asians and Turks selling produce as well as the traditional East End barrow boys. One of the best finds on the street is the Turkish Food Centre, where you can buy loose Turkish Delight and freshly baked Turkish bread.

Leadenhall Market

London EC3
Open: 7 – 4pm Monday to Friday

Sir Horace Jones completed the existing arcade which houses the market in 1881, although there has been a market on this site since the 14th century. Nowadays it is more like a number of static market shops which extend on to the pavements. The food sold is of top quality and consists of delicatessen products such as, cheeses, chocolates, fish and (following tradition) poultry. It's a great place to wander around at Christmas time to see the wares displayed in a festive manner.

North End Road Market

London SW6
Monday to Saturday 9 – 5pm
Wednesday 9 – 12.30pm.

A good, thriving fruit and vegetable market, which also has good value cheese, egg and fish stalls.

Late-Night London

After Twelve

London is a city which continues throughout the night and there's always someone, somewhere, who wants to eat after midnight. Here's a guide to some good places you could try.

Bagel Bake

159 Brick Lane, London E1.
Tel: 0171 729 0616.
Open 24 hours.

Ed's Easy Diner

12 Moor Street, London W1.
Tel: 0171 439 1955.
Friday and Saturday open until 1.00 am.
A mock 1950's diner – have mayonnaise with your chips for a change!

Camelli

128 Golders Green Road, London NW11.
Tel: 0181 455 2074.
Thursday open 24 hours, other days closed between 11.00 – 12.00 am.

Haagen-Daz

14 Leicester Square, London WC2.
Tel: 0171 287 9577.
Friday and Saturday open until 1.00 am.
Indulge in a late-night ice cream in the centre!

Harry's Bar

19 Kingly Street, London W1.
Tel: 0171 434 0309.
Open from 10.30 pm. – 6.00 am.
Great for breakfast after a hard night's dancing!

Instanbul Iskembecisi

9 Stoke Newington Road, London N16
Tel: 0171 524 7291.
Sunday: 5.00 pm – 5.00 am.
Monday to Saturday: 2.00 pm – 5.00 am.
A Turkish menu to delight night owls.

Mayflower

68-70 Shaftesbury Avenue, London W1.
Tel: 0171 734 9207.
5.00 pm – 4.00 am.
Late Chinese eating.

Men's Bar Hamine

84 Brewer Street, London W1.
Tel: 0171 439 0785.
11.45 am – 3.00 am Monday to Friday
11.45 am – 2.00 am Saturday
A good Japanese noodle bar.

New Diamond

23 Lisle Street, London WC2.
Tel: 0171 437 2517.
Noon – 3.00 am.
Chinese food.

Ranouch Juice Bar

434 Edgware Road, London W2.
Tel: 0171 723 5929.
9.00 am – 3.00 am.
A Lebanese Café serving their native food. The freshly squeezed juices are excellent.

Yung's

23 Wardour Street, London W1.
Tel: 0171 437 4986.
Noon – 4.30 pm.

Fish and Chips Around London

A good basic batter and crisp gold chips is the hallmark of successful fish and chips. As a late-night snack they are unrivalled – sometimes just nothing else will do! So, for those certain occasions, here is my selection of the best fish and chips around London.

Sea-Shell
49-51 Lisson Grove, London NW1 6UH.
Tel: 0171 723 1063.
The original Sea-Shell fish and chip shop, good at what it knows best.

Upper Street Fish Shop
324 Upper Street, London N1.
Tel: 0171 359 1401.
An excellent portion of fish and chips in pleasant surroundings.

Toff's
38 Muswell Hill Broadway, London NW10 3RT.
Tel: 0181 883 8656.

Brady's
513 Old York Road, London SW18 1TF.
Tel: 0181 877 9599.
A well-known spot for quality fish and chips. Now they're opened another restaurant in the Fulham Road which will no doubt be a similar success.

Shops and Shopping

London is so well served with a wide expanse of shoppping areas that it is very difficult to pick out the best overall centres. The individual shops and outlets mentioned in this chapter represent the best of the shops available in London. Each has its own focus, and many are stocked from the fantastic (and historic) wholesale markets of central London. These include meat from Smithfield, fresh fruit and vegetables from Covent Garden and Spitalfields and fish from Billingsgate.

The markets are centres of excellence, and the wealth of knowledge that can be gathered from the traders is enormous. Few chefs now venture down there due to the pressures on their time, but a visit very early in the morning is well worth the effort of getting up. Shopping for food in London, whether it involves browsing the capital's luxurious food halls or enjoying the exuberance of its markets, is above all fun, and witness to the vitality and creativity of the food scene in the capital today.

Fortnum and Mason famous for their food hampers, also have a showcase food hall in Piccadilly.

Shopping and Specialist Food Suppliers

FOODS OF EVERY DESCRIPTION can now be obtained somewhere in London. The shopping opportunities offered by the capital are enormous, and are often surprisingly inexpensive. A wealth of specialist food suppliers enable the requirements of almost any cuisine to be met, from Indian spices to Moroccan pastries, Jewish kosher meats to Chinese fruit and vegetables. London also has a plentiful supply of fresh produce in its colourful street markets; mainstream supermarkets, too, are reflecting new eating trends and stocking an exciting, ever-expanding range of 'exotic' fruit, vegetables, sauces and spices. For those who wish to obtain something quickly or in comfort, a wide range of mail order specialists are available in or near the capital.

Fresh Fruit and Vegetables

Fry's of Chelsea
14, Cale St, London SW3.
Tel: 0171 589 0342. (see page 52)
Paul Fry has been helping me to locate ingredients for some time now, and he's always helpful and willing to look out for something specific. His shop on the corner of Cale Street, snuggling behind the King's Road and the Fulham Road, has a 'villagey' feel to it. The produce is well displayed and there's always friendly service to welcome you. He delivers locally and is very willing to take any special orders. A good local greengrocer needs support, as they are under threat from hungry supermarket stores. Its a true pleasure to shop here, in what is really a mini Covent Garden market. Fry's always reminds me on my early morning pick up of the huge number of varieties of fruit and vegetable I see at Nine Elms.

Brian Lau-Jones
36 Heath St, London NW3.
Tel: 0171 435 5084.
The perfect greengrocer for Hampstead, combining just the right mix of everyday essentials with eclectic exotica.

The Wood Fruiterer
51a St Johns Wood High St, NW8.
Tel: 0171 722 0977.
All the staples are here, plus persimmons, prickly pears, cape gooseberries, fresh dates and loquats. There is a good range, too, of dried nuts, fruits and pulses.

D. McKay Fruiterers
19a Harrington Road, London SW7.
Tel: 0171 584 1929 *or*
38 Thurloe St, London SW7.
Tel: 0171 589 4987.
Both shops offer a sparkling display of fruit, vegetables and flowers. They provide all the basics and a good selection of tropical fruits, imported vegetables and fresh herbs.

Michanicou Brothers
2 Clarendon Road, London W11.
Tel: 0171 727 5191.
Here you find an excellent array of vegetables, such as acorn and butter nut squash, baby turnips, sugar snaps and chanterelles. Friendly service and free local delivery.

Daisy Buchanan's
5 Paddington St, London W1.
Tel: 0171 486 3678.
A cheerful shop with good basics and some interesting seasonal exotica.

Butchers

Lidgate's
110 Holland Park Avenue, W11.
Tel: 0171 727 8243.
A family butcher's shop, still run by part of the family, David Lidgate was the founder Chairman of the 'Q' guild butchers. All 'Q' Guild butchers (including Randall Butchers on page 220) have very high standards of produce, preparation and service. This shop is well worth a visit. Try some of their pies, as Lidgate's are constantly winning awards for pies made to their own recipes. Be ready for a big queue at Christmas, however – orders have to be put in early for the special 'bronze turkeys' which are fabulous.

A. Dove and Son
71 Northcote Road, SW11.
Tel: 0171 223 5191.
A family-run concern, this traditional butcher's shop, complete with sawdust on the floor, stocks a great variety of meat sausages, bacon, Aberdeen Angus beef and great game when in season. In a prominent corner location on this popular market street, it's a butcher's that is well worth visiting, if only to pick their knowledgeable brains on how to prepare and cook their wares.

Randalls
113 Wandsworth Road, SW6.
Tel: 0171 736 3426. (see entry on page 220)

Slater, Cooke and Bisney Jones
68 Brewer St, WC1.
Tel: 0171 437 2026.
Another fine shop with excellent produce.

Curnicks
170 Fulham Road, SW10.
Tel: 0171 730 1191.
Another traditional butcher's shop, again complete with sawdust sprinkled over the floor. This is very much a working shop that hangs its meat well. The staff are very knowledgeable and happy to pass on good advice.

Frank Godfry Ltd.
7 Highbury Road, N5.
Tel: 0171 226 2425.
Another family-owned business. A prize 'Q' guild butcher who knows his meat, Jeremy Godfrey has supplied fantastic meat for food photography for me. He's very open and approachable and willing to get any meat that his customers require.

R. Allen and Co.
117 Mount St, W1.
Tel: 0171 499 5831.
Meat and game of the finest quality are sold here. Located on the same premises for over 140 years, this shop always has an impressive array of meat or poultry displayed in its large windows.

M.Moen and Sons
19 The Pavement, SW4.
Tel: 0171 622 1624.
A good local butcher's with an excellent stock of meat and poultry.

Shopping and Specialist Food Suppliers

Fishmongers

Bibendum Crustacea.
Michelin House, 81 Fulham Road, London SW3.
Tel: 0171 589-0864.
This is an upmarket stall, reflecting the stylish fish demands of the clientele. Attached to the Bibendum Oyster Bar, this stall does sell a lot of shellfish, especially native and rock oysters, lobsters, crabs and clams. All the produce is set out on the back of a classic French van that's a joy to see in itself.

Chalmers and Gray
67 Notting Hill Gate, London W8.
Tel: 0171-221-6177.
(see page 16)

Richards
21 Brewer Street, London W1.
Tel: 0171-437-1358.
This well-known shop moved some years ago from its established position on Berwick Street. Fortunately, the same character, quality produce and knowledge can be found at this excellent fishmongers in their new shop.

Covent Garden Fishmongers
37 Turnham Green Terrace, London W4.
Tel: 0181 995 9273.
The celebrated taxi driver turned fishmonger, Phil Diamond, owns this popular fishmonger's shop.

Harvey Nichols Food Hall
Knightsbridge, London SW1.
Tel: 0171 235 5000.
(see page 228)
The fish counter is excellent, with knowledgeable fishmongers – they're also very helpful in ordering special fish when needed.

Harrods
87 Brompton Road, London SW7.
0171 730 1234.
(see page 228)
The fish counter is well worth going just to look over, as are all the other food halls within Harrods. The oyster bar next door sells great oysters, and the wide variety of fish available is always very fresh.

Bakeries and Cheese Shops

Clarke's
122 Kensington Church Street, London W8.
Tel: 0171 229 2190.
Set up by Sally Clarke next door to her restaurant,
I think this is the best bakery in London. Her
breads are delicious and include sour dough,
walnut and olive. This delightful shop always
smells absolutely fantastic; it also sells other
savouries, home-baked shortbreads, tarts, etc. to
enjoy in the shop over a cup of coffee. Clarke's
own preserves and chocolate truffles are sold as
well as Neals' Yard Cheeses (see below).

Dunns
6 The Broadway, Crouch End, London N8.
Tel: 0181 340 1614.
These master bakers make fabulous bread. A
family of bakers' they have been based here for
more than a century.

Asda
Clapham Junction, London SW11.
Tel: 0171 223 0101
Set up by Yorkshire Bakeries, I am very
impressed with the bread baked here on the
premises. It is baked from flour and yeast, not
from commercial bread mixes as most other
supermarket bread is. This bakery section is a
delight – watch out for their new Cheese and
Pickle, as well as the delicious Muesli, bread.

Cheeses
13 Fortis Green Road, London N10.
Tel: 0181 444 9141.
This charmingly old-fashioned cheese shop is
jam-packed with over 150 different cheeses.

Jeroboams
24 Bute Street, London SW7.
Tel: 0171 225 2232. *or*
51 Elizabeth Street, London W1.
Tel: 0171 823 5623. *or*
6 Clarendon Road London W11.
Tel: 0171 727 9359.
These shops have built up a fantastic reputation
over the past 10 years. They contain cheeses
from all over the world, explained and extolled
by knowledgeable and enthusiastic staff.

Neal's Yard Dairy
17 Shorts Gardens, London WC2.
Tel: 0171 379 7646.
The best cheese shop in London – an experience
simply to go inside. Its cool atmosphere and the
large whole cheeses decorating the shop are a
cheese-lover's dream. All the cheeses are British
or from Ireland. The dairy matures some of the
cheeses on the premises or on its own farm in
Kent. Taste with the guidance of informed
and enthusiastic staff, and you'll be in
seventh heaven.

Paxton and Whitfield
93 Jermyn Street, London SW1.
Tel: 0171 930 0259.
(see page 33)

The Real Cheese Shop
62 Barnes High Street, London SW13.
Tel: 0181 878 6676 or
96a High Street, Wimbledon, London SW19.
Tel: 0181 947 0564.
A great selection of cheeses from all over the world.

Shopping and Specialist Food Suppliers

French Specialist Shops and Pâtisseries

The House of Albert Roux
229 Ebury Street, London SW1.
Tel: 0171-730 4175.
This delightful House is a mixture of *traiteur*, *patisserie*, *boucheries* and *fromagerie*, with fresh fruit and vegetables often imported from France. A good shop for sourcing difficult ingredients.

Traiteur Pagnot
170 Regents Park Road, London NW1.
Tel: 0171 586 6988.
A very French haven in North London, the shop exudes delightful food smells. With its working kitchen downstairs, this is an excellent place at which to buy their freshly made foods over the counter or through their home-catering service.

Cannelle
166 Fulham Road, London SW10.
Tel: 0171 370 5573.
A stylish exterior reveals elegant and exciting cakes in the patisserie inside.
or
221 Kensington High Street, W8.
Tel: 0171 938 1547.
or
26, North Audley Street London W1.
Tel: 0171 409 0500.
A great patisserie which produces French breads and croissants to an excellent standard.

Filenic & Filerre
57 & 87 Old Brompton Road, London SW7
Tel: 0171 584 2967.

A pretty little French *salon de thés* for the home-sick local French community.

Bagatelle Boutianne
44 Harrington Road, London SW7.
Tel: 0171 581 1551.
This is charming and wholly dedicated to its French origins and products.

Cullens Patisserie
108 Holland Park Avenue, London W11.
Tel: 0171 221 3598.
(see page 222)

Madeleine
5 Vigo Street, London W1.
Tel: 0171 734 8353.
A great pâtisserie with produce baked on the premises.

Boucherie Lamartine
229 Ebury Street, London SW1.
Tel: 0171 730-3037.

Villandry
89 Marylebone High Street, London W1.
Tel: 0171 487 3816
This well-known pâtisserie includes the only supply of *Pain Poitaine* from Max Potaines bakery.

Bally Lamartine.
116 Mount Street, London W11.
Tel: 0171 499 1833.

'Les Specialist St Quentin'
256 Brompton Road, London SW3.
Tel: 0171 225 1664. (see page 66)

Italian Specialist shops

Salumeria Napoli
69 Northcote Road, London SW11.
Tel: 0171 228 2445.
A traditional Italian deli complete with an authentic canopy set outside. It sells good cheeses, breads and pastas.

Luigi's Delicatessen
349 Fulham Road, London SW10.
Tel: 0171 352 7739.
A wonderful, packed shop with an instantly recognisable red painted exterior – a legend at this end of the Fulham Road.

Speck
2 Holland Park Terrace,
Portland Road, London W11.
Tel: 0171 229 7005.
A modern authentic delicatessen with pasta made on the premises. A delightful and considerate owner, who has opened his doors early to me on several occasions so that I can pick up my shopping en route to a day's food photography.

Lina Stores
18 Brewer Street, London W1.
Tel: 0171 437 6482.
(see page 76)

G. Gazzano and Son
167-169 Farringdon Road, London EC1.
Tel: 0171 837 1586.
A very good and authentic Italian deli.

Carluccio's
28a Neal Street, London WC1.
Tel: 0171 240 1487.
(see page 73)

Di Lieto Bakery and Delicatessen
175 South Lambeth Road, London SW8.
Tel: 0171 735 1997.
An excellent place for Italian breads.

L. Terrorri and Sons
138-140 Clerkenwell Road, London EC1.
Tel: 0171 837 1712.

I. Camisa and Son
61 Old Compton Street, London W1.
Tel: 0171 437 7610.

Jewish Specialist suppliers

Carmelli Bakers
128 Golders Green Road, London NW4.
Tel: 0181 455 3063.
Long opening hours in this great bakery.

Ridley Bagel Bakery
13 Ridley Road, London E8.
Tel: 0171 923 0666.
Jewish-style foods are sold here, as well as other typical delicatessen items.

Kosher King Freezer Centre
235 Golders Green Road, London NW11.
Tel: 0181 455 1429.
A good source of kosher foods.

Shopping and Specialist Food Suppliers

Country Market
36 Golders Green Road, London NW11.
Tel: 0181 455 3289.
A smart kosher supermarket in Golders Green.

Menachem's,
15 Russell Parade London NW11.
Tel: 0181 201 8629.
A good kosher butcher and delicatessen.

Chinese Specialist Food Shops

See Woo
18-20 Lisle Street, London WC2.
Tel: 0171 439 8325.
It seems like a back-street supermarket, but it does have a very good selection of Chinese ingredients. Frozen won-ton wrappers are always here in plentiful supply. The basement of the shop (down a very narrow staircase piled with boxes piled with boxes and clutter) sells a good selection of authentic 'Chinese restaurant style' crockery.

Loon Fung Supermarke
42-44 Gerrard Street, London W.1
Tel: 0171 437 7332.
The large, late-opening supermarket on the main street in Chinatown displays its fresh fruit and vegetables in boxes out on the pavement. A good selection of meat, fish and dry goods are located around the busy and sometimes chaotic store.

The Garden
51 Charing Cross Road, London WC2.
Tel: 0171 434 0737.
A well-known bakery, popular with local Chinese.

Wing Yip
395 Edgware Road, London NW2.
Tel: 0181 450 0422. *or*
550 Purley Way, Croydon.
Tel: 0181 688 4880.
Not specifically Chinese, but supplying Oriental goods, this is a large wholesale-type store. The newer site in Croydon incorporates a restaurant area to enjoy good Chinese dishes.

Indian Specialist Food Shops

Deepak Cash and Carry
935 Garratt Lane, London SW17.
Tel: 0181 767 7819
This is a huge warehouse-type store. It contains a good selection of dry ingredients, as well as plenty of fresh fruit and vegetables.

Drummond Street, London NW1.
Several shops in this area provide specialist foods, including the two below:
Ambala Sweet Centre at 112, which makes brightly coloured and very sweet cakes.
Vinron Europ at 119, an excellent supermarket for spices and condiments.

There are many other individual shops in this area which are worth looking around. I ended up in the basement of a small halal butchers at the end of the street one morning, picking through red and green chillies for a photographic shoot. Most of the shops in the street don't open until 10.30 a.m, however, so don't expect to do any early shopping. The restaurants in this street are excellent, and it is well known for its Indian bhel puri houses.

Other good areas for Indian foodstuffs:

Ealing Road, Wembley.

This is where Indian families come to stock up. In particular look out for:
VB & Sons (0181 902 8579).
Fudgo (0181 902 4820) for home-ground spices.

Southall

Here Indian and Pakistani grocery shops predominate. Look out for:
Sira Cash and Carry (0181 571 4529).
Gifto (0181 574 8602) and **Dokal** (0181 574 1647). If you have a sweet tooth, search out **Ambala's shop** here and also for **Friends Sweet Market.**

Tooting, London SW17 Has several Indian shops and greengrocers on Tooting High Road. **Everfresh Ltd.** at 204-208 Upper Tooting Road has always an amazing selection of fruit and vegetables at very reasonable prices, especially if they are bought in bulk. With specialist products such as Peneer (Indian cheese) available, it's a fascinating experience to look around. Opposite at 197 Upper Tooting Road the **House of Fresh Fruit** offers another good selection of reasonably priced spices.

Taj Stores, Brick Lane, E1, is a useful source of specialist Indian foods, ingredients and dishes.

Greek specialist shops

Greek shops across the capital provide great authentic ingredients. Some in particular to look out for are:

A. Ellinas

146 Ballards Lane, N3.
Tel: 0181 346 0904.
Great authentic products including olives, cheese, vine leaves and pastries.

Milla and Co.

200-202 St Ann's Road, N15.
Tel: 0181 802 7654.
Great Greek supermarkets.

Paul's

62 Camberwell Church Street, SE5.
Tel: 0171 703 0156.
A tiny, usually packed shop.

South-east Asian specialist food shops

South-east Asian supermarkets are useful to buy all the ingredients for this cuisine. Fresh produce such as lemon grass, is now quite widely available in large supermarkets, but things like kaffir lime leaves can still be quite tricky to find.

The Sri Thai

Shepherd's Bush Road, London W6.
Tel: 0171 602 0621.
This is one of my favourite shops. I work a lot with a photographer who lives just around the corner, and it was she who introduced me to this

Shopping and Specialist Food Suppliers

fabulous shop. The owner and his wife are very welcoming, helpful and knowledgeable about their ingredients. With a large selection of all types of foods, their pastes, fruit and vegetables and home-made snacks are my favourite foods. They have a great variety of home-made pastes in their fridges and, with a new delivery every week, I know that Thursday is the best day to go as the stock is newly arrived from Thailand. The easiest way to locate the shop is by the pink awning outside and the bunches of fresh orchids sitting outside the window. The moment you walk into the shop, smells and atmosphere (with Thai music often playing) evoke memories of my visit to Thailand. The whole family takes part in the business with the fresh produce sorted in boxes in the back.

The Hopewell Emporium

2F Dyne Road, NW6.
Tel: 0171 624 5473.
This fascinating shop specialises in Indonesian foods. Sambal oelek (chilli sauce) and ketjap mantis (Indonesian soy sauce) remind me of the shops I've visited in the market of near Medan in central Sumatra. The palm leaves remind me of the palms I've seen growing there – but I have to note that they don't import the oil palm fruit which I saw lorry-loads of, driving around. Southern Asian foods are also available here.

Maysun Food Market

869 Finchley Road, London NW11.
Tel: 0181 455 4773.
An Aladdin's cave of Chinese, Japanese, Thai and Indonesian foods. Even though they don't sell fresh fruit and vegetables, there are plenty of other fabulous ingredients. Well worth a visit.

Other Specialist Shops

Oils and Spice Shop

Butlers Whay Building, 36E Shad Thames, London SE1.
Tel: 0171 403 3434.
A great emporium of spices and oils. With an enthusiastic tasting introduction to any of the oils and vinegars, it's an excellent culinary experience.

The Conran Shop

Michelin Building,
Fulham Road, London SW10.
Tel: 0171 589 7401
The food section of this shop in the basement is always interesting and eclectic. Although only selling dry goods, it is well worth a visit.

Algerian Coffee Stores,

52 Old Compton Street, London W1.
Tel: 0171 437 2480.
Established in 1887 by an Algerian family this store is now owned by Italians. The amazing varieties of teas and coffees available make selection very difficult.

L'Etoile de Sous

Goldbourne Road, London W10.
Tel: 0181 960 9769.
Moroccan specialist shops are few and far between but this Moroccan-run bakery produces a wide range of authentic pastries. There is also a small selection of Moroccan foodstuffs at **Le Moroc.** (95 Goldbourne Road, London W10. Tel: 0181 968 9783.)

Green Valley

36 Upper Berkeley Street, London W1.
Tel: 0171 402 7385.
This is a huge Lebanese emporium stocking Middle Eastern foods. It's delightful to see with the huge number of foods on offer.

Snammins Abbas

74 Green Lanes, London N4.
Tel: 0171 499 7177
This has one of the best fruit and vegetable selections in London.

Reza Patisserie, Meats and Greengrocery

347 Kensington High Street, London W8.
Tel: 0171 603 0924.
This used just to be an Iranian deli, but now it's a much larger shop which is well worth a visit.

Specialist Mail Order Supplies

Cool Chile Company

P O Box 5702, London W10 6WE.
Tel: 0973 311 714 *or* 0171 229 9360
This has a vast selection of dried chillies from Mexico.

Taste of the Wild

65 Ovenstand Mansions,
Prince of Wales Drive, London SW11 4EX.
Tel: 0171 720 0688.
This mainly supplies wild mushrooms gathered in Britain in season and across Europe. Other seasonal wild foods which are supplied include garlic, elderflowers and seaweed.

The Real Meat Company

East Hill Farm, Heytesbury, Warminster, Wiltshire DA12 0HR.
Tel: 01985 840 501.
(see page 221)
This company supplies meat from animals which are reared to high welfare standards on closely monitored farms in the West Country. It doesn't claim to be organic, but no preventative drugs are used and all feeds are specially prepared.

Food Ferry

Tel: 0171 498 0827.
Based in south London, the Food Ferry delivers your weekly shopping load with a flat rate delivery charge of £3.50. You can order from a huge listed product catalogue containing 2,500 lines of brand name goods. They will deliver the same evening between 5.30 p.m.-7.30 p.m. or 7.00 p.m.-9.00 p.m, provided that the order is placed before 11.00 a.m.

The Fresh Food Company

P O Box 5710, London W10 5WB.
Tel: 0181 969 0351.
This was set up about five years ago by Thoby Young (who still runs the service), when he started bringing fresh fish from Cornwall overnight. An organic fruit and vegetable box, boxes of organic meat and dairy produce can now also be delivered. All produce (except fish!) comes from Soil Association registered farms. Ordering must be done a week in advance.

Shopping and Specialist Food Suppliers

Supermarkets around London

We cannot forget the supermarket culture which now dominates much of the population's shopping around the city. The variety of ingredients and products now available is enormous, and, given the pressure of limited time, it is not surprising that most shoppers favour a one-stop shop. There are several stores I regularly use and each one has its own special character.

The Shepherds Bush **Safeway** I know very well, and along its aisles it has it has a good Cypriot section. There is a well-stocked Indian section amongst the other usual products.

The **Waitrose** shop on the Kings Road is a good venue for fresh fish. Their herb, fruit and vegetable selection is vast; new ideas coming up on their dried fruit and nut section recently included sun-dried papaya. It's a great shop to keep an eye on, as all their new products are always well thought through and interesting.

Sainsbury's new venture into 'Special Selections', places an emphasis on the more specialised end of the food market. Foods are sourced from all over the world – one product which caught my eye was the Hokey Pokey candy from New Zealand which is used in the popular ice cream over there. The Cromwell Road Store and the Townmead Road Store in Fulham are my personal favourites.

Tesco has revolutionized the possibilities of city centre shopping by introducing Tesco Metro Stores. Small stores in High Street locations are very popular in the centre of the city; ingenious planning has sited one at Hammersmith tube station, one on Oxford Street and one in Covent Garden. Tesco's range of products is tailored to each individual store's clientele.

Asda needs a mention too, as it was the first supermarket to pioneer 24-hour shopping. Even though shops such as PDQ on Shaftesbury Avenue, Hollywood Stores on the Fulham Road, and a few others offer 24 hour availability, the opportunity to shop at supermarket prices was a welcome and ingenious step. The Clapham Junction store is also open 24 hours at Christmas and deserves a mention for its great bread.

Last but not least, the flagship **Marks and Spencers** in Oxford Street at the Marble Arch end, has a fantastic food hall in the basement. Recently they have reverted to selling the fruit and vegetables loose as well as packaged to give the customer more choice. Choice is also been increased by the butchery 'Traiteur' type counter in the store.

Other celebrated department stores, such as Harrods, Fortnum and Mason and Harvey Nichols, have luxurious food halls which are famous in their own right. These are discussed in more detail on page 228. They are an invaluable source of out-of-season, exotic or high-quality produce – but at a price!

Glossary

Techniques Explained

a point: reduce a sauce or liquid; a culinary term meaning to boil down in order to concentrate flavour and thicken a liquid to the consistency of a sauce.

al dente: an Italian cooking expression. Literally translated, it means `to the tooth' and it is used to describe foods, particularly pasta, rice and now vegetables, that are cooked until firm to the bite but not soft.

anglaise sauce: make a thin, pouring egg custard.

bain marie: a large shallow vessel, usually a deep roasting tin, containing hot water so other dishes or taller pans can be placed in it, with the water coming not more than half way up. It is designed to keep delicate dishes such as custards hot without overcooking them. It also allows the dishes to cook with a gentle heat. The bain marie can cook on top of the hob or in the oven.

bake blind: the technique used to bake a pastry shell of uncooked shortcrust pastry. The pastry is rolled out and used to line a tin or dish. The base of the pastry should be pricked with a fork and then lined with greaseproof paper. Add baking beans or rice and cook in an oven at about 180°C, 350°F, gas mark 4, for about 10 minutes depending on the size of the pastry shell. Remove the greaseproof paper and the beans and replace in the oven for a further 5-7 minutes to cook the pastry without letting it go brown. The pastry case can then be filled.

beurre manie: a French culinary term for a mixture of flour and softened butter that is worked together to form a smooth paste. It is used to thicken sauces, gravies and soups by being whisked into the boiling mixture in small nuggets of the paste, whisking until smooth and thickened.

chicken bouillon: a typical recipe for chicken or fish:

1.5 litres (2½ pints) water
4 tablespoons lemon juice or white wine vinegar
2 teaspoons salt
1 carrot
½ stick celery
1 onion, sliced
6 parsley stalks
3-4 sprigs fresh tarragon
dill or chervil (optional)
6 black peppercorns

Put all the ingredients except the peppercorns into a covered saucepan (not aluminium). Simmer for 45 minutes, then add the peppercorns and simmer for 10 minutes more. Strain before using. It will keep refrigerated for about a week. Makes 1.25 litres (2¼-2½ pints).

court bouillon: a slightly acidulated savoury liquid, prepared primarily for cooking fish, but also vegetables and veal. It gives flavour and also keeps the flesh a good colour. A court bouillon is made by boiling shallots, celery, parsley, lemon juice, wine or vinegar, a few sprigs of herbs and seasoning in vinegar water for 10 minutes.

deglaze the pan: to boil stock or wine with the left-over sediment in a roasting or frying pan, to form a sauce or a gravy.

demi-glacé: this is a half glaze. A sauce reduced by boiling until it is almost thick enough for glazing.
how to bone a guinea fowl (or chicken): use a sharp

pointed knife, to work this close to the bone and take care to keep the outer skin as whole as possible. With its breast bone laid down on the work surface, cut the bird along the back bone, piercing the skin. Resting the knife against the bone and keeping it flat, work the flesh away from the back bone on both sides. Trim the flesh away from the thigh bone and lift out the thigh bone. Be careful not to pierce the flesh. Chop of the leg at the knee joint (leave the wings intact to give a better shape). With the edge of the knife, scrape all the meat from the leg bone. Lift out the leg bone and reserve other bones for stock. Very carefully scrape the meat off the rib cage. When all the meat has been scraped off, lift out the carcass.

how to joint a chicken: using a very sharp knife split the chicken through the breast bone right down the centre. Open out the two halves and lay the chicken skin side down on the work surface. Cut through the backbone with a sharp knife, cut the thigh away from the wings and breast of the chicken. Use kitchen scissors to cut off the wings and cut the rest of the chicken into smaller pieces.

how to shuck (open) oysters: wrap your left hand in a cloth, pick up the oyster flat side up and curl your fingers over it. With your right hand, push the blade of an oyster knife (or a short stubby knife) between the two shells at the hinge end. Lever it open. With the tip of the knife, free the oyster from the shell and tip it into a sieve placed over a basin, so that the juices are saved and separated from the oyster itself.

julienne: the term used for finely shredded vegetables like thin matchsticks. It is also used to describe any other ingredient which may be thinly shredded e.g. cooked chicken etc.

parisiènne potatoes: peel potatoes; then, using a melon baller, cut the raw potatoes into balls (use any left over potato to make into mash) Deep fry for 10-12 minutes until golden.

pâte glacé: a sweet shortcrust pastry.

velouté sauce: a sauce which is good served on vegetables, chicken, meat, fish and the basis for many variations.

25g (1oz) butter
2 tablespoons flour
350 ml (12fl oz) warm stock (chicken, veal, or fish according to the dish for which the sauce will be used)
salt and freshly ground white pepper
few drops lemon juice
1 egg yolk
1 tablespoon single cream

Melt the butter in a heavy saucepan and stir in the flour. Cook over a low heat until straw coloured. Remove from the heat and cool a little, then add the hot stock and stir until smooth. Return to medium heat and stir constantly until boiling. Lower the heat and cook very gently for 15 minutes, stirring frequently. Season with salt, pepper and lemon juice. Add the egg yolk to the cream in a small bowl. Stir in a little of the hot sauce then stir this mixture back into the sauce. Cook until the sauce is glossy and a little thicker, stirring constantly; but do not boil.

Index

Index

Index

Index